P9-DMY-828

Play and Meaning in Early Childhood Education

Doris Pronin Fromberg
Hofstra University

Allyn and Bacon

Boston ▪ London ▪ Toronto ▪ Sydney ▪ Tokyo ▪ Singapore

Series Editor: *Traci Mueller*
Editorial Assistant: *Bridget Kane*
Production Editor: *Michelle Limoges*
Production Manager: *Susan Brown*
Composition and Prepress Buyer: *Linda Cox*
Electronic Composition: *Peggy Cabot, Cabot Computer Services*
Manufacturing Buyer: *Suzanne Lareau*
Cover Administrator: *Kristina Mose-Libon*

Copyright © 2002 by Allyn & Bacon
A Pearson Education Company
75 Arlington Street
Boston, Massachusetts 02116

Internet: www.ablongman.com

All rights reserved. No part of the material protected by this copyright notice may be reproduced or utilized in any form or by any means, electronic or mechanical, including photocopying, recording, or by any information storage and retrieval system, without written permission from the copyright owner.

Between the time Website information is gathered and then published, it is not unusual for some sites to have closed. Also, the transcription of URLs can result in unintended typographical errors. The publisher would appreciate notification where these occur so that they may be corrected in subsequent editions.

Library of Congress Cataloging-in-Publication Data

Fromberg, Doris Pronin.
    Play and meaning in early childhood education / Doris Pronin Fromberg.
        p.   cm.
    Includes bibliographical references and index.
    ISBN 0-205-29650-5 (alk. paper)
        1. Play.   2. Early childhood education.   I. Title.

 LB1139.35.P55 F76 2002
 372.21—dc21   2001022434

Printed in the United States of America

10 9 8 7 6 5 4 3 2   06 05 04 03 02

CONTENTS

PREFACE

This book about play and meaning in early childhood comes to light at a time when play and meaning are in the shadow of political pressures for early education to focus on a narrow curriculum devoted to technical skills in the three R's and transmitted informational facts. However, the narrow type of academic "transmission" education continues to fail many children. The way that children put their experiences together resembles a moving web of connections more than a stored set of stationary drawers or a growing pile of packages. If schools could reduce curriculum to a list of everything that children might need to know, youngsters would not have enough space or hours in a lifetime to add it all up. Children's learning is generative, not just additive.

Young children's play opens a window onto the ways that they understand the world and grasp fresh meaning. This book looks through that window to see how to match the process of teaching to the ways in which children develop meaning. The view through the window of children's play is definitely not straight or static; it is a vista that celebrates the creativity of children's play themes as eloquent representations of their sociocultural and personal-cultural experiences.

Educators and students of curriculum will find *practical ideas* for including play and meaning in early education. Students of child study, the nature of meaning, and sociocultural perspectives on play will find *reasons* to use play and meaning in early education. Educational policy makers will find *information* about the nature of play and meaning in the lives of children, and *guidance* concerning the nature of early childhood curriculum. The practical ideas, reasons, information and guidance concerning play and meaning are introduced under the following headings: dynamic themes curriculum; political and social influences; a recommendation to shift from an academic to an intellectual emphasis on dynamic curriculum; a dynamic theory of play and meaning; and the mutual influence of theory, research, and practice.

Dynamic Themes Curriculum. To provide an alternative to a uniform, narrow, additive kind of curriculum, educators need to reconfigure early education. In a transformed early-childhood education, teachers will build on children's strengths as players. To do this, teachers must select, flexibly sequence, and cluster activities that can support young children's capacity to make new connections. Cyclical change, indirect progress, and synergy are all examples of ways to connect physical, social, and artistic experiences. This book refers to these three underlying experiences as dynamic themes; children who have equivalent experiences that share an underlying dynamic theme may participate in those experiences through different social, physical, or artistic surface forms.

Varied experiences that represent the same dynamic theme are like melodies transposed into different keys or played by different instruments; we might also think of different subject-matter disciplines as different musical keys. The latter sections of the book and the resource appendices discuss how children and teachers can interact to develop meaning; these sections describe a variety of practical ways to implement a dynamic curriculum that focuses on meaning and young children's play.

Political and Sociocultural Influences. Our cultural contexts and perspectives shape our expectations of what is relevant in teaching and learning. Today, there is a political pressure to achieve uniform outcomes related to universal standards in predictable forms, and to raise standardized test scores. Policy makers take the position that raising standards will influence educational outcomes so that graduates can become gainfully employed. But who defines "higher" standards? Policy makers often assume giving harder work to young children in school is the answer to society's problems. They believe that checking off a uniform list of skills and information will remedy the contemporary ills of society.

In today's "tougher" educational arena, teachers and children focus on results (teaching and learning for the sole purpose of preparing for a standardized test) rather than on the reasons behind what they do at schools (Kohn, 1999) and the practical applications of what has been learned. Standardized tests repeatedly measure what is easy to test rather than what constitutes relevant learning.

Shift from Academic to Intellectual Emphasis on Dynamic Curriculum. Our rapidly changing world requires us to shift from an academic to an intellectual emphasis as we think about early education. The image of an unpredictable future invites human beings to adapt to change, think flexibly, persevere, make connections, network with others, integrate skills, and take responsibility for their actions. Young children's power as players sows the seeds that society will need in the future. To grow, those seeds need a supportive community culture and supportive educators, including teachers, parents, *and* policy makers.

This book takes the position that play is an integral condition for early learning and that meaning is the shared center of learning and play. All children do not develop in uniform ways. Each child is unique. Therefore, these pages create a dynamic bridge between how children develop in both different and similar ways, and why and how professional early childhood educators might interact with particular children to help them integrate meaning.

Dynamic Theory of Play and Meaning. This book also responds to the question of why teachers should think of early-childhood curriculum design as the flexible pursuit of dynamic themes. We look in turn at children and research as bases for developing a theory of play and meaning, and we examine the theory in order to better interpret how children play and learn. The chapters that follow explore a theory of play and meaning in early childhood education that builds on research and the overlap of three theories—script theory, theory of mind, and chaos/complexity theory. These theories underscore the generally predictable and specifically unpredictable nature of play and the development of meaning.

Mutual Influence of Theory, Research, and Practice. Researchers have found that children's play influences their development of skills in language, cognition, social competence, and creativity. Teachers who understand the research and theory about how young children play and learn will be better able to select from among diverse experiences to help young children balance and expand new challenges and independence.

After presenting research, theories, and the practical application of the theory of play and meaning, the book offers a paradigm shift for curriculum designers. Some readers may prefer to focus on the practical Sections Three and Four, which follow the introductory chapters. Others may prefer to read straight through to consider research findings and the confluence of theories that influence the author's proposed theory of play, meaning, and teaching.

Whatever path you choose in reading, remember that teachers need to know how to maintain relevant challenges for youngsters. Love alone is not enough to protect children from a paralyzing sense of failure and powerlessness. Play offers a territory in which children can construct and represent the world and cultivate knowledge of their own power.

Acknowledgments

Thank you to Hofstra University for giving me the time to develop this project and to Dean James R. Johnson for supporting a special leave with research funds to study children at the Hofstra University Arnold and Joan Saltzman Community Service Center's Lindner-Goldberg Child Development Institute. Institute director Donna Tudda's support, the skill of head teacher Alma Rocha, and the powerful child players in the Institute added to the project.

I also greatly appreciate the suggestions of constructive anonymous reviewers and Karen VanderVen, along with the involvement of Traci Mueller of Allyn and Bacon. Melvin Fromberg and Deborah Fromberg were conscientious and generous critics who made this project a family affair. They only added to the project, whereas I am responsible for any limitations that readers may find.

D.P.F.

SECTION ONE

Vision Informs Dynamic Theory

This section outlines the domain of play and meaning in early childhood from the perspectives of teaching and the development of individual children within sociocultural contexts. Chapter 1 considers the need for a dynamic theory of play and meaning in early childhood and discusses how such a theory may influence teaching. Chapter 2 develops a multifaceted definition of play as one condition for learning. Chapter 3 describes how children play from infancy through the primary grades and considers some chracterics of play that span human development. Chapter 4 discusses research studies about play as integrated learning that influences children's social, intellectual, and language development as well as their development of imagination and creativity. Chapter 5 summarizes the implications of brain research for nurturing the growth of meaning in early education.

1 What Is Worthwhile Learning?

Is it enough for children to learn to decode, understand print, and pass standardized tests but not seek out literature outside of school requirements? Is it enough for them to successfully memorize answers to informational questions on standardized tests but hesitate to question the events around them or express personal opinions? Who values narrowly defined uses of skills and information for their own children or for themselves?

Astrophysicist Michio Kaku's (1997) projections of the future suggest that the world needs people who can do three important things: (1) envision more than one answer to a question—even a question designed to elicit a single correct answer; (2) take imaginary leaps and act on them; and (3) adapt to rapid change. Kaku also predicts that computers may become so miniaturized that they may be as expendable as scrap paper is today. In addition, he believes that quantum mechanics will transform and extend human travel into outer space and that biotechnology will continue to redefine body parts and health—all within this century. The world will need people who can think flexibly, collaborate with others, and feel comfortable with the predictably unpredictable.

Many of these human qualities are already detectable in the play of young children. Indeed, a major strength of young children is their capacity to play, and to build an understanding of the world through their play. How can educators help children build on their strengths so as to prepare themselves for the future?.

Toward a Dynamic Theory of Play and Meaning

A dynamic theory of children's reality speculates about how they develop and represent their understanding of the world during play. Moreover, recognizing how play influences the development of conceptual, linguistic, social, and creative meaning helps us understand how children learn in general and how adults might interact with them in more meaningful ways.

As it turns out, there is a relationship between play and meaning or understanding. Children play naturally as they construct meaning. However, many educators caution children to "finish their work before they play." The attitude of work first, play later, devalues play. The word *meaning* is also controversial. Different people mean different things when they talk about "meaningful education" and "meanings" that matter. Although schools do want children to learn new ideas and skills, educators disagree on what knowledge and skills are worthwhile and how children should be taught.

This book focuses on how young children develop meaning through play. By understanding the ways in which children develop their play and meaning, educators can better match teaching with learning. Traditional education focuses on teaching children in what we'll see below is a linear manner, but children develop meaning in nonlinear ways. This book argues that teachers must match children's nonlinear ways of learning with nonlinear ways of teaching. It also provides strategies for accomplishing this matching.

Linear Academic Teaching

Educators who engage in linear academic teaching typically transmit to children an adult conception of knowledge in uniform, narrow, and additive ways. Recently, many teachers have engaged in this model of teaching. They have responded to political pressures to "raise standards," teach more, teach sooner, and measure results by the standardized testing of children's memorization of facts and use of discrete skills. In the linear model, the administration asks all teachers in a school or district to use didactic recitation and uniform content; children memorize single correct answers and learn isolated skills to apply at a later time. Solitary paper-and-pencil tasks predominate. Teachers often deliver the linear curriculum with warmth, and try to gain children's involvement through enthusiasm and rewards. For example, they engage children in the uniform construction of crafts projects that the teachers themselves have designed for children to follow. Frequently, the information that teachers ask children to remember proves as trivial as the crafts projects. Thus, skills education (the "three Rs") in the linear model often lacks significant meaning; the information discussed in the classroom may have little or no relation to the questions that children have about their world and environment. For example, city children may be more interested in what happens to the rain flowing into the sewer than in how the rain forest functions. The linear model of teaching has predominated in the United States and has failed to educate all children equitably.

Nonlinear Intellectual Teaching

Teachers who engage in nonlinear teaching expect knowledge to develop when children construct meaning while interacting with other people and the physical world. These instructors take a holistic approach and center their teaching on issues that engage children in questions about their social and physical world. The nonlinear approach integrates skills as children learn meaningful content through direct experiences and their capacity to imagine. The questions they pursue together may have more than a single correct solution. The skills children use are embedded with meaningful ideas that provide personal motives for using and practicing those skills. For example, when children add and subtract the number of blocks or other materials necessary to construct a bridge, they are using mathematics in their play. (See Dunn & Larson, 1990, on design technology.) Children collaborate with one another and their teacher in groups of varying size, and have time to work both alone and with others. This model of teaching occasionally has been fashionable in word but rarely practiced.

Ethical Teaching

It is collaborative, humane and ethical to match meaningful instruction with how children actually learn. It is collaborative because it respects different children's unique pathways to learning, thereby empowering children while also engaging teachers in sensitive scaffolding. "Scaffolding" (Vygotsky, 1962) is the process by which teachers challenge children at the "tangents" (Allport, 1955) of their development. Scaffolding denotes a way in which one or more persons can build up support structures for another person. In a play situation, it is a way to offer a helping hand that might expand the scope or extend the depth or time that children spend in fruitful activity. Other children as well as teachers can offer scaffolds. This is a humane and ethical outlook because teachers adapt to a child's potential for experiences. Teachers who are respectful of children's various perspectives convey a sense of ethical caring (Goldstein, 1999).

Meaning

When you understand something, you understand its meaning. Meaning is the center of human experience and the shared center of learning and play. It is an internal, personal experience. More than just concepts or ideas alone, meaning also consists of emotions and motives. Some meaning involves more powerful or weaker emotion; human beings grasp specific meanings with different degrees of perceptual strength or motivation. Motivation is both an emotional and cognitive reaction to meaning, and it influences how much attention we pay to particular experiences. Therefore, meaning is not "delivered" (in linear terms). Rather, it develops in nonlinear, unpredictable ways when children engage in focused interactions with others and the physical world. Like music, it is a direct experience.

Nonlinear learning consists of diverse connections that are evident in children's sociodramatic play (when children act out imaginary events with other children or an adult). For example, children use body language, gestures, and then verbal language to engage in pretend play. An implicit choreography takes place in sociodramatic play as one child enters into and "becomes" a role while another responds in a complementary role. Child 1: "Wah! My leg is broken." Child 2: "Stop moving. I need to put on this bandage." A different Child 2 might have responded: "I've told you not to jump off the roof. Bad, bad. Now I have to get some splints." Yet another Child 2 might have responded: "Don't move. I'm calling 911" or "Poor baby. There, there." Different children, or the same child at a different time, might respond in numerous ways to a session of "Let's Pretend." The particular response reflects the child's event knowledge, his or her past experiences, and the influence of the other child. However, whatever the response, all the players implicitly agree that this collaborative, oral playwriting is relevant and meaningful to them.

Meaning also develops through imagery and the use of analogy and metaphor. We use metaphor and analogy when we recognize part of a familiar image in a new encounter, thereby facilitating meaningful recognition and connection. For example, hugging a doll or pillow is analogous to hugging a person, an implied metaphor. In some ways, the analogue (doll or pillow) is similar to the person (the referent), and in some ways it is different. Using an analogy is one way to teach a young child how a thermometer works. For example, a teacher could ask the child how he would lie in bed on a cold night. The child might then curl up in a ball to demonstrate. Then the teacher could ask the child how he would lie in bed on a hot night, and the child might stretch out his limbs away from his body. The teacher could then compare the child's body positions with the way mercury in a thermometer expands and contracts in response to temperature changes. Comparing the analogue (body positions) and the referent (mercury in the thermometer) entices the child to perceive the thermometer in a new way. "Metaphor involves the transformation of one thing seen as another" (Belth, 1993, p. 48). Imagery and metaphor form a basis for meaningful thinking. The imagery in metaphor is dynamic and flexible (Prawat, 1999) as well as "unpredictable" (Belth, 1993, p. 48).

Overview

The preceding definitions of terms are elaborated throughout the book and culminate in Figure 15.1, A Paradigm Shift in Early Education: Implications of Nonlinear Dynamic Systems Theory.

Section One continues with Chapter 2, A Definition of Play: Conditions for Integrated Learning; Chapter 3, A Vision of Play in Early Childhood Education; Chapter 4, What Research Says about Play and Meaning in Early Childhood: Play as Integrated Learning; and Chapter 5, Brain Research and Meaning.

Section Two, titled Nonlinear Theories That Function Like Play: Theory Informs Practice, points out the connections between children's play and meaning and nonlinear theories that include script theory, chaos and complexity theory, and theory of mind.

Section Three, Integrating Dynamic Practice, discusses what the nonlinear dynamics of play and meaning imply for teachers' use of dynamic themes as a basis for meaningful curriculum in early education. Teachers who closely observe children develop a repertoire of experiences that they can adapt to match young children's potentials. A collection of experiences built around sample dynamic themes—broad images such as cyclical change—appear in different forms in Chapter 12 and extensive Resource Appendices.

Section Four, Dynamic Issues, considers advocacy and family involvement as well as related present and future issues.

An Invitation

This introductory chapter invites you to consider a dynamic theory of play and meaning that can influence a holistic, nonlinear approach to early childhood education. The chapter contends that our society's unpredictable future necessitates the retention—even cultivation—of children's nonlinear strengths as players and as creators of meaning. When educators match children's learning strengths by focusing nonlinear early education on meaningful themes, children can also learn linear skills in functional, intuitive, and intrinsically motivated ways.

2

A Definition of Play

Conditions for Integrated Learning

Imagine that you have received a gift of the automobile of your dream. Imagine the color, make, and model. The keys and registration are in your hand. The gas tank is full. But—there is no oil in the engine. The engine needs the lubricating oil in order to function. In a similar way, the human body needs lymphatic fluid in order for the bones, organs, muscles, and skin to function (Fromberg, 1998). In a sense, young children's play serves as a kind of lymphatic process or lubricating oil for constructing meaning.

Both play and meaning are dynamic processes; that is, they develop and change. This book considers play as one of seven conditions for learning that also include induction, cognitive dissonance, social interaction, physical experiences, revisiting, and competence (Fromberg, 1995). These conditions for learning contribute to the dynamic processes by which young children can make comparisons and experience relationships. Figure 2.1 briefly defines these conditions, all of which describe the active participation of young children in the development of meaning. *Teachers who use the seven conditions for learning can simplify learning or make it more challenging as they interact with young children.*

Although the seven conditions for learning in early childhood provide the integrated context in which young children build meaning, the remainder of this book focuses on play. Teachers who take a nonlinear approach to early education value play as an integral and significant focus of each day. They see play as a domain in which children feel empowered.

What Is Play?

Play is multifaceted. It changes constantly, and unfolds differently in different settings. For example, a young child's play in a department store differs from play in a classroom block corner, play at a beach, or, in the case of children in Africa, play beside the field in which mothers are working. Children play alone, with

FIGURE 2.1 **Conditions for Learning in Early Childhood Education in Addition to Play**

Induction

The inductive process takes place when children *compare* things and ideas. If children have only one thing or idea available, then they need to rely on memory and rote learning instead of constructing new meanings. Here are a few examples of the inductive process:

- It is easier for young children to learn the name of a new shape or color when the size and shape of several differently colored objects are the same and only the one variable—the new color—stands out against a background of a familiar color.
- It is easier for young children to learn contrasting sounds of letters in word patterns (for example, mat, fat) when the letters exist in relationships with other letters.
- Young children develop mathematical concepts when quantities exist in relationships, such as "larger than" and "smaller than."
- Children of preschool age have learned underlying cultural messages (for instance, fatalism or optimistic striving toward the future) through the oral and written stories that they hear or read in their families (Janiv, 1976).
- Kindergarten children can induce the underlying approach in an artist's style by comparing several paintings by the artist.

Cognitive Dissonance

Cognitive dissonance is a three-part comparison between prediction, experience, and comparison of the prediction with the experience. For example, films and family influence our predictions about marriage. The comparison between our prediction about marriage and our actual experience with it may have unexpected gaps—marriage may be better, or worse, than we anticipated. Young children often predict that a large piece of styrofoam is more likely to sink than a small washer, or they expect that a larger magnet would attract more paper clips than a smaller magnet. *The relationship between the expectation and the findings generates a moment of surprise, a kind of transition or bridge within which meaning may arise.*

Social Interaction

When children have repeated opportunities to compare their own views with those of other children, such as taking turns or deciding who wears a firefighter hat, they learn about the perceptions and feelings of others. The *transition* from a personally centered view to a decentered view reflects a growth of meaning. (See Piaget et al., 1965.)

Physical Experiences

When children directly compare familiar and new objects or qualities by handling them, they have the chance to build additional meaning. *The sensory touching itself is not educative; it is the process of comparison, the underlying relationship, that helps children find meaning.*

Revisiting

When children revisit objects or situations, they have an opportunity to demonstrate that they have extended their understanding over time. Intervening experiences serve to put an earlier experience into a *fresh relationship.* [See Piaget & Inhelder (1973) and documentation from the Reggio Emilia schools (Edwards, Gandini, & Forman, 1998).]

(continued)

FIGURE 2.1   *(continued)*

Competence
When children are busy worrying about their competence or coping with a sense of inadequacy, they find it difficult to focus on new meanings. [See Bruner (1966) on coping and defending and Goleman (1995).] They are more likely to feel potentially successful when they can experience a sense of challenge in a task, comparing some degree of risk with a reasonable chance of attaining success. The degree of challenge, or the underlying *relationship* between challenge and risk, can smooth the process of building meaning.

others, with objects, and with their imaginations. The unpredictable surface forms change as children play, but the relationship between reality and fantasy functions in predictable ways.

"*Play* functions as both a verb and a noun. Rather than a category, property, or stage of behavior, play is a *relative* activity. . . . [T]he shifting functions in different settings" may contribute to problems many researchers experience in defining play (Fromberg, 1999, p. 27).

Because play is relative behavior, scholars have studied it from the differing perspectives of historians, philosophers, linguists, anthropologists, and psychologists [Footnote 2.1]. From these varied perspectives, scholars and researchers have considered the child as solitary, playing with objects or imagination; as well as a social player with one or more peers, children of different ages, parents, and other adults. They have also considered the contexts in which play occurs, the content, the interaction of context and content, and the cultural environment. They have considered the player's experience as "optimal" (Cszikszentmihalyi & Cszikszentmihalyi, 1988) when the player "is unaware of time passing," with play being "satisfying and focused enough in the present to transcend the moment" (Fromberg, 1998, p. 191). There have been both psychological-individual and cultural-social perspectives on play. Scholars have divided social play into structured games-with-rules and sports, as contrasted with the more evolving forms of sociodramatic play. They also have differentiated play from exploration. Despite these varied perspectives, play emerges as meaningful behavior that is both representational and interactive. A working definition of play follows:

Play Is Voluntary

Whichever age group you visit, you might easily identify when children are playing; it seems so evident. When children are playing, they usually appear to be

[Footnote 2.1   Historian Huizinga; philosophers Dewey, Ellul, and Langer; linguists Cazden, Chukovsky, Kirschenblatt-Gimblett, and Weir; anthropologists Aldis, Bateson, Blurton Jones, Schwartzman, Smith, and Sutton-Smith; and psychologists Almy, Monighan-Nourot, Scales, & Van Hoorn; Bretherton; Bruner, Jolly, & Sylva; Fein; Freud; Peller; Piaget; Pulaski; Singer; Vygotsky; and Werner.]

fully engaged and focused on their activity. It is typically an activity that they have chosen. Often, children will select an activity because they want to "hang out" with the other children who are participating. Therefore, the voluntary nature of play exists *in relation to* a particular context.

Play Is Meaningful

Young children's imaginative play has roots in the context of their life experiences. Even when they are playing fanciful roles or using props that suggest other times and places, children integrate such themes as preparing imaginary food, eating the food, going to sleep, and waking up. A toddler, for example, may put her own pacifier on the doll's mouth and giggle at the game. The pretend play of young children is meaningful in that it has connections to their own experience. Meaning is thus a dynamic process. *The diverse surface forms in which children represent their meanings conform to specific underlying processes.*

Play Is Symbolic

Children at play actively do things that represent their images of the world. They may move furniture to create a shoe store, ride in an imaginary space ship, or cook an imaginary meal. Children of preschool and kindergarten age often plan their play together: "You be the doctor, and I'll be the baby." They spend a minimum amount of time and energy planning and negotiating what and how to play and devote a maximum amount of time immersed in the play. (The reverse may be true for intermediate age children, for whom planning itself may be the focus of play.) Therefore, play is symbolic in that it represents youngsters' experience. *The underlying play structures facilitate the diverse surface forms in which children represent their experiences.*

Play Is Rule-Governed

Children often make explicit their rules of engagement by directing or asking one another to undertake particular roles or activities. Children often share an unspoken understanding about how to respond to one another's statements and actions that they monitor with gestures, facial expressions, and the pace at which they act. Many of the play rules emerge as children build the path of their actions together. *There is an ongoing, dynamic relationship between underlying rules and multiple meaningful representations.* In effect, they organize themselves within the play framework.

Play Is Pleasurable

Children pretend to mend broken bones in hospital or veterinary play as they re-create accidents, illness, death, and funerals. Despite the serious themes, the children experience a sense of satisfaction that transcends the moment. The sense of pleasure may come from immersing themselves in the action or emotion, or the sense of control that comes from an awareness of engaging in pretense. Young people feel a sense of power because they make all the play decisions. Sharing these experiences with others helps to validate and sometimes modify potentially troubling events and feelings. The *relationship* between the play frame and the satisfaction of the play content contributes to the sense of pleasure.

Play Is Episodic

Children respond smoothly to one another's actions because they appear to be sharing similar unwritten "scripts" that they have developed together. However, their play often proves episodic. It need not have a beginning, middle, and end in order to provide a sense of satisfaction and immersion. In short, children emphasize activity rather than "outcomes" (Dewey, 1933). *The emphasis on activity is an ever-changing process.*

The Continuum of Psychological–Individual and Sociocultural Perspectives on Play

The context in which children find themselves influences the content of their play. Context may include the physical environment, time, other children or adults, and acceptable and expected cultural conditions. Because context helps to define play, various theorists tend to see the functions of play somewhat differently. They have considered the distinction between the content and context of play as a characteristic of defining play; researchers have wondered about the dynamic relationship between the unstated rules of play and the many different ways in which children can represent those rules.

Figure 2.2, The Continuum of Psychological-Individual and Sociocultural Perspectives on Play, presents contrasting views of how play functions. These theoretical positions emphasize different ways of looking at the same activity. The psychological perspective is represented by the work of Jean Piaget, whose definition of play evolved from the developmental stage-based structure of his cognitive theory of child development and research on the object play of solitary children. The work of social psychologist Lev Vygotsky and anthropologists Gregory Bateson and Helen Schwartzman focus on play's interpersonal dynamics and represent the sociocultural perspective. The different perspectives propose distinctly different processes, influences, relative benefits of play, and possibilities for intervention. However, they all see children as taking an active role in forming their own play symbols.

Play as a Context and Categorization Frame

A definition of play needs to include the cultural context in which play takes place because of the different perspectives on play that scholars take. Some

FIGURE 2.2 The Continuum of Psychological–Individual and
Sociocultural Theoretical Perspectives on Play

Psychological–Individual	Sociocultural
Predominating Process:	
Assimilation (Piaget, 1962)	Adaptation
Distorts reality	Allusion and transformation of reality (Schwartzman, 1978, p. 330)
Transition between egocentric thought and development of reciprocity	Bridge the joining of objects and actions with representation in thought
Orientation to Time:	
Past	Future
Benefits of Play:	
Consolidating experiences	Advancing of development, "zone of proximal development" (Vygotsky, 1978, pp. 99, 102)
Relation to Self:	
Focus on oneself	Subordinate self to rules of the game
Impulsive (Piaget, 1966)	Self-controlling
Isolated wishes	Generalized affect
Role of the Teacher:	
Passive or managing	Sensitive scaffolding

Areas of Overlap Between Psychological–Individual and Sociocultural Perspectives on Play:

Process of cognitive conflict
Wish fulfillment (Freud, 1959, 1960)
Players as active
Sense of mastery and empowerment
(Corsaro, 1990; Eisen, 1988; Opie & Opie, 1976)
Intrinsic motivation

investigators generally contend that what may be play in one time and place may be ritualistic or religious, frivolous, or technical behavior elsewhere (Csikszent-mihalyi, 1976; Kirschenblatt-Gimblett, 1979; Lancy, 1984; Scales, Almy, Nicolo-poulou, & Ervin-Tripp, 1991). The cultural context also determines who may, or is likely to, engage in various kinds of play (Geertz, 1976; Morgan, 1982; Whiting & Edwards, 1988).

Our culture teaches us what to expect and how to categorize reality and pre-tend play (Bateson, 1971, 1972, 1976, 1979). Gregory Bateson specifically identifies the concept of a play frame that functions as a territory or context for play. He suggests that children demonstrate by their verbal or nonverbal behavior that they are able to categorize play and not-play as they enter into and step outside the framework of play situations. By planning their parts and actions together, children communicate about their communication (metacommunication). The process of metacommunication takes place outside the play frame. In this way, play is progress in the child's "evolution of communication" and "metacommunication" (Bateson, 1976, pp. 121, 125). The metacommunication that takes place in social play makes it possible for children to pretend together because without this type of communication, they would be playing by themselves. [Footnote 2.2] These verbal rituals that help children to categorize themselves and others as players in the play frame make it possible for them to transform relationships within the system (Garvey, 1979, 1993). For example, one child may change from being the doctor to being the patient.

When children use an object to bridge the gap between real and make believe, such as using a block as a telephone, or when they interact with others to define a play territory together, they are engaging in symbolic representation. Engaging in the symbolic representation of play seems to advance youngsters' development (Leslie, 1995; Nelson et al., 1986; Reiber & Carton, 1987). Young children at play behave in more complex ways than they do outside the play situation. We can see this when we look below the surface structures of children's play at the underlying rules of play that the children use (Garvey, 1979).

Exploration and Play

A definition of play needs to account for the distinction between exploration and play. Exploration is an attempt to find out about new experiences; play is an attempt to find out what players can do with their new experiences. (See Collard, 1979, and Hutt, 1976 for extended discussion of exploration.) Young children's exploratory behavior precedes play (Wohlwill, 1984), and their manipulation of concrete objects may help the transition between exploration and play.

For example, with flashlights, kindergarten-age children explored how the light beam appeared to change when it was closer to or farther from a wall or when the beam touched their open or closed fingers. Only after they had exhausted their explorations were they able to play with the flashlights to create shadows and project them onto a sheet. The exploratory physical activity might have served as a transition from exploration into play.

Some preschoolers with pretend supermarket props first explored all of the things that they could do with the cash register, and other children explored how various play containers fit into the cabinets and on shelves before they were able to "play store." Primary-age children may spend a major amount of time

[Footnote 2.2   Bateson's view of metacommunication is not the same as metacognition, Piaget's (1976) notion of mature self-awareness. In contrast to Piaget's (1962) position that play reflects development, there is conjecture that young children also acquire knowledge and develop cognitively as they engage in social play (Bretherton, 1985).]

exploring the rules of a game, deciding who will do what and with whom, before they actually play the game.

The term *functional play* is an alternative description of exploration. It is mainly "sensori-motor or practice play" (Klugman & Fasoli, 1995, p. 198). When exploring and using new experiences, children may engage in complex behavior. For example, when they engage in sports, they are refining physical skills. During group sports, they are also learning and practicing important social planning skills and cooperation. In a way, learning such important skills "without being taught," as a by-product of the play, are lessons that learners own.

Constructive play, such as building with blocks, involves prediction and more complex problem solving than functional play (Ibid.). Children's *dramatic pretend play*, which may or may not involve others, or *sociodramatic play*, which involves social interaction and communicative representation, also differ from exploratory, functional, or constructive play.

During sociodramatic play, young children represent and construct meaning. Because of its generative nature, this kind of play is the focus of Chapter 6. As children engage in sociodramatic play, they act out their developing understandings of the world in general and the conventions of play in particular. To provide a shared context for the sections that follow, the next chapter presents an image of how children's play develops in their early years.

The Many Dimensions of Play

Play is one of seven integrated conditions for learning and serves as a kind of lymphatic function in early childhood education. Play formats include solitary or social play with objects and others. Sociodramatic play is a particularly powerful form in which children use both imagery and communication about their imagery in seamless ways. Although their imagery grows out of particular personal and cultural contexts, their capacity to engage in metacommunication seems to exist across cultures. Children move comfortably inside and outside the play framework. Teachers who plan for varied forms of play in early childhood engage in ethical practice because they adapt to the needs of children and support young children's sense of competence and power.

3 A Vision of Play in Early Childhood Education

Imagine visiting nonlinear classrooms for young children in child-care centers and public school in the United States. The following sample anecdotes indicate the increasing ability of children to integrate representational art and literacy forms, display independence, and collaborate with others as they mature.

Imagine Classrooms

How Do Infants Play During Their Waking Hours?

The six-month-old lay on a carpet under a table. A mirror was attached to the underside of the table. The teacher had attached a knitted ribbon loop to the infant's ankle. When he moved his leg down, the ribbon pulled down a soft, red stuffed toy. His entire body shook with excitement as his legs and arms waved in the direction of the toy. When he raised his leg, the toy moved higher. With repeated play, he began to pull his toes closer to his mouth. There appeared to be a *transition point, a phase* during which the infant grasped the meaningful connection between his movements and the recurring closeness of the toy.

Two other infants were sitting next to each other on a mat. They were shaking, slapping, mouthing, dropping, and picking up plastic rings. Three other infants were sleeping in a dim alcove. One infant was at the diapering table with a teacher who was touching his nose, ears, toes, and naming body parts in a singsong voice. Four other infants were alternately crawling on the carpeted floor toward playthings on a low shelf or sitting next to, or on the lap of, a teacher who was pointing and naming objects in a cardboard picture book.

Do Toddlers Ever Stop Moving?

As individual toddlers finished their meal, they began to pull playthings from a low shelf. Several children walked around the open, low-pile carpeted space with pull toys. Several children sat with a teacher in a construction activity with miniature animals. The children piled animals into a central "zoo" and alternately walked toward the shelf of pull toys. Four other children stood at a table on which the teacher had taped paper. The teacher commented, "Jenny's using a red crayon; Hal is writing with a brown crayon. . . ." In a kitchen play area, one child pretended to pour liquids; a teacher, attempting to build on the child's pouring activity, invited the child to serve her some tea. The contrast of the teacher's comments and suggestions offered a bridge, *a phase transition*, to expanded play.

When Will Preschoolers Get Closure?

Five children were pulling kitchen equipment out of the housekeeping area. Two children were stuffing the equipment into shopping bags and announced their departure for a picnic. In less than six minutes, the picnic evolved into a parade when the youngsters were joined by several other children wearing dress-up clothes. A teacher, seated at a table with children who were rolling out and marking play dough with pine cones, remarked, "Your parade is so careful. You are leaving space next to the water table, the blocks, and the play-dough table. Where will you finish? What will you do next?"

Four three-year-olds were at a water table. They were squeezing sponges, pouring water into containers of different shapes that were the same size, using a funnel, a spoon, a ladle, and a baster. From time to time, one child picked up the funnel that another appeared to have discarded but rediscovered as soon as the other child began to use it. The teacher said, "Let's take turns. When Rose finishes using the funnel, then you can have it back. Show us how you were squeezing the sponge so well. Oh, you are so strong." The repeated reminders about taking turns, coupled with the chance to play, helped the preschoolers to make a *transition* from self-interest toward the community's right to have turns.

How Much Literacy Can Kindergarten Children Use in Their Play?

The housekeeping area has been transformed into a hairdressing shop. The children had created the following signs:

> hr cataz [hair cuts] 2$ 99c
> shampo
> karlazz 2$ and 99c [curlers]
> prmz 2$ [perms]

Both boys and girls moved into and out of this sociodramatic play and took turns as customers, receptionists, haircutters, and cashiers. They enacted cutting hair, giving permanents, having manicures, making appointments, writing down appointments, writing out receipts, using the play cash register, and making change.

At the same time, four other children were playing with a balance scale, trying to balance a series of objects against wooden cubes; pairs of children wrote down their predictions and compared their results. Two other children were playing checkers and two were playing Kalah. Players of this African game plan ahead to empty pebbles in each of their pots.

Six children who were building with blocks rolled small trucks down an incline and discussed how to build together. One child wrote a sign, "Dajs Hl" (Dangerous Hill), and attached it to the ramp with tape. Three children wrote in their journals; two others marked the water level on a tape attached to a jar under a leaky faucet. A few children sat in the library corner looking at books. The teacher circulated and provided materials, support, and appreciation. She had taken many *transitional* opportunities to build on their activities by encouraging them to represent their experiences through drawing, talking, and writing about their activities.

How Elaborately Will Primary-Age Children Construct Their Buildings?

Five seven-year-olds were building with a Lego™ set that included motors. They discussed with their teacher ways that they planned to complete their mall. They planned to create signs and flyers.

Three children took apart an aquarium motor on a plastic mat while a fourth child held open the pages of a book that had photographs of a similar motor. Then the teacher circulated, stopping to talk with children engaged in various other activities.

Two children were playing chess. Two were playing a card game. At the same time, two others were using a computer to create tickets for their family breakfast.

Four children were outlining scenery and making costumes for a play that they had developed from the story "The Pied Piper." Several children were reading books in the library corner, and one was reading in a pup tent.

Six children were writing and drawing in their journals; two were discussing the writing: "That couldn't really happen. Ponies can't eat off window sills." These children had internalized the reciprocal roles of author and editor, and helped each other to reflect on their "products."

What Are Some Characteristics of Play That Span Development?

Some characteristics of play cut across different ages. Play integrates brain functions and blends the rational and the imaginative, the intellectual and the emotional, the linear (logical) and the nonlinear (imaginative, intuitive, and aesthetic), the mundane and the creative. As a *process*, play serves as a lymphatic system that lubricates, transports, and transforms the transitions of one phase of understanding into another. As a *product*, play—especially sociodramatic play—enhances development in language, cognition, social competence, and creative fluency.

Play Looks Simple

Play may look simple, but it is actually complex human behavior. Infants in a high chair play with gravity as they repeatedly push food, a spoon, or a toy off the table top with delight. Their intent is play and their delight is the sense of competence they experience when their predictions are fulfilled and the object falls down. Adults may get annoyed at having to replace or "cleanup" the items that infants drop, but they might be mollified to learn that playing infants are building a model of physics from the perspective of a high chair.

Play Usually Looks Like Fun

Children who can speak tell us that they were playing, were having fun, and that play is easy for them to do. However, players can also deal with serious subjects. They might play out the fantasy of getting even with a bully or re-enacting the death of a relative or public figure. They might also mimic adult work behaviors in sometimes serious or officious ways.

Play May Look Trivial to Some Adults

Children at play appear to engage in effortless behavior. This creates a public-relations nightmare for early childhood education because some adults may not perceive play as a significant condition for developing meaning. However, researchers have found that play skills are related to the development of social competence, intelligence, language development, and creativity (Fromberg, 1999). In particular, children who engage in sociodramatic play and use less realistic props to represent ideas have stronger academic achievement (Smilansky, 1968).

Children learn by observing and interacting with one another. Therefore, play serves as a frame that holds a picture of what children understand. Their play demonstrates the ways that they have learned to communicate, solve problems about developing a story line, take turns, and share various perspectives.

Play Takes Different Forms

Construction play with objects is mainly physical, when children build with blocks or sand or put together puzzles. Children practice using playthings with increasing skill and a growing sense of competence. An example of physical play took place when Ally, a toddler, repeatedly waddled toward and away from the mirror, giggled at her image, and gurgled with pleasure.

During *pretend play*, children may play alone with toys, household objects, or rocks and twigs while creating an imaginary story. For example, Deb, a preschooler, created a corral with twigs and rode a broomstick horse around the corral; she transformed her essential image of riding into a pretend action.

With *sociodramatic pretend play*, children create and act out imaginary events with other children or an adult. For instance, they may pack a valise and pretend to take a trip. Or they become characters within their imaginary community, whether members of a family, a farm, a spaceship, a shoe store, a post office, a wedding party, or a funeral. They also play card games, board games, ball games, circle games, chasing games, and construction games.

Play Is Legitimate School Activity

Many adults believe that children should work rather than play in school. The adults' implicit view of work usually is linear. In contrast to this linear perspective, it is worthwhile to envision John Dewey's continuum of fooling . . . play . . . work . . . drudgery; he believed that a balance between play and work could serve learning (Dewey, 1933, pp. 284–287).

Another view is that children should work first and have time for play as a reward or a relief from work. This view poses two problems. First, offering a reward for activity that is voluntary diminishes it as satisfying in itself (Kohn, 1996). For example, one child who was a highly self-motivated early reader became disenchanted with reading when the first-grade teacher offered rewards for reading (Haberman, 1995). Second, work feels fulfilling when it is meaningful. Sometimes activity that begins as required work can become self-selected because it is intrinsically satisfying; such satisfaction defines "functional autonomy" (Allport, 1958).

If autonomy were a goal of education, then children would need to build inner motives for becoming thoughtful and ethical citizens in a caring community. Teachers in a caring and ethical community support children's sincere motives and efforts; they welcome multiple forms of representation. Meaningful learning for young children in a nonlinear-oriented intellectual classroom is a powerful experience that includes surprises, delights, and novelties. Teachers and children become comfortable with ambiguity and "predictable unpredictability." They become respectful of one another's uniqueness.

The Disciplined Freedom of Play

Play is a legitimate and important part of early childhood education both inside and outside of school in group as well as solitary settings. It is not the child's work in itself, nor is it a medium for learning in itself. We can think of play as an oscillating model that moves between process and product; it is neither process nor product but an integration that transcends both the process and the product perspectives. At the same time, play is a form of disciplined freedom. It continues throughout the life span and is valuable in itself as well as a vehicle for transporting and integrating development.

4

What Research Says about Play and Meaning in Early Childhood

Play as Integrated Learning

This chapter selectively reviews research into the impact of play on meaning in early childhood. The findings can guide educators' and policy makers' decisions about providing resources for children's school play.

Play Influences Development

Can play either influence development or support what children already have experienced? (See Figure 2.2.) If you take the position that play influences development, you can intervene sensitively in ways that keep play vital. If intervention becomes directive or intrusive, then play will dissolve. If you take the position that play is trivial, then you risk marginalizing it.

However, the body of research on play points to the supportive influence of play in the development of three competencies: social competence, cognitive development, and language development. Some researchers have mixed findings concerning the relationship of play and creativity. Although children's play influences these competencies in unified ways, the limits of language direct us to consider each perspective in turn.

Social Development

Children who play with one another learn that others have views that may differ from their own. They also learn that others have feelings that are similar to their own. They are "decentering" from themselves (Piaget et al., 1965). Therefore, in their social interaction they are building their "theory of mind," the sense that others have their own ideas and feelings. This insight constitutes an influential aspect of multicultural education.

How Do Children Participate?   Young people learn from observation and negotiation that there are a variety of ways to enter and to extend a line of play, and to develop ideas together. These strategies indicate social competence. Therefore, observations of social pretend play offer adults a window into children's social competence.

While participating in play, children use a variety of strategies to gain entry into an ongoing enactment. A kindergarten-age child, for example, attempted several approaches to shoe-store play. She entered the play frame, said, "Hello," and left. She circled the area, returned, and said, "How do they fit?" and then left once more. She circled the area again, returned, said, "I need a new pair of sneakers," and left. After she circled the area yet again, she returned, took a shoe box from the shelf, sat down, tried on a shoe, and asked, "What other colors do you have?" This child appeared to follow a "circle of safety" strategy. Verbal in group meeting times, she was unwilling to risk rejection. She repeatedly took the limited risks of short approaches, and gradually added to her comfort level before fully entering the play. Her entry strategy let her creatively contain the risks while remaining within the play frame.

Here are some examples of children who successfully entered into ongoing play by simply becoming players:

1. A four-year-old (CH 2) had a successful entry exchange in the blocks area: CH 1: "I am building a spaceship that only I can go in." CH 2: "I am going to build the engine of this spaceship."
2. A different four-year-old boy entered the family center and said, "I want to make pancakes." A girl responded, "You can't make pancakes when the party's over." The boy replied, "I'm cleaning up the table. Do you want to help me?" (They cleared the table together.)
3. When a child announced, "This is a firehouse!" another child entered the play by announcing, "Excuse me, fireman. There is a fire in my house!"
4. Two boys were playing in the blocks area. The following exchange took place: Girl: "David, can I play with you?" Walt: "Why?" (The three children began building together.) Girl: "Here, you can have my piece of wood." Walt: "OK, but only one girl, two guys, and one girl." The girl's original yes-no question (metacommunication) did not bring her success. Nevertheless, she did succeed when she modified her approach to fit into the play frame.

An unsuccessful attempt occurred when one four-year-old boy asked to enter hospital play. When another child said, "No," the boy went crying to the teacher, who suggested that he talk to the other child. However, he withdrew and went to the library corner.

Play entry strategies give children an opportunity to learn about the influence of their actions. Interestingly, those children who had mastered the entry structure of engaging in the play theme were more successful than the children who attempted to enter by asking a yes-no question.

Entry into a play frame is a transition between the phase of not playing and the phase of playing. Children also learn to make phase transitions when they have opportunities to observe others. In addition, interaction with older children, siblings, and adults apparently influences the complexity of children's play (Dunn & Dale, 1984; Farver & Wimbarti, 1995; Haight & Miller, 1992; Howes with Unger & Matheson, 1992). Those children who appear to be skilled players tend to plan and organize play cooperatively for longer periods of time with greater flexibility and fluidity (Fagot, 1997; Fein, 1985; Jones & Reynolds, 1997; Trawick-Smith, 1994). Children who acquire successful play skills get along well with their peers and have learned to negotiate by giving as well as getting. They know how to let other children feel involved and competent.

When Do Children Participate in Pretense?   In one study, children as young as toddlers engaged in pretend play by acting as if they were another object or person before they engaged in coordinated social pretend play during the third year of life (Perner, 1991). As young children's language develops within the context of social play (Eckerman & Didow, 1989), their play becomes increasingly imaginative. The connection between language development and social play supports the idea that there is an ongoing integration of development (Shore, 1990).

Although children's sociodramatic play competence and complexity increase through five years of age, play appears to decline among six-year-olds, possibly influenced by school practices and the children's internalization of imagination (Cole & LaVoie, 1985; Voss, 1987). Children between five and seven years of age appear to shift their focus to the purposes of actions rather than the pretend actions themselves (Forbes & Yablick, 1984). Even a casual observation across numerous classrooms revealed that few primary classrooms housing six- and seven-year-olds have provisions for sociodramatic play areas. Instead, play appears to be defined by—and separated into finite periods for—educational games, outdoor sports, gardening, and arts curriculum. Often, the games, sports, and arts were presented as "rewards" or relief from "significant" work, such as paper-and-pencil tasks or quiz-like worksheets that demanded a single correct answer.

Social competence within the play frame, a context in which other players might scaffold children's strategies, has close links with children's cognitive development. In effect, the increasing complexity and extent of children's play reflects their growing theory of mind, a cognitive process. *These findings suggest that teachers need to sensitively scaffold children's entry strategies and level of play complexity by observing opportunities for timing transitions from one phase of play to another.*

Cognitive Development

Young children's play with others as well as with objects influences their cognitive development. In both cases, the key to competence is flexibility in dealing with ongoing object construction or social construction. Developmental progress can take place more easily when a child uses alternative approaches and perspectives.

Realistic and Unstructured Playthings.   In block play, practice time for building helps children construct their conceptions of the three-dimensional world. Play with blocks supports the development of mathematics by helping children to imagine, plan, predict, and enact various structures. Mathematicians and chemists (Kean, 1998) use similar mental images in their work. At the same time, researchers have found that children who play with realistic toys first find it harder to use their imaginations. They represent ideas more continuously than do children who begin to play with unstructured toys (McGhee, Etheridge, & Berg, 1984). Children who use *unstructured* toys engage in more extended collaborative script building than those who use high-specificity props (McLoyd, 1983; Wanska, Pohlman, & Bedrosian, 1989).

Floor blocks and other unstructured, three-dimensional construction materials strengthen the imagery that children need in order to deal with scientific and mathematical concepts. Playthings that have more than one use also help children to consider alternative ways to draw inferences in other situations (Heath, 1983).

Play with a *variety* of objects and toys supports the children's capacity to pretend by substituting less realistic objects for prototypes (Copple, Cocking, & Matthews, 1984; Fein, 1975). Young children progress through the processes of decentering, decontextualizing, and then integration (Bretherton, O'Connell, Shore, & Bates, 1984; Fenson, 1984, 1985). *Decentration* refers to a progression from focusing on the self toward a focus on others. *Decontextualization* refers to the growing ability to substitute objects and then symbols for their prototypes, and to become more inventive. Children increasingly *integrate* language with a combination of action sequences. For example, a preschooler might pretend to feed, bathe, and put a doll to sleep with accompanying language. Language becomes increasingly predominant.

A now-classic study began with the observation that young, low-income preschool children who had academic difficulties also played with less complexity, symbolic substitution, and language skills (Smilansky, 1968). After teachers intervened personally and selectively with these children in order to stimulate their sociodramatic play, the children became more flexible planners, used language more elaborately and expansively, increased their use of pretense, and lengthened their play episodes. Another study found that the imagery of a similar population of low-income children was very rich but became evident outdoors at the later ages of six to eight years (Eifermann, 1971).

In another study, toy demonstrators taught low-income mothers of toddlers play skills in order to assist their toddlers in enriching their play repertoire (Levenstein, 1992). These children had significant increases in their IQ scores. The same findings occurred when these procedures were repeated with different low-income groups. Discussion of these findings suggested that children's play was connected to their problem solving, academic skills, and classroom attitudes as well as IQ.

A related study with three-year-olds used doll play, props, and story stems (problem narratives) (Buchsbaum & Emde, 1990). The researchers found that the children could offer coherent and varied "prosocial choices in a moral dilemma" (p. 150) when the task was relevant and emotionally accessible to them. The researchers suggested that the built-in oral-script theory to which the children responded was powerful because it grew from children's experience-based knowledge.

Individual Variations.   Nature and nurture both contribute to children's symbolic competence and their ability to represent experiences through play. Researchers have identified "patterners" (object-oriented) and "dramatists" (symbol-oriented) (Gardner, 1982), whose behavior reflects a combination of underlying "mental structures" and personality (Taylor & Carlson, 1997). Both styles lead to general symbolic competence, similar to the notion of "introverts" or "extroverts" (Adler, 1923).

Children also seem to be high or low fantasy in their play (Connolly & Doyle, 1984; Moran, Sawyers, Fu, & Milgram, 1984; Singer, 1973). High-imagination children can wait quietly for longer periods of time and engage in fantasy play (Singer & Singer, 1979). They also use more analogies, tell more imaginative stories, and prove more tenacious than low-imagination children. High-imagination children have parents who model, welcome, and provide opportunities for fantasy play. *Schools appear to value children who can wait quietly and persevere. Children may feel disempowered if their teachers attempt to influence these dispositions in a direct, linear way. Caregivers who value and provide opportunities for fantasy play and who use nonlinear approaches may support children's self-organized and self-directed capacity for patience, perseverance, use of analogies, and imagination.*

Gender.   Block play, often a pastime of boys, contributes to the development of visual-spatial skills that in turn are important to the development of mathematical concepts (Fagot & Leve, 1998; Maccoby & Jacklin, 1974). If block play and group sports help children to develop visual-spatial skills, then all children need equitable access to these construction activities. In one study, when teachers placed themselves in the block area, girls were more likely to play and spend more time there (Serbin, 1978).

Research suggests that girls tend to balance their own perspectives with others (Sheldon, 1992), while boys tend to be more interested in seeing their ideas accepted (Black, 1989). Moreover, boys often lead girls into play topics, and girls' block constructions can be more sophisticated when they play with boys (Pellegrini & Perlmutter, 1989).

Other studies indicate that boys also engage in more rough-and-tumble play, games with rules, and games that call on spatial relations than girls do (Paley, 1984; Pellegrini, 1987). Boys seem to engage in more group sports and games in larger groups that require strategic planning, whereas girls tend to participate in more "chumships" (Maccoby & Jacklin, 1974). Some researchers have found that boys are more playfully exuberant, teasing, clowning, and humorous than girls (Bergen, 1998; Honig, 1998).

These findings suggest that teachers and parents who would like to see equitable access to visual-spatial learning can contribute to girls' play in particular. Namely, they can plan, bridge, and encourage girls to participate in building with blocks and engage in group games and sports. "Bridging" means that adults enter the play frame, invite girls to enter, observe them, and perhaps begin to play with the girls if necessary. The adults then withdraw to an observer's role as soon as possible. Adult playfulness and a sense of humor can also support children's sense of play as well as their willingness to participate.

Language Development

Language and cognitive development are intertwined. When children play with others, they get opportunities to expand their knowledge as well as refine their language skills. For example, children engage in more literacy activities and increase their literacy skills when play-area props include literacy materials such as writing tools, signs, posters, banners, books, labels, receipt and appointment books, price lists, and magazines (Christie, 1991; Morrow, 1997; O'Brien & Bi, 1995). Similar findings relate to emergent numeracy (Cook, 1996). Other research showed children using more varied and extensive language when play props suggested varied themes (Bagley & Klass, 1997; Dodge & Frost, 1986; Levy, Schaefer, & Phelps, 1986).

The body of research in this vein indicates that an important interaction exists between language development and sociodramatic play. Children practice literacy skills together, practice collaborative oral play writing, provide an audience and feedback on literary "voice" for one another, and expand their vocabulary and event knowledge. Children thus test their predictions as they develop oral scripts together; prediction is also essential to the process of reading.

In addition, story comprehension improves when children have a chance to role play the events of a story (Pellegrini & Galda, 1982). Investigators suggest that when children maintain the play frame through talking about their roles, they can imagine both their own role and their peers' interpretation of roles (Galda, Pellegrini, & Cox, 1989). They thereby demonstrate their growing theory of mind.

In these ways, children scaffold one another's play, a perspective that supports Lev Vygotsky's notion that "play creates a zone of proximal development" (Vygotsky, 1978, p. 102). This "zone" is the growing edge of learning in which children can absorb challenge and balance risk and a chance of success. Young children at play exercise their greatest self-control and behave "in advance of development" (Ibid., p. 129).

Children also enjoy playing with language itself, because it supports their sense of their own power (Freud, 1960/1916; Kirschenblatt-Gimblett, 1979). Sometimes language play takes the form of creating metaphors, poetry, riddles, jokes, and scatalogical language.

Within the play frame, children experiment with language conventions as well as word meanings. Humor is a form of playing with language and reality in a risk-friendly "as-if" environment (Bergen, 1998, p. 334). Children who play with language may also attempt to test the limits of appropriate use by erupting with toilet and body-part words, chants, reference to poison or death, teasing, and off-color language (Davidson, 1998).

Young children's play with language, their communication with one another about their play, and their practice of different voices during play are all connected. Language play reflects children's use of syntax, expressions that represent more mature people, various story forms, and new meanings. Thus, children create analogies and use mental imagery and mental models. They compare and contrast ideas and relationships that help them to make new connections and infer new meanings. *Teachers who welcome children's sociodramatic play and collaborative work help to support language development.*

Creative Development

As a haven for controlled risk-taking and an attempt to see what's possible, play is a creative process. Consider the view that creativity is the process of making the familiar "strange," while learning new meaning is a way to make the strange familiar (Dewey, 1933).

We might even infer that sociodramatic play supports general creativity in problem solving more than mere verbal instruction can. Children model for one another alternative approaches and ways to solve problems. Observations of young children in their natural group settings suggest that pairs and trios of children were most effective in stimulating each other's imagination (Bruner, 1980). Research also suggests that children's working in a group might reduce aggressive behavior (Farver, 1996). These observations support the idea that *children who are stimulated to play more imaginatively show an improved ability to make new connections.* As children resolve problems together during play, they also build their sense of competence (Gitlin-Weiner, 1998).

> Unlike creativity in adults, where a societal criterion is imposed, creativity for children usually means that the play or activity is original for this particular child, based on a personal or individual criterion. . . . Domains of creative play include arts and crafts, designing miniature play scenes (which may then result in imaginative play), and using musical instruments or audiovisual equipment (Johnson, 1998, p. 149).

Researchers have found a relationship between direct tutoring and encouragement to use thematic play with children's later creative use of unstructured props (Dansky, 1986; Feitelson & Ross, 1973; Freyberg, 1973). Greta Fein (1985) saw "pretense as an orientation in which the immediate environment is deliberately treated in a divergent manner" (p. 21). Elliott Eisner (1990) envisioned a shared representational power and significance between art and play. Anthony

Pellegrini (1998) found a relationship between flexible, rough-and-tumble players and their social problem–solving flexibility.

However, there is ongoing debate about these findings concerning the connection between play and creativity. Some researchers have questioned the impartiality of particular researchers, their definition of children's behavior as play, and the validity of research procedures (Simon & Smith, 1985a, 1985b, 1985c; Smith & Whitney, 1987). In turn, their concerns have been challenged (Dansky, 1985, 1986). An additional study that aimed to eliminate researchers' bias and retested preschoolers found that mainly boys' rather than girls' play was connected to creativity (Clark, Griffing, & Johnson, 1989).

It is thus worthwhile to further study divergent play, children's flexible use of alternative approaches, and their development of fluent and original ideas. The nonlinear, dynamic nature of such creativity defies compartmentalization and demands a connected, holistic conception. Indeed, recent research on the human brain, discussed in the next chapter, suggests that the brain is our ultimate holistic, covert connection maker.

The Influences of Play

Researchers have found that young children's play positively influences their development of social competence, language, and cognition, though findings concerning the impact of play on creativity are mixed. Social, linguistic, and cognitive meaning is the significant center of young people's play as well as their education. Children's sociodramatic play, in which their meanings predominate and in which they employ their personal power, serves as a particularly significant force in integrating their development.

Children feel powerful when they play. Their sense of personal power grows out of the dynamic political and cultural context in which they acquire experiences. They feel competent within the "predictable unpredictability" of play.

The varied forms that play can take demonstrate an underlying "grammar" of play. When we focus on the processes by which events shift during play, changes take place, and children make new connections, we can envision how children learn. Recognizing how young children construct meaning gives educators an opportunity to rethink and transform their relationships and ways of communicating with children. Recent research concerning how the human brain develops, the subject of the next chapter, supports these perspectives.

5 Brain Research and Meaning

Research on how the human brain functions offers additional support for the findings about play covered in Chapter 4. Neuroscientists have used various electronic scans to study how the human brain functions. There is plenty of agreement among them on how early childhood teachers might work with children (Calvin, 1996; Jensen, 1998; Shore, 1997; Sylwester, 1995). The discussion that follows suggests experiences that teachers can influence.

Influence of Enrichment and Connections

Enriched educational experiences create stronger structural connections and pathways within the brain. Teachers can influence children's brain development through varied forms of enrichment, including linguistic, artistic, scientific, physical, and social dimensions. The parts of the brain that children use when they play are *integrated* mainly in the **connections** between the amygdala (predominantly emotional center) and neocortex (predominantly thinking center). The same parts of the brain also affect attention, potential attitudes toward learning, creative thinking, problem solving, and the arts. Strengthening the amygdala strengthens these interrelated capacities. The term "emotional intelligence" has become a popular way to think about the significance of these connections (Goleman, 1995).

Enriched experiences can increase and strengthen the connections between neurons, as if establishing increasingly sturdy paths along which connections may travel. Play is a powerful integrator of experience and can support the growth of connections. Rich experiences also provide opportunities for wholesome repetition and connection making to take place. Children have the chance to organize their own sequence of behaviors and integrate learning when teachers provide for play and playfulness.

When children at play develop their own sequence of activities, they engage in creative behavior, "what Luria [a Russian psychologist] called a kinetic melody" (Calvin, 1996, p. 100). "Kinetic" suggests movement, and "melody" suggests connectedness; in effect, connected movement. This image of connected movement is consistent with the seven integrated conditions for learning in early childhood, including play (see Figure 2.1); the perception of movement permits learning to take place whereas a static or isolated fact may camouflage meaning.

Sudden movement, whether by a change of pace, direction, or emotional tone, can overshadow other meanings. For example, when humans feel stress or fear, the brain gives priority to coping with it. At such times, connections in the brain are reduced to survival. Under stress, the brain consumes its fuel, glucose, to cope rather than to learn (Jensen, 1998, pp. 19, 57). *Teachers who support play and reduce children's stress enhance children's problem-solving skills and learning.*

Influence of Feedback and Stress

Feedback is a form of enrichment. The brain receives internal feedback from the child's perception of current experience. The brain also receives external feedback from others and the ways in which they behave toward the child. In contrast to coping mechanisms,

> . . . the ideal feedback involves choice; it can be generated and modified at will. . . . Immediate and self-generating feedback can come from many sources: having posted criteria for performance, checking against personal goals, using a computer, or when the student checks with a parent or teacher from another grade level (Jensen, 1998, p. 33).

(Discussion of the relevance of choices continues in Chapter 9, Beginning with Nonlinear Environmental Design.) The feedback through oral and body language that children provide to each other during sociodramatic play encourages fresh perspectives.

Brain growth is more critical to brain development than solutions to particular problems. The brain integrates experiences across many of its regions. Stress may inhibit attention, self-motivation, thinking, and learning. When children engage in play, their self-motivation, attention, and problem solving intensify, and their stress level decreases. Natural body chemicals that foster a sense of well-being flow during such play. *Thus the wholesome balance of play with work in early education can influence children's positive attitudes toward school.* (Chapter 13, Present and Future Issues: The Power of Play, continues discussion of the play-work continuum.)

Influence of Early Experiences

Early experiences have far-reaching implications for connection making. During their first two years, children establish their emotional interaction patterns. Early secure attachment to a significant human being influences a child's later capacity to play flexibly, elaboratively, and collaboratively (Coplan & Rubin, 1998, p. 372). These observations are examples of "Sensitive Dependence on Initial Conditions." Neuroscientists generally agree that children who miss early opportunities for experiences have difficulty making up the loss later. Young children's brains are much more active than adults' brains. For example, if a fear reaction predominates across the brain owing to early abuse, it may establish associations that hinder children's later learning.

During the first two years of life, the brain also absorbs the sounds of language. Children hear contrasting patterns of sounds and their repetition in the context of use and thereby induce the underlying structure of their native language (Brown & Bellugi, 1964). *Children need to hear much responsive language from their earliest days of life.*

Influence of Personal Meaning

Personal meaning can support the development of connections. Meanings are diverse and cut across many parts of the brain. Meanings emerge from connections that include feelings, emotions, intensities, patterns, concepts, feedback, and relevance in different contexts. When children perceive that events are personally relevant to them, their neural connections proliferate and situations and ideas become part of their long-term memory. Meaningless things, such as irrelevant telephone numbers, will not typically become part of long-term memory; we have enough trouble remembering a telephone number that we have researched only a moment ago!

Contrasts between familiar and new experiences are particularly important as children acquire learning. *Teachers of younger children have the great task of coordinating and sequencing activities from which children can perceive and create patterns.* Interdisciplinary, cross-disciplinary, and extra-disciplinary curriculum models help children develop meaningful connections because they provide multiple opportunities for children to "tune in." (Chapter 12, Dynamic Themes: Weaving the Strands, extends this discussion.)

Connections

Neuroscientists have found that the human brain functions as a network of connections, particularly during problem solving and learning. Rich experiences in the form of variety, feedback, and secure and supportive early encounters optimize brain functions.

We have an opportunity to rethink and transform the nature of teacher and child relationships and communication when we study the processes by which events shift, changes take place, and children make new connections. *The teacher within this dynamic theoretical perspective can become a creator of experiences that generate transitions from unfamiliar to familiar meaning.*

Nonlinear Theories That Function Like Play

Theory Informs Practice

There are three nonlinear, dynamic theories that function like play: script theory, chaos and complexity theory, and theory of mind. Although the theories come from different perspectives [Footnote II.1], they represent a combination of relationships between underlying forms that manifest themselves in a variety of surface forms. Comparing these theories highlights the power of nonlinear processes and lets us build a nonlinear model of teaching practice on a nonlinear, dynamic theory of play and meaning. Matching teaching to learning processes in this way helps children feel and be competent in an unpredictable world.

However, attempting to grasp the nonlinear processes that play and meaning share is like trying to catch water in your hands. Instead, we need to capture "snapshots" of the flow. Let's first consider models that deal with relationships between underlying structures and their surface representations:

Underlying Structure	Surface Variety
A musical scale offers a limited number of notes	but there are many ways in which the notes can be related to one another in their sequence or through different rhythms.
An underlying alphabet	changes into different meanings as the letters are combined to create different words.

[Footnote II.1 Script theory comes mainly from the work of psychologists (Nelson et al., 1986) who have collaborated with linguists and specialists in artificial intelligence (Schank & Abelson, 1977). Chaos and complexity theory grew from work in the physical sciences (Gleick, 1987; Holte, 1990) and expanded to encompass the social sciences (Robertson & Combs, 1995; Waldrop, 1992), including the nature of play (Fromberg, 1999; VanderVen, 1998). Educators have also theorized about nonlinear relationships in models of learning (Belth, 1970; Fromberg, 1977, 1995; McLuhan, 1963). Studies of theory of mind come from the fields of child development and cognitive science (Astington, 1993; Astington & Pelletier, 1999; Bartsch & Wellman, 1995; Harris & Kavanaugh, 1993; Rosengren, Johnson, & Harris, 2000).]

An underlying set of grammatical rules	change into different meanings as words proceed in different orders.
Children use an underlying set of rules in play	to represent a variety of emergent meanings.
An underlying set of images in the physical world, such as cyclical change or synergy,	take unpredictable forms within different physical or social environments

In these examples, the deep forms are predictable, and the surface forms unpredictable. As discussed in Chapter 6, *it is the transformation between the deep and surface forms that generates meaning*. Chapter 6, Sociodramatic Play and Script Theory, also discusses children's capacity to use underlying sociodramatic play structures to represent their variety of experiences in both predictable and emergent ways.

Chapter 7, Chaos and Complexity Theory, explores the similar, predictable processes in the physical and social world that appear in unpredictable forms.

Chapter 8, Theory of Mind, considers the connections children make that help them develop an awareness of their own minds and others' minds.

Taken together, research findings and nonlinear theories provide a dynamic image of physical, social, and personal meaning. Educators who support children's use of dynamic play can extend and enrich children's development of meaning. *Teachers of young children must therefore bridge the distance between adults' and children's knowledge in ways that children perceive as meaningful (Dewey, 1933).*

6 Sociodramatic Play and Script Theory

Sociodramatic Play as Representation

There are symbolic parallels among play, the arts, and mathematics. For example, a philosopher makes the point that mathematics consists of games with rules (Whitehead, 1958), and adults perceive representation in the arts as their forms of play (Fromberg & Bergen, 1998). From these perspectives, the act of representation, "seeing" what you can do or make, shares a characteristic with play.

Sociodramatic play takes place when a child engages in pretense with one or more other children or adults. It can occur almost anyplace. It can deal with any subject matter within the context of children's lives and imaginations. Children represent their understanding of the world and other people in their play. *Therefore, sociodramatic play is an oral form of representation alongside written narratives, mathematics, and the arts.*

Script Theory and Narrative Structures

Both indoors and outdoors, children play out a variety of themes that represent everyday life. They also embellish their play with imaginary characters and incidents. Their sociodramatic play is a powerful, collaborative learning opportunity that may influence their social competence, language development, cognitive development, and creative fluency.

When young children engage in sociodramatic play, they participate in oral playwriting. They serve as audience, voice, and oral co-editors for one another.

The content of play grows out of children's lived experiences. Therefore, any experience that you might imagine children have had might become integrated with their collaborative script building. As children weave themes into their oral scripts, they reflect the multicultural experiences they have had. They use culturally specific gestures, hand motions, shrugs, inflections, and expressions. They might act out the behaviors of nurturing or abusive parents, older siblings, or neighbors. They might act out drunkenness (Mall, 1995), weddings, waiting rooms for community services, shopping for food or clothing, funerals, missile attacks, surgical procedures, transportation of goods, firefighting, or the behavior of media figures. The range of topics is as unlimited as the variety of life experiences and children's imaginations. (Appendix A offers a sample of young children's sociodramatic play themes.)

Script theory (Nelson et al., 1986; Schank & Abelson, 1977) refers to children's capacity to enter one another's oral scripts on the basis of minimal cues or plans. Young children instantly become the roles that they play within the emerging scripts. They engage in different degrees of oral script development, depending on their developmental age and language skills. Many scripts tend to be played out in episodic ways, without a typical story line that has a beginning, middle, and end.

The goals that children have stated may shift and proceed in different directions. They make also grow, depending on the children's interactions and ongoing negotiations. Youngsters interact with "shared predictability and collaborative novelty" (Fromberg, 1999, p. 32). *The transformational relationship between predictable underlying structures that surface in diverse content forms is similar whether children engage in sociodramatic play or in learning through experiences that represent underlying dynamic themes.*

Shared Predictability and Collaborative Novelty

The transformation between deep structures and surface forms becomes apparent in the unpredictably novel ways in which children have tried to solve problems for one another. Cycles of metacommunication (planning the play) and play imagery take place. In the two examples that follow, a third party attempted to resolve tension:

Example 1:

(For half an hour, Sophie kept pleading with Bette to let her wear a dress from the costume center.)

SOPHIE: "Bette, please, are you done with it? I have to see your dress. Are you done wearing that dress?"

BETTE: "No. I had it first."

SOPHIE: "You should have left it on the wire. Bette, you have five minutes" [amending her statement after seeing Bette's angry expression], "ten minutes you have to take it off."

SOPHIE: [a minute later] "It *is* ten minutes."

DORA: "Here, Sophie, I got you a dress." [Dora helps Sophie put on a different dress.]

SOPHIE: [smiling] "Thank you, Dora." [After putting on the dress, they move together toward the customer service desk.]

SOPHIE: [returns three minutes later, to Bette] "Are you done with that dress yet?"

DORA: [valiantly trying to distract Sophie again] "The babies are tired. Give me your baby to sleep. I'll take the baby home. OK?"

SOPHIE: "Bette, are you done with that dress yet?"

DORA: "The baby's tired. Can I get something for the baby?"

SOPHIE: "Bette, Bette" [8 times], "are you done with that dress?"

DORA: "Which baby is this one?"

BETTE: "It's time to get the baby in the bathtub."

SOPHIE: "Bette, I was waiting patiently for five minutes. You didn't take it off."

BETTE: "Well, it's my favorite dress."

SOPHIE: "Well, it's my favorite dress."

BETTE: "Next time, when you pick dramatic play, you can have it next time."

SOPHIE: "Well, I'm not gonna pick dramatic play."

BETTE: "I'm gonna wash my baby like this."

In this episode, Sophie attempted several creative strategies in order to obtain the dress that Bette was wearing. Dora was also creatively trying to distract Sophie from her great need for the dress. She offered her an alternative dress and then tried to engage her in playing with the baby doll. Bette offered Sophie the unacceptable alternative of wearing the coveted dress during a later play session. Sophie and Bette stepped out of the play frame in order to talk about time and ownership (metacommunication), whereas Dora remained within the imagery of the play frame in order to redirect the play. Dora's strategy revealed her attempt to understand Sophie's motivation.

Example 2:

The grammar of play is apparent in another episode of children's play in which children used both metacommunication and playing within the play frame (or play imagery) to build the narrative script in a negotiated, emergent way.

[Bob and Carl in the blocks area were alternately building and extinguishing a fire with a flexible hose. Bob and Carl resolved their disagreement about who would wear a hat by transforming the hose into a telephone into which they would speak and then listen to each other. Ann came over and began to build.]

BOB: "Hey, this is our house."

ANN: "I'm building something."

CARL: "She can come in our house. She can come in our firehouse." [metacommunication]

ANN: "I'm making a firehouse." [negotiating the script within the play frame by describing her enticing play activity.]

CARL: "You're the fire girl. We're the firemen." [metacommunication]

BOB: "Yeah, two guys and a girl. No more girls." [metacommunication]

Example 3:

In contrast with the preceding episodes, the entire oral script that follows takes place within the play frame. (David had been deserted in the house play, so he created a picnic theme that took him outside the house area where he invited others, including Ed, to play. In his absence, Ed and Frank entered the house area and planned a picnic by preparing food and putting on hats.)

ED: "I'm getting this sandwich" [an elaborate construction] "ready for the picnic."

DAVID: [returns, smiling broadly at Ed] "We didn't know you're coming in here. You're loved." [He gives Ed a hefty hug] "Hey, Ed, Frank" [with toy camera] "hey you, let's take a picture. Say 'cheese.'"

ED: [after the photograph, picks up a crutch] "Oh, my aching leg."

Metacommunication May Predominate

Young children's negotiations sometimes reflect their command of social leverage. In the following example, negotiation through metacommunication may predominate and reduce occasions for the script to build.

IAN: "If you give me those shoes, I'll give you a Power Ranger set."

JON: "I don't like Power Rangers."

IAN: [using hair dryer and curling iron as guns] "Bank robber . . . Jon, can I use those shoes for the last and single time?" [appeals to the teaching assistant]

TA: "Jon, five more minutes and then share. I'll tell you when." [Ian appears to shelve the issue of the shoes. The children then have a smooth transition into other play, only later to have the same sharing and control issue arise over a wheelchair]

The same underlying metacommunication and imagery thus can surface with different degrees of emphasis as well as different content.

Seamless Negotiation Between Imagery and Metacommunication

Young children also share information during their sociodramatic play, seamlessly moving between being the players (imagery) and commenting on the play (metacommunication). The following episode took place during an outdoor snack time, when Ken picked up a cigarette butt from the ground.

KEN: "My daddy smokes cigarettes. I smoke cigarettes." [After looking at the other children's puzzled and shocked faces, he shifts his comment.] "I don't smoke."

LEN: "Ken, can I tell you something? If you do smoke, you die."

KEN: "If you smoke real cigarettes." [puts cigarette butt from the ground into his mouth]

LEN: "You could die like that."

KEN: "Take me to the hospital, Len. Take me to the hospital. Pretend there was a hospital." [lies on a sculpture]

MEL: "And I'm the doctor."

LEN: "I'm the doctor. It's Doctor Collins."

KEN: [jumping down from the sculpture] "Watch this."

LEN: "If you do that you will break your knee."

KEN: "I can jump into the sky."

Other examples of the interaction between play imagery and communication about roles follow (italics indicate metacommunication):

Example 1:

CH1: "We're going for a walk."

CH2: "Can we go out to dinner, please?"

CH3: *"They have to be the mom. Pretend we have two moms. You be the mommy. You can both be my mom."*

CH1: *"They have to be the mom."*

CH2: *"You can be her."*

CH1: *"Please pretend you both be my moms."*

CH2: *"OK . . .* I'm not wearing these shoes. There are no high heels on a farm."

CH1: [using a rake] "This is a farm."

CH3: "You forgot your hat. *You're a farmer."*

Example 2:

CARL: *"Can I drive, Don?"*

DON: "Blast off."

CARL: *"Get the helmet and let's go back into the rocket."*

DON: "We need to call Earth." [picks up an invisible phone]

Example 3:

CH1: *"Pretend you are waking up, just you, not him."*

CH2: "I had the worst nightmare."

CH1: "Mom, you have to put on your space suit."

Example 4:

CH1: "Can you get me a jar?"

CH2: "Sure. I'll see if it's in the refrigerator."

CH1: *"Pretend that I just took it away, OK? Right?"*

Linear and Nonlinear Imagery Processes Interact

Children have to communicate about their communication (metacommunication), a linear process, when they attempt to shift the framework of their playing field and sometimes to negotiate entry into play. They use imagery and metaphor, nonlinear processes, when they represent a material or situation in place of another material or situation within the setting of pretense. Children do not solve their negotiation and communication problems in a linear, step-by-step way. *They integrate their nonlinear imagery and metaphors with their linear metacommunication skills to solve problems. In this way, sociodramatic play serves as an ultimate integrator of both linear and nonlinear experience.* Sociodramatic play also makes accessible the dynamic process by which young children integrate new meaning and extend their knowledge; teachers who consider these processes by flexibly planning experiences with dynamic themes in mind are likely to reach children with diverse learning needs.

Diverse Cultural Context and Content

Beyond teachers' planning, cultural contexts also define what the content of children's play will be, whether children play at all, and where they play. Of course, imagination and fantasy also stimulate play and indeed may eclipse outside, cultural constraints. Thus cultural context focuses children's experiences and expectancies concerning what is important, possible, welcome, tolerated, or disdained.

Knowledge of cultural content develops as children acquire social and personal experiences in a particular family, neighborhood, community, and larger society, including media. Therefore, children's understanding of events *integrates* their culturally specific and personally specific experiences.

For example, a five-year-old who had been on several family vacations returned from Disney World and announced, "This was the best vacation." Her mother reminded her that she had also made the same statement about visiting with the forest rangers in the national parks. With a moment's reflection, the girl announced that both vacations were "best" but that the forest rangers were real.

If this child had not been privileged to participate in such varied events, but had access only to television, she would have struggled to sort out such distinctions. In a similar way, children need direct contact with people from other cultures who live both similar and distinctive lives. Teachers who plan varied experiences that celebrate the dynamic theme of human differences and similarities help youngsters extend their knowledge.

For example, kinship structures are different for children who come from highly mobile, nuclear families as contrasted with families who have extended connections within large, traditional networks. These structures can generate different behaviors. To illustrate, some parents may sort objects on the basis of their use and level of safety, while others keep together all containers that are made of glass or all containers that are made of cardboard, regardless of their contents (Janiv, 1976). Mythologies and expectations may also differ in the stories that elders tell children. The stories of some cultures emphasize interpersonal relationships and a sense of the inevitability of "fate," while others teach children that individual striving can change a person's future. Cultural orientation also influences whether children tend to focus on a figure or the background, the logical or the figurative, the single or the multiple interpretation, collaboration or competition (Erickson & Mohatt, 1982; Heath, 1983; Nisbet, cited in Goode, 2000). Multicultural content appears in children's play through the use of gestures, language expressions, and attitudes toward issues that arise.

In itself, the act of engaging in sociodramatic play helps children to appreciate one another's perspectives and contributions. As the youngsters develop an oral script together, they sometimes add to one another's multicultural knowledge within the framework of pretense. The broad variety of young children's experiences also provides event knowledge that they then represent in their pretend play. Some underlying emotional, moral, and cosmic issues surface across the range of young children's play themes. However, regardless of which props they use, children's scripts depict their *personal* event knowledge. Whether they focus on hospital play, space travel, automotive repair, or supermarket play, they often create subsidiary scripts as well that include familiar content, such as nurture, eating, sleeping, and emergencies. While they use teacher-provided props and related literacy materials, they continue to play out their own wishes, fears, and fantasies.

Emotional, Moral, and Cosmic Issues

A survey of more than 120 sociodramatic play themes of 400 children between the ages of two and six years included emotional, moral, and cosmic issues. The emotional issues encompassed power, control, authority, wish fulfillment, anxiety, separation anxiety, humor, joy, jealousy, sharing, fear, and nurturance. The moral issues that extended beyond human interaction came mostly from television and also from folk literature. They included conflict, competition, cooperation and sharing, and good in relation to evil. Among the cosmic issues were birth (including fear, anxiety, separation anxiety, jealousy, and conflict), death and mourning (including punishment, separation, fear of the unknown, and acceptance), humor, war, crime and conflict, and construction in relation to destruction. Children have represented these types of issues within many different thematic contexts. For example, pretend death and birth have taken place with grocery store, hospital, and spaceship props. The issues of conflict and good in relation to evil have taken place in housekeeping play, the blocks area, and the outdoors, fueled only by imaginations.

Group Identity and Stereotypes

As children play, they plan, negotiate, disagree, solve problems, offer and receive nurture, offer and receive both attention and disapproval, and celebrate. Gender stereotypes appear rarely but are potent when they do arise, taking the form of remarks such as, "Those are girls' colors," "They can be boys' colors too," "Girls can't play," or "Only this fire girl." As the example below shows, children may also indicate awareness of skin color:

[Two children in the housekeeping and costume area have engaged in a performance. CH1 has been in the "audience" as the parent of the performers, participating as an observer and on-cue applauder. CH2 is engaged nearby in a parallel activity. CH1 then gets into a costume, takes the play microphone, and begins to perform.]

CH1:   [to CH2] "Come on, Mr. Brown."

ADULT: "His name isn't Brown. It's Smith."

CH1:   "Come on, Mr. Smith Brown."

CH2:   "My name is not Brown."

CH1:   [walking toward him] "You have a brown face."

[turns away to CH3] "Come on out." [CH1 invites CH3 to begin performing in her new costume. Despite the adult's valiant attempts to involve CH2 with the other children, CH2 returns to the parallel play activity.]

The significance of skin color varies for young children[6.1]; although young children generally play with one another based on mutual interest in the activity's content and degree of action.

Play Grammar

Regardless of the play context, youngsters' mutual development of the various oral script themes that they use during their sociodramatic play follows an

---

[6.1]Researchers have found that children between three and six years of age become aware of skin color (Clark & Clark, 1939; Goodman, 1964; Porter, 1971).

implicit "play grammar." The grammar, a representation of script theory, reflects the underlying grammatical relationships in the play. The capacity to communicate pretense through play signals appears to be part of the brain "wiring" (or potential) of normal children. It develops through children's social and physical interactions within a particular cultural context.

The seamless weaving together of shared novelty magnetizes young children, however briefly, as oral playwriting partners. The oral playwriting experience is both intimate and transcendent, and linear and nonlinear. Yet, the experience can unravel if the power balance shifts between players or their joint rhythm is disturbed. Sensitive teachers keep these considerations in mind, therefore, when they attempt to intervene. *The adult who can enter seamlessly into young children's oral playwriting demonstrates respect and validates the children's power to engage in this collaborative narrative.*

The underlying grammar system that emerges in play mirrors some nonlinear concepts in contemporary chaos and complexity theory. Children's theory of mind—their growing awareness of their own and others' thoughts, beliefs, deceptions, and intentions—also develops within nonlinear, emergent human interactions. The extended discussion of these dynamics—chaos and complexity theory and theory of mind—continues in the next two chapters.

7 Chaos and Complexity Theory

Many everyday experiences that we take for granted serve as the subject matter of chaos theory. Chaos theory explores nonlinear, dynamic, seemingly random experiences, and phenomena that, though different on the surface, manifest underlying regularities. For example, the weather, the behavior of crowds, or adult and child antics may look chaotic on the surface, but on closer study they reveal deeper patterns. Consider the weather. We often have difficulty predicting the weather within a few days. However, those of us living in northern climates expect that it will be warm in summer and cool in winter. Or what about waves? When we see waves at the seashore, they seem to break in predictably unpredictable ways. However, a photograph from a satellite reveals considerable regularity in the long phase movements of distant "scroll waves" (Briscoe, 1984; Sullivan, 1985).

We cannot always know when and how these regularities will take place. Indeed, we typically accept and live with them. *In a similar way, children negotiate their play activities by moving in and out of the play frame in both predictable and unpredictable forms, as described in the preceding chapter.* When we have a broader view and greater distance in space or time, or look at many samples of young children's play, we see deeper regularities more easily. In any case, those things that make being human interesting, puzzling, and significant are the nonlinear aspects of life—such as emotions, aesthetics, and other directly experienced and immediate events.

The introduction to Section Two set forth the relationship between deep imagery systems and surface forms of representation, such as the alphabet, grammar, and rules of games. Chapter 6 described the imagery systems, grammar, and rules of sociodramatic play. Chaos and complexity theorists also recognize systems that transform deep images into many varied surface forms that represent these images. The term *isomorphism* is a shorthand way to refer to these underlying relationships that may take different surface forms; analogies help humans infer the isomorphic connections. Young children directly and intuitively experience isomorphic relationships because their analogical thinking and isomorphic imagery is powerful and fluid. A few concepts from chaos theory may help us view everyday events differently, particularly children's nonlinear play and nonlinear teaching.

Sensitive Dependence on Initial Conditions

Definition

Most of us believe that if we put forth more effort, then we will accomplish more—and vice versa. In nonlinear terms, however, a small input may lead to a large output.

The term *Sensitive Dependence on Initial Conditions* (SDIC) refers to the "limited predictability" (Casti, 1994, p. 113) of the nonlinear relationship between initial events and their later manifestation. Examples that follow represent different nonlinear forms of reality and show how much more can happen when a seemingly small, initial event takes place.

Examples

- Missing a school bus by a few seconds translates into being late to school by two hours, because there's no other bus for an hour or no more buses at all that day.
- A butterfly flapping its wings in one part of the world may influence a tornado in another part of the world (Lorenz, cited in Peitgen, 1990), because weather systems have an underlying instability (Casti, 1994). Wind, temperature, moisture, and the Earth's relation to the moon and sun are among the many forces that interact to influence and augment the initial movement of small, flapping wings. Therefore, there is a "stretch" between the initial conditions and the "chaotic" transformations that later transpire. (It might help to imagine this stretch in the same way that an analogy is a stretch between the referent and its comparison; for example, "She [referent] married a lemon [analogue].")
- A single choice may turn around a lifetime of possibilities. A young child who chooses to attend a sibling's violin lesson, for example, may develop a passion for music. A seemingly small humiliation or success early in life might mean the difference between benevolent or hostile expectations of others in adulthood.
- A teacher who is highly directive and controlling may actually have less control over children's aggression when he is not present, whereas a teacher who permits more child involvement in planning and choosing may exert more influence on children's productivity, autonomy, and self-directed responsibility.

Relation to Play

When young children play effectively, they learn through observation and practice how to enter a play frame sensitively. For example, in Chapter 6, Dora successfully redirected, even if temporarily, the focus of energy away from the struggle over the dress to attention to the doll baby. When David, mentioned in

Chapter 4, felt deserted in the house area (an initial condition), he left the area and set in motion a flurry of fresh activities that subsequently expanded the house-area activities. Thus, initial conditions in play are subject to change through the influence of other players. These initial conditions are neither predetermined nor random. Within the play framework, the general process of oral script development is predictable, but the specific product is not.

The shared event knowledge of the players is an initial condition that might influence the direction and depth of the play. If players can adapt to each other's different knowledge backgrounds, then they are more likely to extend the play.

The predictability or grammatical structure of play constitutes a kind of "attractor" in chaos theory. When weaker, the attractor (or underlying grammatical system) permits more random and unpredictable representations. Nevertheless, these representations still retain their relationship to the underlying attractor. Although play may have weak ties to reality, children's creativity becomes apparent in their fantasy play. They create connections by using analogies. The creative process functions best when there is greater stretch between the analogue and the referent. Children's play and their grasp of meaning are therefore unpredictable. In a similar way, *different children doing the same thing at the same time may have different experiences; the same children doing different things at different times may have equivalent experiences.*

The variety of play themes and negotiated solutions in particular play episodes are unpredictable, although the underlying rules of play and the scope of the oral scripts are generally predictable. *Children generate play scripts that depend on the initial conditions of the play context and the player's experiences. The play evolves unpredictably within the predictability of the underlying enplotting (planning)-enacting (doing) rules of play.*

Self-Organization of Systems

Definition

Another chaos-theory concept, self-organization of systems refers to the tendency of a gathering (for example, a mob, a cocktail party, elements in a weather system, ingredients in a recipe, leaves in a stream, atoms in a cloud chamber, molecules in gases, liquids, and solids) to evolve and develop a coherent process.

Examples

Tornados are self-organizing systems; shifting winds, or a small, circular shake of liquid in a bottle, seem to organize in an increasingly coherent and turbulent way. The climate of each classroom is also a self-organizing system. For example, when young children make reasonable choices among activities and can pace their participation, they tend to take more responsibility for their own self-direction when the teacher is absent. In a parallel way, when five- and six-year-olds enter a burst of spontaneous giggling, the giggling tends to spread and grow in a self-organized manner until the energy eventually dissipates. There appear to be "predictably unpredictable" attractions between the mix of children and the class-room climate.

Problem solving is another self-organizing process. Brain studies confirm that people do not solve social and complex problems one part at a time in a linear way. Rather, during problem solving, brain cells function in holistic, self-similar ways making connections and creating networks.

Relation to Play

Youngsters organize and solve many problems that arise during play. They collaboratively plan their sociodramatic play scripts (a process of metacommunication when they talk to, signal, or prompt one another). They then play out the oral script using their individual imagery. The oral sociodramatic play scripts consist of conventions and rules that generate an infinite set of surface combinations. *The grammar of play is thus self-organizing.*

Teachers who consider the self-organizing capacity of young children can adapt varied experiences for different children. They understand that different physical or social experiences can represent the same underlying dynamic theme, such as cyclical change. They can be secure in the knowledge that young children will induce the imagery.

Problem solving during sociodramatic play entails a combination of logic (metacommunication) and intuition (imagery). The networks of neurons in youngsters' brains organize the logic and intuition in self-similar patterns on different size scales as fractals, discussed further below.

Fractals

Definition

Like the networks of neurons in the brain, fractals describe self-similar patterns that appear on smaller to larger size scales. "Fractals are curves that are irregular all over. Moreover, they have exactly the same degree of irregularity at all scales of measurement" (Casti, 1994, p. 232).

Examples

Fractals describe jagged perimeters such as rocky coastlines and broccoli. The different scales, smaller and larger, are self-similar. Another example of a self-similar relationship is that children feel more comfortable with mathematics and achieve more when they work with a teacher who feels more comfortable with mathematics (Karp, 1988).

Relation to Play

Children of different ages with different language skills who enter similar oral sociodramatic play scripts retain the underlying grammatical structure of the play frame. *As they develop as players, children retain the play grammar but play for longer periods of time with different degrees of thematic coherence and linguistic complexity.* In these ways, the degree of expanded development, a fractal image, follows a similar underlying grammar of play.

Children build meaning during the transitions between the self-similar system of rules and their representations; the transitions oscillate between metacommunication and imagery. Complexity theory considers these transitions of meaning.

Complexity Theory and Phase Transitions

Definition

A part of chaos theory, complexity theory proposes a process—in particular, phase transition—by which learning takes place. Phase transition refers to the "bridge" between one state and another, the transition system that includes the time before insight and the crossing over to meaning.

Examples

Children watch the world around them carefully, to capture the precise instant when a light switches on or when heated water begins to boil and bubble, to know how far they need to move a magnet before it will no longer attract a key, and to identify the exact spot to stand on the see-saw in order to tip it to the other side.

A phase transition, like the fulcrum on the see-saw, is that turning point when one state changes into another, such as moving from up to down; turning from on to off; shifting from calm to turbulent; moving from in to out; changing from a liquid to a gas; transmuting from a milling group to a mob; defining a puzzle then finding its solution; being naive and then knowledgeable; and so forth. Effective teachers try to create the learning conditions, including play, within which phase transitions can take place.

Relation to Play

Play features a dynamic phase transition between reality and pretense; metacommunication and representation; and enplotment and enactment. *Phase transitions are areas of opportunity for teacher or peer intervention; they are the moments during which meaningful, extended, and expanded development for children may take place.*

Phase transitions serve as "attractors" that draw children to a change of focus. For example, when children identify or change a play theme or direction, they appear to grant a "warrant" that signals an agreement to proceed together (Cook-Gumperz, cited in Van Hoorn, Nourot, Scales, & Alward, 1999, p. 227). "The boundary between two or more attractors in a dynamical system serves as a threshold of a kind that seems to govern so many ordinary processes, from the breaking of materials to the making of decisions" (Gleick, 1987, p. 233).

The phase transition process helps children to bridge non-meaning and meaning. Phase transitions also help children to become aware of other people's meanings and move toward building a theory of mind, the subject of the next chapter.

Chaos Theory and Phase Transitions: Some Final Thoughts

This chapter discussed the nonlinear nature of chaos and complexity theory using several definitions of concepts, examples, and their relationship to play. Chaos theory attempts to understand the "predictable unpredictability" of everyday events. It is a body of theoretical work that focuses on the processes and relationships that unfold in the physical and social worlds.

Learning takes place during phase transitions, the "tipping points" between one state of being and another, ignorance and knowledge, or self-involvement and caring. Teachers who respect the power of play in children's learning attempt to tip the oscillating balance between irrelevance and meaning, boredom and engagement. They help children negotiate freedom and independence, and responsibility and impulsivity, by sensitively scaffolding rather than controlling for its own sake. Chaos and complexity theory, along with script theory, confirms the generally predictable but specifically unpredictable nature of children's play and construction of meaning.

CHAPTER

8 Theory of Mind

"Theory of mind" refers to a person's capacity to be aware of his or her own as well as others' internal experiences. By interacting with others, young children gradually realize that they have thoughts, beliefs, intentions, and feelings. They also infer that others have thoughts, beliefs, intentions, and feelings as well. Researchers are divided about exactly when children construct a theory of mind, though most agree that it's between the ages of two and four years.

Researchers study how children represent real and imaginary thought, and how they think about thinking, motives, beliefs, false beliefs, and deception (Astington, 1993; Astington & Pelletier, 1999; Bartsch & Wellman, 1995). Their work points to the isomorphism between children's narrative structures in sociodramatic play scripts and youngsters' developing theory of mind (Ibid.; Garvey, 1993; Harris, 2000; Harris & Kavanaugh, 1993). Children represent implicit meaning in explicit forms during sociodramatic play, making their theory of mind accessible to study. It is apparent that taking a role, such as becoming a younger sibling or an adult medical worker, suggests that the player imputes thoughts, feelings, beliefs, and intentions to the role that they are playing. During their play, children show that they can interpret and predict the behavior of others. The act of pretend play itself involves an as-if/if-then relationship in which the player behaves "as if" he or she is another person and predicts that "if" he or she behaves in a certain way "then" the other player will respond in an expected way. In effect, when children explore and play, they build mental models, images of how things work and what they might expect other children and adults to think and do.

The growth in a child's ability to tell a story ties in with the growth of a typical four-year-old's theory of mind. Researchers suggest that young children can narrate events first with action sequences, then reaction sequences, and then episodic narratives in which they set and attain goals (Benson, 1997).

Four-year-old children's responses to adult questions suggest that they have a sense of what the adults might think is acceptable behavior. For example, Kay and Ira sat on the couch in the pretend hospital waiting room. They held hands, moved near each other frequently, built with blocks together, and hugged on the block-bed. When Kay sat alone, she pulled on her lip and looked off into the distance. In the hospital center during one play session, the following events took place:

[They play at kissing, "mwah," in the direction of others who continue to play around them. Then, drawing closer to each other, they hug.]

IRA: [treating doll patient] "The baby has blood pressure."

KAY: "I can't believe it."

IRA: [applies tissue to the doll patient, then uses a crayon box to pound on the doll patient; kisses toward the air, then Kay does the same]

KAY: "Oh, there's another fire."

PAUL: "Are you playing doctor? We're playing fire." [smells empty liquid detergent container and then uses it as a hose]

IRA: "Look! It's over there." [Puts his arm around Kay, lying on the floor and hugging, while directing Paul to put out the fire.]

KAY: [pointing to Ira] "He died." [She rubs Ira's back. He opens his eyes, wiggles, and smiling, they hug. Sixteen minutes later, when they separate, she rises from the floor, and gets on the examining table.]

JUNE: [wearing surgical shoes, doses Kay with a spoonful of medicine]

IRA: [at the same time, wraps a bandage around Kay's ankle, studies her head, then touches her forehead as if to test her temperature] "Say the eye chart." [After she recites the eye-chart letters, they sit on the couch and kiss.]

JUNE: [wearing a stethoscope] "Who wants to be a police?"

PAUL: "Ira, do you want to be a police? Someone's dead." [pointing to the doll]

TEACHER: [to Ira and Kay] "How are you doing?"

IRA: "We're playing hospital. We're not playing fire anymore."

[The preceding day, when the teacher saw them hugging and asked what they were doing, they informed her that they were playing fire and were "saving each other." On another day, when they were discussing being boyfriend and girlfriend, the teacher entered the area and began to help children with their surgical costumes, then invited them by name, at which point Ira and Kay joined in the costume process.]

IRA: [He gets on the examining table. Kay waits on the couch with her left knee crossed over her right knee.]

PAUL: [pointing to doll] "Will water keep her alive?"

JUNE: [with stethoscope] ". . . healing her." [turning to Ira on the examining table] "I have to operate."

KAY: [to June] "Is Jim your boyfriend?"

JUNE: [nods] "OK. Ready to operate." [cuts gauze and wraps it around Ira's arm]

KAY: [soothes Ira's forehead, puts on surgical shoes, and sits on couch with her fingers to her mouth, pulling on her lip]

IRA: [After the "surgery" is finished, he comes to the couch, removes a prop box from the couch, sits beside Kay, and ruffles her hair. She smiles at him. He hugs her and she places her head on his shoulder.]

KAY: [to June, who has placed a band on Ira's wrist and squeezes in next to Ira] "No, don't sit there." [June places her arm around her patient, Ira, while Kay and Ira hold hands.]

During seventy-five minutes of these synopsized events, the following themes swirled around Kay and Ira, in some of which they took part: eye chart, broken arm, several broken legs, multiple examinations, surgeries, medical dressings on children and dolls, dress-up activities, mother and baby doll patients, sick baby dolls, a dead baby doll, telephone messages and emergencies, waiting-room activities and recording of medical data, writing of prescriptions, feeding of ice cream, packing of picnic food, hiding in a closet, pretending to be a baby in a cradle, and sleeping in a cradle.

These four-year-olds appeared to comply with their teacher's efforts to distract them, but were aware of her intention to attract them toward play themes other than boyfriend-girlfriend. Their behavior suggests that they had a working theory of mind. Similarly, toddlers can knowingly, with humor, offer a "wrong" name, preschoolers can offer a "wrong" gender, and children of primary age can offer a "wrong" answer to a question (Wolfenstein, 1954).

When children purposefully distort what they know to be true, they reveal their power to understand the difference, an achievement of self-awareness and a theory of mind. Young children, therefore, reveal their theory of mind as a system of relationships between underlying images and the many meaningful surface forms that represent these images. The concluding statement that follows pulls together the preceding chapters that dealt with research and theory and looks ahead to implications for the practical implementation of nonlinear theory in nonlinear early education.

Toward a Dynamic Theory of Play and Meaning

So, how do script theory and narrative structures, chaos and complexity theory, and theory of mind help us understand young children's development of meaning?

- Script theory involves the *relationship* between the underlying rules of play (metacommunication) and the variety of surface forms of imagery that children create together.
- Theory of mind involves the *relationship* between self-awareness (metacognition) and an awareness of the thoughts, beliefs, and motives of others.

■ Chaos theory involves the *relationship* between predictably unpredictable phenomena in physical, social, and aesthetic experience.

These theories have in common a *nonlinear relationship* between underlying forms, rules, images, and attractors, and the variety of emergent surface forms. There is a transformational, generative relationship between the underlying and surface forms. *The three theoretical perspectives focus on the dynamic, nonlinear nature of meaning.* The commonality among these theories adds credibility to the practice of nonlinear early education.

Valuing Predictable Unpredictability

The linear view is that theory "solves problems" (Schrader, 2000, p. 397) in order to "to resolve ambiguity, to reduce irregularity to uniformity, and to show that what happens is somehow intelligible and predictable" (Schrader, 2000, p. 397, citing Laudan, 1984, p. 13). The nonlinear view of a dynamic theory of play and meaning welcomes predictable unpredictability as the basis for addressing the question ("solving the problem") of what is worthwhile learning. In early education, the experience of ambiguity is not harmful, but useful.

It is uniformity that does not serve early education. The predictable in early learning is its predictable unpredictability. The dynamic theory of play and meaning celebrates ambiguity, predictable unpredictability, and the place of meaning at the core of early education. Within the dynamic processes of play and meaning, young children demonstrate their power as agents in their own learning.

The dynamic theory of play and meaning coincides with neuroscientists' current findings about the dynamic, holistic ways in which the human brain functions. Neuroscientists have accepted that the brain solves problems holistically, as do young children at play.

As children interact with the physical world, other children, and adults, they experience phase transitions that lead to fresh perceptions. Children perceive new meaning as first-time figures emerge from a background of familiar experiences. Their brains process these fluid experiences in fractal, holistic ways. Children use and expand their event knowledge as they develop oral scripts with others. The feedback that children receive during interactions with the physical world and others during play, and during their other daily life experiences, helps them to develop a theory of mind. *Play serves as a lymphatic system for the development of meaning through the holistic processes of the brain.*

The Nonlinear Dynamic Theory of Play and Meaning

Figure 8.1, Nonlinear Dynamic Theories Weave a Nonlinear Dynamic Model of Teaching Practice, offers a visual rendition of the *permeable and fluid integration* of the nonlinear dynamic theories. Together, the three theories confirm the active ways that young children develop meaning through play. The dynamic relationships that define these theories reflect the way we perceive meaning; the young

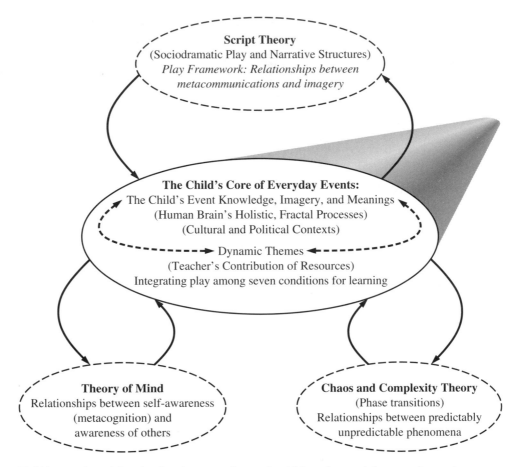

Fluid integration of theories flow in a recurring cycle within and around the core of everyday events; theories are modified by the study of everyday events.

FIGURE 8.1   Nonlinear Dynamic Theories Weave a Nonlinear Dynamic Model of Teaching Practice

child's display of meaning during play confirms the implicit dynamic relationships. Event knowledge flows in a recurring spiral within and around the core of everyday events. Young children acquire event knowledge and a theory of mind within the chaotic flow of daily experiences that include play and other conditions for learning.

The theories depicted in Figure 8.1 support the idea that isomorphic relationships represent the "chaotic" way the physical and social world functions, the way that children develop a theory of mind, and the way that children build oral scripts as they engage in sociodramatic play.

The distinct *core of everyday events* in a child's life includes the event knowledge and imagery that she develops within the limits of a particular cultural and political context. Event knowledge grows as young children have a variety of experiences at home, in the community, and at school. By collaborating with one another, children represent their combined event knowledge during play. They learn together about one another's event knowledge. Children both represent their own event knowledge and learn from the representations of their playmates' event knowledge.

Teachers can intervene by providing resources, and indirect and direct forms of intervention. (See Chapter 10 for intervention strategies.) Teachers assess children's event knowledge as the basis for deciding if, how, and when to intervene. They influence children's event knowledge by thoughtfully selecting and clustering a variety of experiences from which children may perceive underlying dynamic themes. Phase transitions (children's fresh perception of meaning) result from the match between children's event knowledge and the teacher's relevant intervention.

Play, consisting of an interaction of imagery and metacommunication, is a "breathing model" of how children develop meanings and solve problems. Teachers support, but do not interfere with, the ways that children learn and develop meaning and solve problems.

During the teaching-learning process, it is important to keep in mind that implicit meaning, a holistic function, may appear in explicit representations that may take many forms. The challenge for teachers is to create happenings with children that *balance* both planning and adapting to emerging events. The challenge is to connect adult understanding of humanity's fund of knowledge (Dewey, 1933) with young children's experiential ways of learning. Teachers can meet the challenge by welcoming more than one interpretation of an issue.

For teachers of younger, rather than older, children, the translation of humanity's fund of knowledge requires the creation of many phase transition happenings in ways that cross physical, social, and aesthetic domains. The challenge for teachers is to schedule and provision for play.

The dynamics common to these theories and to children's play make clear the kind of nonlinear curriculum in which young children can build new meaning. *Dynamic themes*, such as cyclical change or synergy, convey meaning in the multiple surface representations of a variety of physical, social, and representational experiences. *There is an isomorphic relationship between dynamic themes and the multiple forms in which children experience them. That relationship is consistent with the dynamics of script theory, chaos and complexity theory, and theory of mind conceptions.*

Section Three, Integrating Dynamic Practice, follows. It opens with two chapters that discuss how to set up a learning environment and organize a context to support a rich dynamic-themes curriculum. The two chapters that close Section Three provide a repertoire of thematically organized experiences.

SECTION THREE

Integrating Dynamic Practice

This section presents practical implementations of a dynamic-themes curriculum. Chapter 9, Beginning with Nonlinear Environmental Design, and Chapter 10, Classroom Organization, recommend physical and social environments. These chapters also suggest ways for teachers to support play-oriented, meaning-centered, child-centered learning. The environmental context supports connection making and facilitates youngsters' exploration and play in ways that light up the underlying dynamic images and themes.

Chapter 11, Building Play into Curriculum Strands: Play Is a Condition for Learning, and Chapter 12, Dynamic Themes: Weaving the Strands, present two ways in which teachers can integrate the seven conditions for learning. Chapter 11 looks at the typical school organization of parallel curricular strands—the physical, quantitative, social, and representational concepts—that children develop by using the integrated conditions for learning. Chapter 12 provides examples of dynamic themes that weave the curricular strands in Chapter 11 throughout a school year.

9 Beginning with Nonlinear Environmental Design

Just as societies, communities, and families set the stage for defining permissible play, classroom design communicates what kind of play is acceptable. The classroom in which each child owns a desk and works individually at it for much of the day signals a linear outlook and a single way to interpret experiences; children's self-organized play in such a setting is rare.

In a nonlinear classroom, play is decentralized into small-group meeting areas. The decentralized classroom uses physical space to communicate that children can organize their activities independently and welcome others to collaborate and play. This chapter discusses how to create a nonlinear environmental design at the beginning of the school year. The nonlinear environment helps to build a caring community of independent and responsible members who are empowered to play with ideas to make new connections. Within this setting, young children have many opportunities to play alone and with one another, and to organize their time within a thoughtfully planned educational environment.

Beginnings

Children learn during play. Therefore, teachers must provide them with a safe environment for play. Effective teachers organize a population of ten to twenty-five youngsters in the artificial confinement of a classroom in ways that can be educational. Children will feel and be secure when they have a shared understanding of the expectations, possibilities, traffic patterns, and scope of their rights and privileges as well as their limits within the classroom. This understanding grows out of the experiences on which their teacher helps them to focus.

Meaningful learning through play takes place mainly within small groups and, with some materials, solitary play. To organize a classroom for mainly small-group and individual work, teachers should plan carefully and be aware of the dynamics of self-organizing groups. There is a natural ebb and flow between areas in early childhood classrooms when some children spend more or less time immersed in an activity. When teachers spend most of their time circulating during the early days and weeks of school, children build a sense of security within their new environment and learn how to pursue their goals.

The next section offers a glimpse at ways to think about the first days of school and the value of teacher circulation in helping children build a sense of responsibility, independence, and caring. The ages listed include different principles that you might generalize to the full spectrum of early childhood. Thus you may want to adapt relevant activities and practices with younger children for older children.

Infants and Toddlers

All settings for infants and toddlers need to have one or more teaching assistants who work with the teacher all day, depending on total group size. Different states require different teacher-child-space ratios.

Infant rooms include framed pictures on the walls at children's eye levels—near the floor, crib, and at the diapering table. These pictures can depict a single object with deep hues. These rooms also include mobiles, rattles that attach to children's wrists with Velcro™ closings, or hand-held rattles. There might be materials with contrasting textures, and containers into which children can drop items or from which they can retrieve objects too large to swallow. Infant rooms also feature push-button and sturdy pull toys as well as "jack-in-the-box" types of toys; small blocks; stacking materials; and abacus-type frames.

Each child's personal storage space is labeled with a name and photograph of the child. The teachers and toddlers wear name tags attached by clips to their clothing.

For children who can crawl and walk, there are areas with larger and smaller, more active and more sedentary activities. Toddlers might have a communal wall on which to draw with crayons hung by strings. There could be an area for pull toys and building blocks as well as housekeeping furnishings. Toddlers (and older children), particularly those who may be struggling with separation anxiety, may find comfort in play dough or water play.

These rooms may have child-sized tables and chairs, although toddlers often choose to engage in most activities on the floor. If your room has multiple pieces, even half a dozen stacking toys or objects in a sensory box, consider placing them on a felt mat or tray to serve as a "playground." The mat may focus players' attention, when a child is not walking off with an object, and simplify cleanup. Less is often more—as long as the play materials provide contrast or aesthetic experience.

Toddlers tend to herd together, so be sure there is plenty of elbow room between defined areas. Have multiple sets of new or revisited materials and objects as well. To eliminate or reduce waiting, prepare materials before the children arrive.

Planning with Infants and Toddlers

Planning with children begins after you greet individual children upon arrival and escort each one, dyads, or triads, to play areas. Family members sit out of the way during an adjustment period and redirect their children to the teacher for assistance. Toddlers often will go directly to an area that they find attractive. A main goal for teachers is to offer a possible next step or material to extend the amount of time or the quality of the play; for example, "What else can you do with that crayon over here?" "Let's see how you can make it wider." "Show me again how you did that."

Sometimes, fewer playthings can help focus youngsters' attention. Teachers can place playthings on low shelves so that children can retrieve them independently. Some teachers change the selection of cabinets or boxes that are available at any one time, a strategy that can encourage toddlers to focus and refocus their attention during an activity period. Boxes sometimes contain particular categories of playthings, such as animal figures or colored cubes, in order to offer a rotating focus. That way, the teacher can create intentional physical contrasts as well as planned verbal interactions that build toddlers' vocabulary.

After all the children have arrived, the teacher might invite smaller groupings of children to gather with an adult. Each adult can then read the group a story or engage with them in a tabletop activity, water play, or a limited selection of construction options. Each adult should keep track of her space and her particular children to maintain a safe setting and a secure feeling for children. This proactive attention can minimize accidents, scuffles, or separation anxiety.

Proactive teacher monitoring is essential for children who are likely to react with aggression in the absence of adequate language skills. Consistent proactive monitoring by an adult might prevent biting or hitting as children refocus their choices. The assigned adult also can separate a potentially clashing dyad.

Verbal Harmony: A Form of Teacher Intervention

While infants are learning to understand language, they benefit when the teacher provides a running, cheerful description of what they are doing: "Oh, you're picking up the red ring and putting it on the pole; now you're picking up the blue ring and adding it to the pole; now you're picking up the green ring and putting it on top of the blue ring. You have one-two-three rings. Let's see which ring you will pick up next." Such verbal harmony is useful during daily routines as well as play activities; for example, "Now it's time to put on your bib. Up we go onto the feeding table. There's a hungry Bobby. In goes the spoon of potatoes" or "Here's your spoon and your bowl of cereal. You certainly can eat those corn flakes by yourself." Verbal harmony during routines, while playful, also helps to build oral language skills, particularly during outdoor play.

An infant experiences as play the ritual of an adult's singing a nursery rhyme while the youngster faces a corresponding picture. Adults can provide this ritual before or after feeding or diapering. Such rituals afford a sense of predictability and security and add to children's language awareness and development. Infants welcome chanting games, for example: "Let's button the button. You touch the button. This is a button, button. Now you touch the button, button. Now I touch the button, button, now you touch the button."

Verbal harmony continues through the preschool and kindergarten years within the context of daily activities. Teachers accompany activities with talk, and model vocabulary and grammar use while appreciating the processes of children's play. The classroom descriptions that follow outline ways to establish a nonlinear classroom beginning in the earliest days of school.

Preschool and Kindergarten

Most preschool settings have one or more teaching assistants; a few kindergartens have one teaching assistant for all or part of the day.

First Day

The teacher and children are wearing name tags attached to loops of twine around their necks. As she distributes the name tags, the teacher shows the children their individual storage spaces, labeled with their names and a colorful sticker. She holds the name tag next to the storage name tag and points out that they are the same.

The whole group meets together for five minutes as the teacher points out those areas that are prepared for their use that day. These areas include the sociodramatic play area, which contains a minimum number of items, and the library corner, which features some beautifully illustrated books whose covers face the room. Play areas also include colored pencils, crayons, and paper at a table; plasticene or play dough that has been softened and placed on smooth boards at another table; peg boards or other small building materials such as grooved blocks or colored cubes; other manipulable material set on a felt surface (which helps to contain the multiple pieces) on the floor or on a table; and a puzzle rack with several puzzles, each of which rests on a felt surface.

A different group of four-year-olds enter their new room at the child-care center in September after having visited it on many occasions for shared activities during the preceding year. For each child, the teacher has prepared a name card attached with Velcro™ to a bulletin board in the group meeting area. In addition, each child and teacher wears a name tag attached by a clip to his or her clothing.

Teacher (smiling and making eye contact): "I am so happy to be here with you today. First we will talk about what you might want to do this morning. Then, you will have a chance to choose an area in which to play."

The teacher, touring the room with the children, points out the empty Velcro™ strips near various centers, such as the sociodramatic center, the block center, the science center, and the computer center. She says, "That's like a ticket to get in. When children fill all of the Velcro™ strips with peoples' name cards, it shows that the area is full and that you need to choose another center until there is an open Velcro™ strip. When you leave, please put your name tag back on the bulletin board, like this, so there will be space for the next person to come in." (Several children take turns showing how they move and remove the name cards at various centers. Note: Some teachers use clothespins instead of Velcro™, and the children practice clipping and unclipping the clothespins.) Amazingly, with reminders interspersed during the first few weeks of the year, the system works, with children reiterating to one another what they are doing.

The use of Velcro™ and name cards for entry into an area encourages children to be independent. Instead of Velcro™, some teachers place a numeral and the number of dots in each area to indicate the number of children who may play. When children look to see whether a Velcro™ spot is open or compare the number of players with the numeral or dots, they are engaging in mathematical problem solving. Other teachers prefer children to take responsibility for deciding when there is enough space in an area.

For some children, the beginning of the school year can be fraught with separation anxiety. Sensitive administrators have created a gradual separation schedule for parents and children. An occasional kindergarten-age child may need a few days to make the transition. Tears or tantrums occasionally accompany separation, even for a child who has enjoyed the school activities. Teachers can respect tears as a form of communication and continue to engage the child in comforting activities. Sensitive teachers take special care to be with the child during transition times when anxiety might resurface.

Planning with the Children

The kindergarten teacher begins to plan with the whole group: "When you use any of the table activities, you will see if there is a chair. If not, then you may choose some place else that has space. You will have a chance to try many different areas this week. Please remember to raise your hand when you are finished in an area to let me know that you are ready to choose someplace else. Everybody, let's see your favorite hand for signaling—raise it and . . . put it down. Wonderful."

"Now, we have space at the clay table. Please raise your hand if you would like to start there. You may walk to the table after you see your name on the chart." (Six children raise their hands. The teacher places their preprinted name cards in six slots of the large planning pocket chart, while the children observe.)

The teacher: "Please raise your hand if you would like to start at the block table. (Six children raise their hands. She places four name cards in the four slots of the pocket chart.) "There is space for four children, and six children want to play. There is not enough space for two children now, but they might come back when there is space later, after they use another area."

She turns to the two children for whom space is not available: "In which other area would you like to begin today, Les? Van?" After all the children are settled in an area, the teacher circulates during the fifty to seventy-five minutes of center time (activity period).

Primary Grades

Few primary grades for children between six and eight years of age have a teaching assistant for part of the day.

The teacher and children are wearing name tags clipped to their clothing during the early days of school. As she distributes the name tags, the teacher shows the children their individual storage spaces labeled with their names. The one-hour to one-and-a-half-hour activity period begins with a whole-group planning session. Part of the function of planning time is to share choices available for that day. The teacher might use a pocket-chart format or list children's names under the prewritten areas of the day, with the number of slots available in each area. Listing the number of slots, based on enough space or materials, minimizes tensions over inclusion or exclusion. The teacher might also organize a "buddy system" so that children can call on one another for reminders or help—another way for them to build independence from adults.

Early in the year, play activities might take place in a library center, a writing or drawing center with space for six to eight children, a sociodramatic play area, a table construction project, an animal center, and a games and puzzles area. Teachers can set out materials before the children enter the classroom in order to reduce waiting time and to permit more interaction with the children.

The teacher's main function during the first month or two is to circulate among the youngsters. That way, teachers can firmly establish the questions that children will need to ask themselves later, when the teacher is working directly with small groups. For example:

"What will I do with this when I am finished?"

"What might I do next?"

"Which buddy might I ask for help before I seek help from the teacher?"

Teachers should assume that different children will engage in similar activities at a different pace and can take responsibility for moving safely to another activity. In these ways, children function with increasing independence and a sense of empowerment.

Planning with Children

Helping children plan their independent play choices adds to their self-motivated participation and their wholesome focus on the play. After the first month or two of the school year, when teachers engage in small-group direct instruction with children, the independence of the remainder of the group is critical to the successful functioning of a learning community. If other small groups are playing independently and fruitfully because the classroom routines have been well and clearly established, significant small-group instruction can occur.

Choices

It is difficult for children to choose an activity if they do not know what it means. Planning time provides an opportunity to share possibilities. The youngest children need frequent small-group and individual planning and replanning. Preschoolers can begin with a whole-group planning session and then progress to some ongoing replanning with teacher support. After a month or two of working together, kindergarten- and primary-age children usually can manage an entire activity period following a whole-group planning session.

For the sake of safety, security, and peace, teachers might remind themselves that children's participating in everything is not necessarily a right but a privilege based on readiness. When considering activity options, it is useful to plan for varied degrees of challenge and complexity or types of projects. It is also useful to renew centers regularly in order to energize children's participation. *There are different degrees of choice based on competence and performance that include:*

What? Among all the available play areas, in which one do you plan to begin?

How many? There is space for four people here. Who wants to join this center?

Either/or: Do you prefer to begin the day in this or that play area?

Now/later: You may choose to do this now or later.

Now: This is the time to be in this center. (The "Now" decision may be based on the fact that a child has never tried something and has had other opportunities and degrees of choice. Or it may be that the teacher has planned to bring together a few children who are ready to learn a particular game or skill, or to review a procedure, because his observations indicate that they need extra help or an opportunity to extend their possibilities.) Teachers use "now" sparingly in the context of a center-based classroom.

Choices give children opportunities to learn self-pacing and self-organization. However, as the teacher circulates she can help children expand or extend their involvement through supportive interventions, such as verbal harmony, brief participation in the play, or expressions of appreciation for children's intent.

Primary-age children's approaches to the world may confound even the most organized teacher's plans. Young children, after all, can be original and creative. They might flexibly change the rules of a game or comfortably complete only part of what the teacher expected. Or their moods may fluctuate from helpfulness to withdrawal or disgust. The teacher's sense of humor and sympathetic appreciation of young children's sometimes erratic development go far to support the progress of a caring community. Smile and circulate! When you circulate, you can take advantage of opportunities to create phase transition "happenings."

The Teacher Circulates

After all the children are settled in an area, the teacher circulates continually during "center time." As she circulates, she quietly speaks to individual children or small groups. This low tone of voice keeps the sound level in the classroom down, lets youngsters concentrate, and shows that the teacher values the children's work. Short of an emergency, she would not call out to children across the heads of others. As she moves around the room, she makes herself available to children who may need her assistance. She helps children in the following ways:

She appreciates:

"You're really thinking about what you are doing."

"What an original idea! I really want to see that when you have done more in that area."

"It's wonderful to see how you are sharing those colored pencils."

"I love seeing that smile."

"How did you figure out that hard puzzle? What did you do first?" "Thanks for showing me your building. Let me get the camera."

She nods and smiles. She makes or returns eye contact and smiles. She pays close attention, evident in her posture, while observing.

He helps children to plan:

"Where will you put the materials when you finish?"

"When you finish, what will you do next?"

"Do you want to save your picture in the folder or hang it in the frame on the bulletin board? "

"Please return the book to the shelf before you go to the table." "Finish up what you are doing. In five minutes, it will be time to begin cleaning up."

"Where could we put that so you can remember to keep working on it this afternoon?"

She helps brings children together:

"Let's see what Pat is doing."

"Pat, how could we help you build in this direction?"

"It looks as if Robin could use an extra pair of hands. Let's see how you might help."

"How could you make it bigger with Lou's help?"

"You're both about finished, so you might want to try this game next."

"When there is space, we need to find a way to include friends."

He engages in some fleeting teaching:

"What other directions might you try?"

"What does this remind you of?"

"When did something like that happen to you?"

"If it doesn't work right side up, what other ways might you try?"

"Let's compare these with one another by lining them up."

For older children:

"How are these the same? Different?"

For younger children, after modeling a few samples:

"In this basket, put together the pieces that are the same color." (For older children: "Put together the pieces whose names begin with the same sound.")

"You've created a rhomboid or oval shape with the clay. Show us how you can make another oval shape that's thinner."

The teacher may remodel a task in a new way. She may ask a child to restate what she is doing. He may remodel standard grammatical usage in context. She may describe or explain an idea that emerges; for example, "That water on the sand looks like the erosion we saw at the beach. How might you reduce the amount of erosion?"

He engages in assessment, noticing:

—which children are impulsive when using sedentary activities and may need more frequent encouragement, task partitioning, and replanning.

—which children need more time to engage in different activities.

—which children are having difficulty with coordination and may need adaptive scissors, textured pencils, or more elbow room.

—which children may need close monitoring and attention during their transitions from one activity to another.

—which children may need tasks with fewer steps or instructions.

—which children can handle fewer choices.

—which children need a reduced field of sight rather than facing others.

—which children need help moving next to another child in a parallel-play situation.

—which children work smoothly together and which need to play in separate areas.

The teacher provides time for children to share their ongoing activities with one another. Children can showcase their finished work by looking at one another's efforts, talking about their drawing or constructions, reading their writing, or parading around the room or into other classrooms with their productions.

By continuously circulating throughout the room, teachers can establish a secure classroom climate and help children become responsible and independent. The activity period during the early weeks of school lets teachers learn about the unique strengths and needs of each child while steadily creating a harmonious environment through modeling and talking.

Building Autonomy and Shared Responsibility

Teachers with a vision of play in early childhood anticipate and prepare the kind of classroom framework in which children can build autonomy, independence, and responsibility. Autonomy emerges when children have strong, intrinsic motives for their activities. You can help them to talk about and celebrate their goals and movement toward them. More autonomy for children means shared responsibility and fewer instances that require teacher intervention. Indeed, autonomous children continue to function compatibly and independently in the teacher's absence.

Therefore, it is worthwhile to invest time and energy at the beginning of the year to help children self-organize. Teachers can circulate among small groups of youngsters, describe activities, appreciate children's efforts, help children plan, bring children together, teach briefly, and assess children's needs. The next chapter discusses additional strategies for organizing the school day.

10 Classroom Organization

How does a nonlinear classroom actually function? This chapter addesses that question by exploring how ethical teachers organize time, space, and intervention.

Schedule

Early-childhood education programs consist of markedly different schedules, including half-days, part- or full-weeks, extended-day part- or full-weeks, full-day daily school days, and full-day daily school or child-care center schedules. However, regardless of program schedule, play is an important provision and condition for learning. Research suggests that a minimum of thirty minutes affords children the chance to create sociodramatic play (Christie, Johnsen, & Peckover, 1988). Some children, though, may need thirty minutes to engage in a safe activity before they can try new things (Paley, 1984). When you consider start-up and close-down time as well as transition times, thirty minutes is perhaps more minimal than experienced teachers would suggest. Fifty- to seventy-five-minute activity periods permit children to pursue several activities in depth.

Transitions Are Problematic

Prolific transitions (for example, every ten to twenty minutes) during a school day suggest a focus on whole-group, linear, teacher-directed activity. Transitions also require a great deal of time spent on the mechanics of start up and close down. For the youngest children and for children with perceptual challenges, these frequent interruptions can make it particularly difficult to shift their focus. For all children, frequent, brief whole-group activities and close-down times implicitly teach that it is not worth investing personal energy in school activities. The youngsters conclude that they won't have enough time to develop and complete projects, and their intrinsic motivation erodes.

When teachers build routines with children for a limited number of transition times, children can develop their independence and sense of responsibility.

For example, rituals during transition times can create a feeling of predictability and a positive classroom climate because children can manage themselves and feel a sense of control over predictable events. Rituals might include explaining where to replace particular materials, how to handle a wet painting, how to replace a scissors pointing down, what to do when a clean-up task is completed, which pathway to take in getting coats, and how to sit companionably in a group meeting area.

To support a positive classroom climate and make transitions less overwhelming for some children, teachers can increase predictability and rituals. Just as teachers provide different degrees of challenge within activity centers, they can expect that some children may need more or less time to change their focus and transition to another activity. For example, an adult may need to shadow a particular child during transitions. Although children may independently pace themselves for some transitions during an activity period, teachers can anticipate their varied needs during a general transition period—another reason to build fewer transitions into the school day.

Scholarship Takes Time

Scholarship takes different amounts of time for different children. Too-brief time periods reduce children's opportunities to develop projects alone and with others. Young children also associate feeling rushed with feeling incompetent.

Children engaged in sociodramatic play—whether in a thematic medical or generic blocks center, sand box, or puppet framework—need time to plan together, negotiate, and develop their oral scripts. They also need time to engage in other classroom representational activities in the arts, construction, and writing. One teacher found that a group of kindergarten boys participated in two-dimensional artwork only after having had time in the blocks center (Paley, 1984).

Time of day may also influence the course of learning. Brain researchers tell us that many, not all, children experience an afternoon lull in energy level. Therefore, consider planning low-energy afternoon activities, such as listening to soothing music through headphones. Add mats to the library area, so the youngest children can nap whenever they need to.

Within any half-day program, planning sufficient time for center-based activities provides plenty of opportunities for teachers to circulate. It also allows teachers time to schedule and respond to small-group and individual instruction. These instructional episodes might take a few seconds or minutes for infants and toddlers, five or ten minutes for primary-age children.

Any teacher can decide to stretch or reduce center time based on what is emerging. Much (not all) of the early-childhood curriculum is play-centered within small groups, because children represent experiences through both play and early learning. In addition, whole-group activities, such as planning, movement education, sports, storytelling, celebrations, special projects, and field trips, expand children's knowledge.

Setting Up Space to Support Play and Meaning

The spatial organization of a classroom communicates who has the power to make decisions. To ensure opportunities for play in which children integrate the conditions for learning in early childhood, teachers arrange for small-group furnishings, nooks, and a balance between individual and small-group settings.

Teachers who claim a lack of resources because they have only one chair and desk for each child reveal that they expect mainly whole-group, teacher-directed, individual activity with little choice, self-pacing, and opportunity for socialization. This claim also suggests a teacher's belief that play and learning centers are peripheral additions to the linear classroom. After all, furniture is movable, and young children comfortably use the floor or move chairs for whole-group activity. Therefore, it is not necessary to have whole-group seating in addition to a full range of play centers.

Imagine a sit-down dinner with no choice of menu or seatmate versus a buffet format with shared options. A buffet and fair-like format in the classroom, with teacher-guided options, offers more opportunities for children to experience a sense of empowerment, choice, and increasingly independent self-organization.

Traffic Patterns

The following guidelines can shape traffic patterns for the indoor and outdoor play of young children:

- Respect, support and expect children to concentrate their efforts, focus, and attention; to engage in scholarship, both indoors and outdoors; to build and practice independent and responsible interpersonal relationships; to independently use their capacities to organize themselves; and to play in areas alone or with a few others. Young children need opportunities to balance privacy and participation, and need teachers to respect their reactivity times.
- Classrooms have artificially defined areas that—by their very presence—provide invitations, information, and opportunities for privacy and participation. (Even a one-room residence may have specific areas for cooking, cleaning, meeting, and sleeping.) Thoughtful planning suggests that areas housing active pastimes would be close to one another, and areas housing more sedentary pastimes would be set apart; wet-use areas would be near a water source, and dry-use areas would be away from wet ones.
- Thoughtful plans that support play also consider traffic patterns. If water is outside the classroom, set up centers that use water near the hallway door. That way, children who need to refill containers or clean equipment do not pass by others' activities. An open area that defines the middle of classroom space invites fast and loud passage; instead, break up central spaces with L-shaped arrangements of tables, low shelves, and other low partitions.

■ When you need space for whole-group activities, use established procedures by which children take turns moving furniture in orderly ways. For example, early in the year everyone in the class can practice pairing off to safely lift and carry a table so as to enlarge open space. It is important to anticipate the needs of children who may require extra space in which to coordinate their movements; for example, to accommodate a sturdy chair with arms or a wheelchair.

The size of a play area also strongly influences classroom dynamics. If children in a preschool classroom are having frequent struggles or crying and disagreeing in the block area, the area may be too small to accommodate the blocks or the number of children. Among toddlers, biting might signal inadequate space or the need for some duplication of materials.

The Sociodramatic Play Area

Consider the particular need in every early-childhood classroom to provide sufficient space for sociodramatic play. For toddlers, teachers might include floor building blocks in an area adjacent to home-center kinds of equipment. For preschoolers and kindergarten-age children, the floor building blocks would be adjacent to the furniture, which may start the year as housekeeping materials but change themes every month or every few weeks. There would also be an open traffic area between these provisions in order to encourage mobility and reciprocity between boys and girls, as well as the integration of construction and oral script building.

The Floor-Blocks Area. The floor-blocks area consists of rectangular wooden blocks of different sizes, as well as cylinders, arches, and partial arches. Sturdy, wooden floor blocks are typically one inch by two or four inches long. These relationships help children develop their visual-spatial and quantitative skills; their understanding of mathematics, physics, chemistry, geography, and the arts depends on such visual-spatial perceptions.

Children transform the blocks by constructing pretend places. They turn the block area into dormitories, mazes, zoos, barnyards, seashores, post offices, fire stations, trains, buses, airports, spaceships, and communities. The Downtown Community School in New York City uses floor blocks as the centerpiece of their play curriculum, beginning with toddlers through the eighth grade. Children represent various community functions that they have observed. Before play begins, teachers and children discuss the children's observations of their community, and the youngsters make preliminary plans for their roles during the construction process. They build and play out emerging ideas, and talk about their buildings at the close of a play session. The block play further stimulates selection of literature, creation of related artwork, writing, and pursuit of scientific and technical problem solving, as well as pretend play.

Teachers have also added the following *props* to the block areas in classrooms: signs; traffic signals; train tickets; strips of oak tag denoting roads; writing materials; miniature animals, cars, buses, trucks, airplanes, fencing, trees, and people; and real tree branches.

Accessories have included inexpensive items such as the following: lengths of clear plastic tubing; ropes; baskets; pulleys; steering wheels or cardboard replicas; empty film canisters; wooden spools; pine cones; and string.

Some teachers have rotated the placement of photographs at children's eye level—images that depict different kinds of dwellings, public buildings, styles of architecture, bridges, and aerial views of islands. As is the case in any sociodramatic play area, *young children usually do best when props representing a single theme are present at one time.* Too many different objects can distract youngsters, whereas a coherent collection helps them to focus their collective energy.

Children who use the floor blocks often begin with physical construction. The youngest children engage in building side by side. Preschoolers will plan together intermittently. When sociodramatic play emerges, talking usually follows the main construction process. Children may use their constructions as the background for their sociodramatic play. For example, a group of four-year-olds, with minimal talk, built a house with the blocks. They designated a section of blocks on the floor as a bed and then proceeded to lie on the bed, playing the roles of an adult and a child who needed to be "put to bed." In short order, the play extended to a series of emergent themes that included pets and pet care, cooking, eating, and building a bridge.

In more complex play, older four- and young five-year-old children used the floor blocks as well as white plastic bars and connecting joints to build a market, employing the blocks as both hammers and shelves. While building and stocking the market, one child made a sign at the writing center, and the following script emerged:

MEL: "Whoever lives behind the supermarket, it's their home, right?"

DOT: "No, it's a supermarket, it's a grocery store."

MEL: "How about we both be the puppy, Nat? Nat?"

NAN: [to Dot] "They're playing puppy store."

DOT: "No, it's a supermarket. Guys, you cannot play this."

NAN: [to teacher] "They're playing wrong."

DOT: [to teacher] "They're playing puppies and we're playing grocery store."

TEACHER: "What could you do? What could be your solution so that everyone's happy?"

DOT: "I know, I know. Well, we can make half pet store, half supermarket."

TEACHER: "I think that's a wonderful idea. See, you know what to do. . . ."

MEL: "No, this isn't the puppy store. The puppy store is over there."

DOT: [runs to the child who is making a sign in the writing center] "Nel! Get over here right this minute."

For primary- and kindergarten-age children, the floor blocks would provide a stimulating sociodramatic area if they also included props that children could use to build a variety of scripts. Children at these ages build their own enclosures with large hollow blocks or interlocking blocks and then play out scripts that range across the spectrum of their concerns, such as home, spaceship, airplane, hay ride, bicycle shop, or dental office.

Few primary-grade classrooms offer floor blocks. However, they may have other construction materials such as Lego™ or Tinker Toys™ or simple Erector™ sets. Some recent futuristic additions to preschool, kindergarten, and primary classrooms include contemporary creations such as the Hoberman Mini Sphere™ (Hoberman Designs), an unfolding structure of plastic parts and pivoting joints. "The hinge system allows a geometric form, like a sphere or polyhedron, to mechanically blossom or contract while retaining its original shape" (Jana, 1998, pp. 22, 26). Zoob™ (Primordial, San Francisco) consists of ball-and-socket, hinge, and flexible saddle joints that can connect in many different ways to construct DNA-like structures of animals as well as other objects. Chaos™ (St. Louis, Missouri) is made of snap-on connectors for plastic chutes and trampolines that can serve as runways for balls; children can make Rube Goldberg–type creations and solve problems in physics. The founder of Chaos™, Jim Rothbart, refers to Chaos™ as "kinetic sculpture." Like wooden floor blocks, these materials let players control the process and product. The process itself is a direct experience that enhances the development of children's quantitative and physical knowledge.

It would be useful for manufacturers to offer generic, wooden hollow blocks along with accessories to suggest various possible themes. The materials could take the form of changeable modules or huge "Post-it note" tablets designating objects such as a cook top for a restaurant, hospital, or home kitchen. Teachers have easily designed their own signs to denote such places as voting booths, post offices, pet shops, farms, and garage facilities. At the same time, they have offered the appropriate prop box or bag full of relevant items to fit the children's theme.

Housekeeping furniture is costly and suggests single-purpose use—unless teachers intervene creatively to change the themes. By joining block and housekeeping spaces, teachers can reallocate funds for generic wooden blocks and other creative equipment and materials.

The Pretend Housekeeping Area and Thematic Variations.   The pretend housekeeping area typically contains child-size kitchen furniture with a cooking surface, sink-type tub, refrigerator, table and chairs, doll's high chair, telephone, and ironing board, as well as bedroom furniture with a doll bed, multicultural dolls, mirror, and dress-up clothes. Some areas have an easy chair or child-size couch, a radio, microwave, tablecloth, vase with flowers, toy cameras, hair dryer, crutches, wheelchair, and drawings and labels designating where objects are stored. The furniture often creates an area bounded on two or three sides and set apart from the larger classroom space.

One researcher noted that children often talk to one another during their play in this area, but that the structure and content of the talk becomes repetitive when housekeeping is the only theme (Cazden, 1971). Researchers found that when alternative thematic centers existed, the play grew more varied, symbolic, and cognitively complex (Bagley & Klass, 1997). Other researchers also have found that children use literacy materials and talk much more and with greater variety when the housekeeping-area props represent such varied places as a post office or a veterinary or medical facility (Christie, 1991). Here are some ways to transform a pretend housekeeping area into varied themes:

- A *beauty parlor* contains a price list, cash register, receipt book, towels, smock, appointment book, and appointment cards. A sign and logo can transform the housekeeping space.
- A *hospital* includes a sign and red cross, rubber gloves, hospital caps, booties, face masks, a stethoscope, play hypodermic, play thermometer, bandages, tongue depressors, forehead lamp, microwave, baby lotion, medicine bottles, telephone, an appointment book, appointment cards, and prescription pad.
- A *space center* includes helmets covered in aluminum foil, gloves, uniform shirts, a keyboard and computer screen, posters of the planets, a model sun and moon hanging from the ceiling, space telephones decorated with foil, and kitchen furniture covered in foil. Literacy materials for four-year-olds and older children can include a sign labeling the area as a spaceship with its name, a schedule of jobs, a schedule for signing up for flight time, an order form for meal delivery, and a list of space clothes with available sizes.
- An *office* includes a briefcase, desk, stapler, Scotch tape™, paper clips, hole punch, adding machine, typewriter or computer, briefcase, and passes.
- *Grocery store* props include signs reading Grocery Store, One-Day Sale, Jean Mart, Blue-Light Special, Buy One Carrot—Get Three Free, Clearance Sale, Fruits, Vegetables, Bakery, and Cashier. Labels can include the price of juice ($2.00) on a juice bottle, Sink, Soap Dish, Ice, Water, Scale, Bread, and Fresh Bagels. The store contains a cash register, baskets and bins filled with labeled merchandise, and price tags, a telephone, catalogs, and actual supermarket flyers and coupons.
- A variation of the grocery store is a *general market* with a labeled customer-service desk containing a cash register, play telephone, scissors, Scotch tape™, wrapping paper, stapler, pens, and receipt books. Labels for the store and its merchandise include toys, electronics, clothing, flyers, and cold drinks.
- A *restaurant* includes a large sign with the name of the establishment, menus, a daily-specials board and price list, uniforms for servers, a pad of bills, and a cash register. It can also become the site for selecting a real

mid-morning snack; children might take a seat and order from the changing list of available snacks, such as celery sticks and peanut butter or pretzels and apples.

■ *A garage* includes a large sign with the name of the garage. There are also child-size or teacher-created automobiles (a cardboard steering wheel and tires), gas pump, air gauge, air pump, jack, road maps, cashier, credit-card scanner, appointment book, receipt pad, pencils, toolbox, and uniform caps.

The Puppet Area.   Another sociodramatic play opportunity can occur in the puppet-theater area, beginning in kindergarten with children who have well-developed speech. A puppet theater might be made commercially or by the teacher and children who decorate a carton box. The puppets might also be made commercially or consist of stuffed socks, paper plates on sticks, other stick puppets, dolls, stuffed toys, or paper bags. Puppet play can sometimes help reticent children give voice to a puppet that they might not easily express by themselves.

Children need well-developed speech to give voice to puppets; otherwise, the play may degenerate into a silent "Punch-and-Judy" event. Kindergarten-age children typically have the language skills to speak for puppets, but they can more likely sustain dialogue if they have planned some of the action beforehand. Becoming the character while simultaneously manipulating the puppet requires coordination, practice, and support.

The Pouring Area.   Young children also use the pouring table (filled with water, sand, rice, salt, oats, or cornstarch "goop") as a place to converse with others and create events. *Accessories* may include the following: sieves and plastic berry baskets; pitchers; transparent hoses and funnels; spoons, slotted spoons, and ladles; basters; soap; containers of different shapes but equivalent volume; and hoists. Children might engage in such themes as farming, boating, construction, firefighting, and inventing.

Younger children with less developed language often find satisfaction in this area; toddlers and preschoolers, more often than older children, engage in these activities. When a water table is present in a kindergarten classroom, children may play with air-propelled boats or try to float objects on varied shapes of aluminum foil or plasticene. Primary-age children might contrive various events with transparent hoses, funnels, and squirt bottles.

The Playground Areas.   Sociodramatic play can also emerge on the outdoor playground or in an indoor gymnasium. Principles and practices for organizing play would be similar in both settings. A suggestion for planning outdoor play space states that,

A good playground should include open spaces for running and chasing; safe, out-of-the-way places for supervised, *friendly* rough-and-tumble play; cozy crannies for a few friends to enjoy together; trees, hills, a stream—whatever blessings nature has donated; animals to pet and learn about informally; gardens where children can grow flowers or vegetables; water tables, water toys, tubs, hoses; sand and sand toys; wheeled vehicles; balls; a workbench and real tools; a variety of arts opportunities; and more! (Vergeront, 1988, p. 22).

Outdoors, children engage in pretense on climbing equipment or in sand-boxes. On climbing apparatus that has rigid parts or ropes, children play out themes such as firefighting with real or imaginary hoses, climbing, rescuing, and so forth. In the sandbox, youngsters play at being workers and patrons in a restaurant with "sand-food." Tricycle paths often lend themselves to transportation themes as well as chase-and-save adventures. Children might also bring a "patient" to an outdoor office for medical help or elaborate on the theme of super-heroes or heroines.

Teachers can transform indoor gymnasiums with thematic changes that suggest farms, zoos, jungles, airports, and multicultural festivals. In neighborhood back yards or on city sidewalks, children pretend to be attackers and victims, or engage in chasing and hiding games. Other playground themes have included nurturing play, with doll carriages and baby dolls on outings. Some children, using twigs or commercial toys, engage in chase-and-attack games that include villains and heroes or heroines as well as victims and saviors.

Other Forms of Play

Sociodramatic play is a powerful conduit for learning, but other forms of play also contribute. These include games, puzzles and mazes, sports, and constructions of various sorts. As we saw earlier, the visual, movement, and poetic arts, as well as gardening, are representational forms that require imagery. They function best in the form of self-motivated, satisfying experiences, as does sociodramatic play.

The *visual arts* include three-dimensional constructions, woodworking as a variant of block building, sculpture, and drawing in which children may function as "patterners and dramatists" (Gardner, 1982). Exemplary early childhood class-rooms offer an art-studio area that contains materials for both two- and three-dimensional constructions.

Movement activities, such as dance and creative use of climbing apparatus, embody similar criteria for play imagery, representation, and emotional catharsis. Music and dance creations need open spaces, which children can produce by moving classroom furniture when dedicated school spaces, such as gymnasiums or yards, are not available. Some young children also joyfully collaborate in using climbing frames creatively and imaginatively. Preschoolers might enjoy socializing on double-width slides. Children with physical disabilities have benefited from raised surfaces that typically are used on the floor, such as an outdoor sand-box or indoor blocks.

With minimal teacher intervention, children can create their personal spatial boundaries; for example, a teacher might invite youngsters to do the following:

Pretend that you are inside a bubble and the other children are inside their bubbles. Imagine the bubble all around you on the sides, on the top, in front, and in back of you. Imagine where your friend's bubbles begin and end. Now let's see how you can keep the bubbles whole.

Indoor and outdoor games and sports, and puzzles and mazes, including garden mazes where available, encourage children to solve problems and play with strategy on their own or by negotiating with others. Sports can be play or work, depending on children's attitudes and adults' roles; competition, though, may overwhelm young children in some situations. Board games have a grammatical structure that might entail a variety of markers that move the game forward. Even if you use a single marker with which all players can identify, you can vary the games by using a die or dice, a spinner, cards, and a mechanical or computer lottery.

Another kind of game would be to propel a vehicle vicariously. For example, four-year-olds have used the keypad on a computerized vehicle to propel the vehicle. Their focus was on gaining proficiency and control of the medium. When the teacher taped the floor with the length of the toy, the children had opportunities to estimate distances and learn about comparative distances and quantities.

Other underlying structures in physical games include tossing and blowing, or propelling objects with air pressure (Kamii & DeVries, 1980, 1993). In addition, card games provide a combination of chance and skill-building strategies.

Preschoolers who are ready for something different can easily learn the card game of Concentration (also called Memory or Pairs). Children turn up two cards at a time in search of a matched pair and turn the cards face down in the same place if there is no match. When they find a matched pair, the two cards are saved in the "Pairs Bank." Teachers can make the Concentration game easily by creating categories of cards such as animal pairs, fruits, shapes, or words. They can also adapt the game by adding or removing pairs of cards. Sensitive and industrious teachers have created customized card and board games. These various forms of play offer children a challenge, an opportunity to take risks, and a chance for success.

Challenge is the essence of phase transitions. The effective teacher creates challenging conditions to help children experience a phase transition, the seat of learning. The phase transition is the area where teaching and learning can take place, the area between the child's potential and the teacher's provision of possibilities. With games, children seem to propel themselves through the phase transitions.

How Might Teachers Influence Children's Development?

Children need opportunities to "play out" what they have learned and to self-direct the process. A teacher might take two or three minutes to show kindergarten-age children how to make "trains" with Cuisenaire blocks (colored rods of graduated size). Teachers can also provide children with opportunities to try out combinations of rods of different sizes, equal in length to a "train," within a game format. Six-year-olds might sit back to back and take turns creating directions for one another as they add different combinations of smaller Cuisenaire rods equal to a larger rod (Davidson, 1977); they might also record their representations and compare them. This back-to-back game format supports direct instruction at the same time that children engage in social, self-directed possibilities.

Effective teachers use many game formats during activity periods, as well as provide plenty of opportunities for children to set and solve their own problems in play centers. These teachers recognize that children need to engage in independent, self-directed, imaginative play.

Play and playful work experiences exist on a continuum of child control. Both forms of experience need incubation time, reaction time, time for revisiting, and time for recycling with variations. Stretches of time sufficient in length for play and playful involvements therefore create an enriched environment that supports children's general development; the time lets them strengthen learning connections within their brains.

Brain research indicates that children need sufficient time to progress through the incubation of imagery and play. Long stretches of time help children to develop their thoughts. There is,

> . . . value in focused learning time followed by diffused activities like reflection. . . .
>
> In the classroom, there are three reasons why constant attention is counterproductive. First, much of what we learn cannot be processed consciously; it happens too fast. We need time to process it. Second, in order to create new meaning, we need internal time. Meaning is always generated from within, not externally. Third, after each new learning experience, we need time for the learning to "imprint" (Jensen, 1998, p. 46).

When teachers understand the power of play to influence children's development, they often look for opportunities to support that process. They use indirect as well as direct ways. *Indirect ways* include the following:

- Arranging time, space, and materials for many forms of play. Teachers may add or remove props. They schedule sufficient time and opportunity for sociodramatic play both indoors and outdoors.
- Including games in daily activities, even within the framework of "work" time. Games help children strengthen and practice new learning. Teachers demonstrate new games and play games with children. Real games differ from exercises or drills. They have elements of challenge but also provide opportunities for children to try out strategies and control their own participation.
- Observing children to assess what they may need for future planning.

- Developing with children a variety of dynamic themes that pervade various experiences and play areas.
- Providing rich activities through trips, visitors, films, and literature that add to children's event knowledge. Teachers also work with parents to extend and expand children's event knowledge.
- Offering children opportunities to re-enact stories.
- Enjoying riddles, humor, and jokes together with children. Teachers who maintain a playful attitude and a sense of humor further support play as integrated learning.

Teachers also can engage in *direct intervention* activities that can influence children's play. These activities include the following:

- *Modeling* fantasy, a helpful behavior, or new direction.
- Taking a brief role in sociodramatic play to influence the tenor and content of the play.
- Asking a question to help children plan, consider an alternative next step, or extend thinking; for example, "Now that you are the judge, what might you do to solve this problem?"
- Asking a question to invert reality; for example, "What if the turkey could tell us how he feels? What might he say to us?" "What if you were in a town where people never hit one another? What could they tell one another when they were angry?" "Did you ask if you could have some?" "What happened when you talked to her about it?" "Did you ask him why he did that?" "Deb has something to tell you. Will you listen to her now?" "What are you planning to build?" (Rather than telling a child what you do *not* want him to do, ask this last question to redirect the child who may be distracting others.)
- Bringing children in sight of each other or next to one another, and inviting a child to enter a play activity by offering her an object or opportunity; for example, "There's space on the boat over here" or "Eva's playing here with you today" or "How can you help him with that?" Teachers can also invite a child to move toward a different area: "It's time to pick another center." "What other center can you go to?"
- Providing, adding, or modifying a prop; for example, re-creating the housekeeping area as a hospital, farm, zoo, airport, bus station, restaurant, or shoe store.
- Removing a prop that has been overly used, takes up too much space, or is a source of contention.
- Engaging in verbal harmony, or describing what children are doing; for example, "Oh, that zeppelin can really carry more people." Or, to respond to a child's comment of "OK," the teacher might say, "Oh, so you suggest that it's fair to divide the tools equally!?" Researchers have also found that such verbal harmony helps preschool-age children learn compound sentences within the context of their self-selected activity (Hart & Risley, 1975, 1995; McCartney, 1984) and games (Fromberg, 1976).

- Validating or celebrating a child's behavior by comments that support his motives and efforts, recording his statements, extending children's oral scripts in role play and retelling, and photographing products. (Validating children's play products adds to their sense of competence and their growing theory of mind.)
- Casually suggesting a possible next step.
- Simply being present, which might extend the duration of productive interactions, or draw girls into the blocks area.

Adults' intervening in the play of young children can be treacherous, because play exists relative to the particular setting in which the play appears. *Sociodramatic play in particular involves a balance between independence and collaboration.* The social interaction among players that transforms play from one phase into another is the transition in which development occurs. Therefore, the best times for teachers to scaffold children's sociodramatic play are when phase transitions are taking place. Scaffolding is a form of phase transition; any form of scaffolding, however, entails the hazard of obliterating the play.

Skillful teachers can intervene in young children's play in ways that help children balance the challenge of working with others while remaining independent. Such teachers intervene in ways that help children retain a full focus on the present, so that the children can transcend the moment. Human beings usually experience this satisfying sense of challenge, independence, immersion, and timelessness as pleasure. Psychologist Mihalyi Csikszentmihalyi (1988) called this sort of experience a sense of "flow." The sense of flow may emerge during such varied occasions as mountain climbing, exercise or dance, musical experiences, immersion in a mutually satisfying conversation, feelings of affection, or the solving of a puzzling problem. A sense of flow adds to the satisfaction that humans experience when they are immersed in play.

Supporting Play and Learning

Scheduling sufficient time and organizing spaces with sensitivity to how young children develop and learn through their play are essential attributes of a nonlinear early-childhood classroom. There is a great variety of play formats within which young children can develop meaningful experiences. It is important to note that spaces need periodic thematic changes as well as opportunities for children to revisit themes.

Teachers can intervene with sensitivity and caring both indirectly and directly in order to support children's play and learning. Just as play is the lymphatic system of the young child's learning, so are classroom design and organization the skeletal system for a classroom's success.

11 Building Play into Curriculum Strands

Play Is a Condition for Learning

When young children develop meaning, they use imagery that follows the non-linear contours of the "what-if, as-if" domain of play. In contrast, these printed pages are naturally linear; one thought follows another. Therefore, the discussion of learning within these pages necessarily follows the structure of language. Oh, if only we could represent and communicate the play and learning processes simultaneously, as in music!

Although we lack the capacity to communicate in the nonlinear form of music or visual arts, let's consider the following discussion of curriculum as a four-strand aggregate of musical voices that we can read as a series of strands. The teacher weaves the strands together in actual practice. Chapter 12, Dynamic Themes: Weaving the Strands, provides examples of experiences that integrate the strands. Integration happens naturally, because literacy activities harmoniously pervade physical and social knowing, while quantitative knowing harmoniously pervades physical, social, and representational knowing.

The discussion begins with (1) *quantitative knowing*, which includes the continuum of experiences that build visual-spatial skills and mathematical perceptions (mathematics, geography, and the three-dimensional arts), (2) *physical knowing*, which includes the continuum of experiences that build visual-spatial skills and scientific perceptions (physical and natural sciences), (3) *social knowing*, which includes the continuum of experiences from which young children build social skills, social perceptions, and a sense of community (social learning, social studies, and social sciences), and (4) *representational knowing*, which includes the continuum of experiences that build communication skills and perceptions of literacy, the arts, and aesthetics.

Knowing is different from knowledge. For example, social *knowing*, a nonlinear experience, contrasts with social *knowledge*, a linear experience that rests on information. Social knowing refers to the meaningful and integrated ways in which young children construct social meanings. Richard Feynman, a theoretical mathematician and physicist, addressed the difference in the following way: "You can know the name of that bird in all the languages of the world, but when you're finished you'll know absolutely nothing whatever about the bird. . . . So let's look at the bird and see what it's doing—that's what counts" (Gleick, 1998, pp. 28–29). By contrast, social knowledge (Piaget et al., 1965; Piaget & Inhelder, 1969) is informational. Children accumulate it when a teacher tells them the names of shapes, colors, animals, tools, planets, dates of holidays, other vocabulary, and printed words or shows them how to play a game.

Young children acquire and retain informational knowledge most readily when it is embedded within meaningful activities. For teachers who feel pressured politically to do otherwise, this book suggests a minimum amount of time devoted to such transmittal activity. Meaningful experiences form the center of early childhood education and should reflect the majority of time that young children spend in school. Too often, schools reverse these priorities. Teachers then struggle with "not enough time," "misbehaving" children, minimal achievements, and professional disappointment. The education of young children, however, is a privilege and joy for teachers who offer experiences that are congruent with a young child's grammar of experience.

Each strand that follows presents a vision of how quantitative, physical, social, or representational knowing develops in early childhood. There are also examples of activities and games in which children and their teachers have engaged. The main criterion teachers use to select experiences is that young children may find meaning in them; teachers use play and the other integrated conditions for learning to support children's construction of meaning. Age designations for sample activities are broadly suggestive. Keep in mind that older children can expand the complexity and extend the scope of activities, games, and playthings that younger children use.

Quantitative Knowing

The development of visual-spatial relationships is the core of quantitative learning. Quantitative knowing that we associate with mathematics develops when young children have experiences with the three-dimensional world, including the arts.

Visual-spatial learning emerges when infants follow movements with their eyes, and when their entire bodies move with excitement; they also begin to learn about quantity by playing with objects in these ways. Adults support this learning by moving objects slowly from side to side across the "midpoint" of the child, thereby engaging her whole brain's attention. Adults make sounds in front of, to the side of, and behind the infant. They sing nursery rhymes and play "Rock-a-bye baby," also crossing the midpoint. Toddlers and preschoolers dance with scarves in ways that also encourage them to cross the object over their midpoint. They also learn about quantity as they experience the duration of time through routine schedules in their daily lives.

Their earliest explorations and play contribute to the ongoing depth and breadth of their understanding, and meanings grow along with the complexity of their play. As young children explore the world, their muscles and senses (the force of feeling on their skin, the intensity of their vision, the amplitude of sound on their ear drums, the magnitude of fragrance, and the variability of their taste buds) give them information that builds their perceptions of quantity. Objects exert more or less pressure on their skin and muscles, and feel more or less rough and smooth; some shapes and colors fill more or less of a child's visual field; some phenomena make louder or softer, more or less comfortable sounds; some fragrance intensities or qualities are more or less approachable; some things taste or feel more or less welcome—and all of these experiences take place over more or less time.

As children grow older, they embellish and transform the types of activities in which they participated at earlier times. For example, whereas infants may engage in dump-and-fill activities, toddlers and preschoolers may try to fit objects or their own bodies into various spaces, such as a cabinet or refrigerator, or stick a leg between the slats of a porch. Some examples of ways in which children play as they mature and suggestions for adult support follow.

Infants

As young children live through their everyday experiences, they increasingly place objects and events in relation to one another. They begin to expect that a certain sequence of events will occur, for example, when their caregiver chants a nursery rhyme while they gaze at a picture on the wall during diapering. The rhythm of the rhyme is a quantitative pattern for which infants build expectancies. The warmth of the caregiver's arm may contrast with the cool plastic mat of the diapering shelf, a relative degree (quantity) of temperature.

Infants begin to connect more vigorous flailing of their legs with the intensified movement of a mobile toy, their grasp of a toy with a rattling sound (an intuitive if-then experience), an approaching smell with a particular person or food, the movement of their head with a face (not yet identified as their own) reflected in the mirror at the side of the crib. They turn their head toward the door when they connect the sound of footsteps or a human voice to a caregiver.

Adults' play with infants supports youngsters' learning of quantity when it provides many opportunities for *contrasts* in sound, touch, sights, smells, and tastes. Following the same sequence of events during the day will help infants anticipate events; sequence is part of quantitative learning and parallels anticipatory behavior in reading later on. Anticipations that are fulfilled feel satisfying and support the infant's sense of security and competence.

For example, in a classroom for children from birth through age three who have cerebral palsy, the teacher developed a series of mats, each of which offered a single contrast. As the children lay on the mats, each one could feel a rough texture with one hand and foot while feeling a smooth texture with the other hand and foot. Other contrasts included warm and cold, hard and soft, and rounded and jagged edges.

Infants first learn to grasp objects; only later do they develop the capacity to let go. As they learn to let go, they tend to repeat the process, a way of predicting outcomes and thereby gaining a sense of competence.

Toddlers

Toddlers learn about quantity as they engage in a variety of characteristic activities, some of which may bring them close to hazards that adults would do well to anticipate. For example, toddlers love to play with objects by *banging* them, *filling* containers with them, *dumping* and mainly *emptying* them, as well as *placing them in their mouths.*

In encouraging youngsters to wash their hands or eat, adults need to allow toddlers time to play with the hand-washing process or to play with their food. *Repetitive play behavior provides a sense of predictability, security, and success.* For example, toddlers may shake talcum powder or salt across a room or unfurl a toilet paper roll. As they play, they learn about the properties of objects, often a matter of inconvenience to adults. Therefore, *they need enough time to manage routines as well as a changing and steady supply of a few objects on which they can focus at one time.*

Toddlers are adept at emptying the contents of low cabinets and shelves and dumping objects off tables. They also explore the possibilities of fitting objects into containers or onto rods, and fitting themselves into cabinets and boxes or under chairs or tables. They begin to play by pouring water or sand into pails with shovels, spooning sand into funnels, or dumping sand through sieves or wide cylinders. They also begin to squeeze liquids out of flexible containers.

Dump-and-fill activities lead to adding and taking apart or reducing by subtracting and dividing. These youngsters' play with water, sand, and play dough offers them opportunities to learn about relative size, shape, length, flexibility, equivalence, and reversibility. In addition, play dough lets them squeeze and compress by rolling or pounding. Children initially interpret the changes as "more" or "less" size, based on perceptual cues. For example, when they begin with equal-size balls and then flatten one, they testify that the flatter one is larger than the spherical one.

Children build toward the experience of conservation through these activities. They therefore need plenty of opportunities to play with malleable materials and reverse the ball-making and pancake-making activities. Toddlers also play with objects by tasting them (weaker or stronger amplitude of taste) and feeling their texture (more or less rough or smooth) on their tongues. They also learn about the topological meanings of in, out, under, over, and through as well as enclosures and boundaries when they engage in large-muscle play activities with objects. For instance, they enjoy crawling into a tent made by a blanket over a table and climbing over and under a simple obstacle course made of tires and boards.

Toddlers can keep rhythm, the beginnings of quantitative patterns. Their social play with rhythm instruments adds to the building of these patterns. Spoken language has its own rhythm as well, and the syllables in words reflect different quantities. When adults repeat strongly rhythmic rhymes in poems and songs in routine contexts, such as during diapering, washing up, or preparing for bedtime, toddlers begin to complete the rhyme. As they play with sounds in this way, they begin to create their own rhymes, sometimes as nonsense syllables. This signals that they are hearing differences and similarities, a benchmark in oral literacy.

Preschool and Kindergarten

Preschool-age children acquire significant visual-spatial learning from construction, mainly wooden floor-block play. Many trial-and-error opportunities help them figure out how to build structures that are both wide and tall. They learn to bridge openings by finding just the right length piece. They learn about fitting their own bodies into and around the structures that they build.

Children of kindergarten age can use similar materials and equipment with additional variables. Like younger children, kindergarten-age youngsters are also incomplete classifiers; this quality becomes apparent as they change the rules of games, shift the focus of sociodramatic play scripts, and sort objects with confident inconsistency. They are beginning to be able to read a picture-word sign in the snack center, select a specific number of crackers, and pour their own juice; to young children, pouring may feel like play.

Primary-Age Children

The growth of reading, writing, and mathematical skills in the primary grades expands the playing field for children. Although sociodramatic and large-muscle play decrease in many primary classrooms, children have not shed their need to play as a condition for their learning, their humanity, and the exercise of their imaginations. At these ages, they can integrate literacy and numeracy learning into their puzzles, games, constructions, and sociodramatic play. They also become more particular about playing games according to the rules.

Physical Knowing

Physical knowing grows from experiences that build visual-spatial skills. It consists of both the natural world of living beings and the physical world of objects. Infants begin to travel the path of physical knowing when they categorize edible and inedible and living and nonliving objects, and when they engage in rolling and tossing. Toddlers observe animal behavior, bath-water drains, and flushing toilets; maneuver pull toys; and jump over objects. Preschoolers and kindergarten-age children sort leaves, shells, and rocks accompanied by teachers' verbal harmony, blow bubbles, and play aiming games with pendulums and other objects. They play with flashlights, textures, melting, and evaporation. Children of primary age play systematically with shadows, pulleys, fulcrums, and levers. They also extend and expand activities in which they engaged when younger, with the addition of their literacy and numeracy skills as well as their finer muscle coordination.

Social Knowing

Social knowing comes from experiences that build social perceptions, social skills, a sense of community, and knowledge. Teachers can help by adding props to blocks and other sociodramatic play areas that represent different times and places. Teachers can also add transparent pipes to blocks, water, and "pouring" areas in ways that support collaborative play; boards or hollow blocks may be too long for one child to handle alone.

For adults to identify what children have learned from their playful social experiences, they can consider the varied perspectives that make up the social sciences:

- For example, geographers study the interaction of the environment and human beings, including *spatial relations* and geographic forms.
- Historians explore the issue of variable interpretation of events by different people, including the development of a relative sense of *time*.
- Economists examine the issue of *scarcity*, including the social issue of building consensus and setting priorities.
- Political scientists study *power* and decision-making, including the issues of voting and influence (Phenix, 1964).
- Multicultural educators consider the integration of social sciences from the perspectives of both *variety* and differences, including underlying shared human experiences (De Gaetano, Williams, & Volk, 1998).

While recognizing traditional interpretations of the social sciences, teachers can also retain awareness of alternative perspectives on how human beings and the environment are served best, how to interpret past and present events, why certain resources are scarce or valued, and whose votes count for what purposes. For example, schools across generations have not questioned the correctness of celebrating Columbus Day as the "discovery of America" rather than defining it as an imperialist European conquest of Native American peoples. Children develop perspective taking during their play, and they need a school climate that values it.

Youngsters' play helps them to construct social knowing as they learn about others' need for space and time, and the reality of limited resources (an economic concept). They also try to influence decisions (a political-science concept) and control their behavior in a culturally diverse world. Social knowing through active interaction and play with others merges emotions with social life.

Some social games let two or more children or a child and an adult interact or engage in parallel activities that have a high potential for imitation and interaction. For example, infants can play give-and-take with rattles when adults remember that infants find it easier to grasp than release an object. These youngsters enjoy peek-a-boo, massages, and tickling. Toddlers enjoy a mirror for two (distributed by Constructive Playthings, 1999); a rocking boat; chase, hide, and retrieve; and stamping together on bubble wrap taped to the floor. Preschool and kindergarten children enjoy simple card and board games, singing games, thematic sociodramatic play; and constructions. Pairs and groups engage in aim-and-toss games (Kamii & DeVries, 1980). Children of primary age enjoy collaborating in play with spinning tops and gyroscopes, then chalking the pathways; sharing yo-yo tricks; and playing with string figures in games such as Cat's Cradle.

These multiple experiences are like vitamins that simultaneously nourish the growth of quantitative, physical, and geographic knowing, because spatial relationships underlie the relevant activities. Spatial relationships also flourish within representational art forms.

Representational Knowing

Representational knowing derives from experiences that build communication skills. Play is one form of representation. Multiple forms of the arts and literacy also represent perceptions and concepts. Many representational activities are integrated with quantitative, physical, and social ways of knowing.

Representations in the arts, including the visual, movement, and auditory arts, transmute into play when children explore processes and construct their own products. Children engage in representational play when they build with blocks and other sculptural materials as well as paint and dance. They also create oral and graphic written poetry, songs, sociodramatic play scripts, and stories. "[S]tories, fantasy, and play take on particular importance when the subject matter is something children cannot touch, like astronomy . . . [and] delving into fantasy makes the study of reality more accessible, and real to children" (Mardell, 2000, p. 28). Novelist John Fowles captures the notion of a broad conception of representation when he says, "We all write poems; it is simply that poets are the ones who write in words" (Fowles, 1969, p. 161).

Writing oral or graphic poetry is actually a form of construction that employs the building tools of images and metaphors. Teachers who model poetry by reading aloud implicitly welcome such play with language. Children may listen to the folk music of poet composers and play by substituting words in songs.

Children become literate as they explore the *functions* and *features* of written language. A *function* is a reason, or a purpose, for using print. Exploration of language is a natural part of play because children need written language to support their play themes. They label things, record medical information, write in appointment books, read menus, use telephone books, order food, and take down restaurant orders. Play provides a natural and meaningful context for exploring the many functions of written language. . . . Once children have a reason to use print, they naturally explore its features (Owocki, 1999, pp. 24–25).

It is worth mentioning that young children, given an array of areas in which to play, may instead choose to attentively leaf through or read a book. The preschool teacher who builds on children's interest in stories by engaging them in episodic role playing helps children to develop their sense of story and practice the syntax and vocabulary that they'll find in books. Some early childhood educators (see Cooper, 1993; Dyson, 1997; Morrow, 1997; Owocki, 1999; Paley, 1981) have experimented with dramatizing and collaboratively retelling stories. These forms of representation build on young children's joy in play.

A bean-bag toss game offers an example of how teachers can make a game increasingly complex and adapt it to the skills of different children. For toddlers, simpy toss and retrieve the bean bag. Preschoolers might stand at different starting points marked on the floor with tape, and pitch the bean bag into a large box or basket on the floor. For children of kindergarten and primary age, teachers can create a target on the floor with sections of different colors. Replicate those colors on a group record sheet with matching stickers available. After each throw on a colored part of the target, place a sticker in the box on the record sheet with the matching color. This game has the virtues of adaptability to the children, noncompetitiveness, opportunity for symbolic representation, and low cost.

Infants

Oral language, visual stimulation, tactile experiences, and kinesthetic events are the early sources of experience that help infants build toward perceiving and representing experiences. Infants' interactions with adults and other children are essential to these developments. An example of an adult's scaffolding with a ten-month-old appears in a dramatic photographic sequence within the Reggio Emilia exhibit catalogue as follows: The ten-month-old and an adult are leafing through a magazine. The preverbal child makes eye contact with the adult and points to a photograph of wristwatches. The infant then touches the adult's wristwatch. The adult holds the wristwatch to the baby's ear. The infant then places his ear on the magazine photograph of the wristwatch (Malaguzzi et al., 1996).

The infant was playing in the same way scientists play. He made an inference and tested his hypothesis. The infant made observations and connections, generalized, and had an experience in cognitive dissonance, the tangential area in which learning occurs. That is, the baby anticipated that the photograph would offer the ticking sound of the actual wristwatch. He then learned about the distinction between objects and photos—a step along the path to personal representation. This episode depicts a phase transition and graphically demonstrates the relationship between an underlying perceptual potential and its surface representation; in effect, adult scaffolding influenced the child's potential for connection making.

Brain-research literature also reiterates the importance of human interaction in infants' ability to develop language and secure human attachments. Visual signals, signs, and oral activities are interrelated. When adults look at objects, infants often follow the adult's gaze. This "joint attention" (Bruner, 1980) creates the earliest "zone of proximal development" (Vygotsky, 1962/1934),

> . . . for cognitive, behavioral, and specifically linguistic development. Thus, communicative interaction between mother and child presupposes a sophisticated control of mutual eye movements. Indeed, there are specific prefrontal mechanisms in pointing and in coordinated eye movement that in humans seem to be instrumental in serving communication and cooperative activity (Velichkovsky, 1996, p. 12).

Joint-attention activities also include looking together at pictures and books.

Toddlers

Verbal harmony during daily activities plays an important role in toddlers' ongoing language development. Adults engage in helpful verbal harmony when they sit with children during snack and meals or while children are playing on the floor or at tables. Toddlers' constructions show increasing control of materials. They pretend with object substitution, and begin to engage in sociodramatic play and construction activities.

Preschool and Kindergarten

Preschool children enjoy listening to favorite stories and are adept at using picture books. They can identify their names and can match identical words. Their drawings, paintings, and constructions show increasing control of the materials. They enjoy playing with words and build a repertoire of songs that play with words. They also build sociodramatic block structures.

Kindergarten-age children begin to do observational drawing, draw their way into writing, and write their way into reading, using invented spelling. (When teachers move or enlarge a writing center from time to time, children sometimes refresh and renew their participation.) Youngsters at this age also enjoy pretense with costumes that help them extend their self-representation into new roles. They revel in singing, dancing, and movement activities as well.

Primary-Age Children

In primary grades, teachers can continue to read to children and make available books that children can read to themselves. Teachers select those books that are likely to be most meaningful to the children. Meaningful content in literature is dynamic in that it deals with issues with which young children can identify. Examples of such issues or themes include:

- sibling rivalry as well as friendship and rejection (conflict/contrast),
- everyday events, such as shopping and wanting more than is possible (conflict/contrast),
- fairness, justice, and retribution (conflict/contrast),
- wishes, hopes, dreams, and imaginary events (double bind or indirect progress),
- human sensitivities to one another and to animals (reverence for life and caring about others' feelings) (double bind or indirect progress),
- feelings in general, including difficult days, conflict resolution (conflict/contrast), and getting lost (change and the unknown),
- life changes such as having birthdays, moving, and separating (part of cyclical change),
- identifying with real or imaginary interests that represent children's personal growth and independence (rites of passage, part of cyclical change) or that might include learning to ride a bicycle; steering or rowing a boat; and propelling trains, aircraft, and space vehicles;
- important people in children's lives, including grandparents, heroes, and heroines (sense of community, part of a sense of synergy), and
- diverse working lives, such as those of sports figures, parents, and others in the community (part of synergy).

Exploring these kinds of issues in literature helps teachers create thematic "backpacks" of children's books and at-home activities that involve families in children's literacy programs.

Sensitive teachers invite children's reactions, opinions, ideas, thoughts, and attitudes about literature rather than test them on details. These teachers are sincerely interested in children's views. Rather than asking children rote questions, they pose questions for which children can legitimately share their own perspectives. They try to help children connect the readings to their own lives and to savor the beauty of language and artwork in books.

Adults consider their own self-selected and self-organized book groups as part of their play lives; shared desserts or meals often form part of the play. The concept of a book group for children is equally relevant. A small group of children select their shared reading after discussion and voting on a book or topic. Following reading, they share their personal reactions and connections to other books and events. The discussion becomes a particularly playful event when the teacher lights a candle to highlight the occasion.

Writing often is another playful way for young children to enter the world of reading. They can be pen pals with youngsters in another class as well as "adopt a class" in another school and become pen pals at a distance. Teachers can energize writing by planning an "author's theater" with children (Dyson, 1997). The young writer sits in an author's chair, and coordinates his friends' role playing of his story.

Field trips within the school and into the community are wonderful opportunities for children to see the many forms that representation takes; for instance, written signs, the printed cost of items, musical and dramatic productions, and presentation of works of art. School groups have visited bakeries, supermarkets, toy stores, and sporting goods and hardware stores; public institutions such as a firehouse, post office, public library, museum, airport, veterinary hospital, and zoo; and theaters, including backstage. These visits add to the event knowledge on which youngsters base their sociodramatic play. In turn, teachers provide props, including literacy materials with which children can represent their experiences in play.

Planning for Varied Representational Forms

It is particularly worthwhile to represent experiences in three-dimensional as well as two-dimensional forms. The following sections highlight relevant areas to consider when planning.

Movement and Dance

Movement and dance activities are early ways in which children play with physical science and quantitative concepts. Through these activities, they explore space, topology, speed, resistance, and eye-hand coordination. These activities also demonstrate children's learning about rhythm, pacing, spatial relations, and aesthetic appreciations and creations.

By moving and dancing, young children learn what they can do with their bodies, how they can move, where they can move, and with whom they can move. Like the imagery of Labanotation—a written form for dance choreographers to record direction, pace, level, and use of space—teachers invite children to keep still or move their entire bodies or parts of their bodies. The youngsters play with moving their bodies at higher or lower levels, turning, and rolling. They experiment with the dynamics of faster or slower, sharper or softer. They use imagery to move in ways that are wide or narrow; stretched out or compressed; and in forward, sideways, or backward directions.

For toddlers, dance might consist of bouncing to rhythm in one place. Children of preschool age play at becoming an animal (moving like a giraffe or a mouse) or object (moving like a wheel or a washing machine). Young children have played with ropes, scarves, hoops, and rope ladders; for example, children with developmental and physical disabilities make scarves dance by swaying their arms.

Preschool and kindergarten children dance together while imagining becoming mirrors, magnets, floating and sinking objects, and animals. They represent the feeling of being hot or cold, and they represent stories. Kindergarten-age children engage in simple partner dances such as "Up on the Mountain" (Landeck, 1950), in which children explore dance figures together and then spin away from each other to "freeze" into different sculptural forms, or "Polka

Klumpakojis" (Columbia Records), in which child-created dance escalates into three speeds, with gleeful results.

Children of primary age have also engaged in simple square-dance calls. These let them represent imagery that can be a precursor to understanding evaporation-condensation or, later, adult concepts dealing with the explosion and implosion of celestial bodies. The different surface forms of the dance may thus represent similar underlying images from the physical sciences.

Visual and Construction Arts

Visual arts can be a source of joy when children retain playful control over materials. Play with three-dimensional activities is worth the effort of planning. It becomes a wellspring for visual-spatial imagery as well as joyful experiences.

Teachers can create invitations to play by setting clay on boards, aligning collage materials in baskets or boxes, offering fresh paint containers, hanging sturdy and accessible suspensions for mobiles, and offering weaving opportunities that match children's capacities. It's best to set out these materials before children need to use them; this eliminates waiting time and maximizes the time that teachers can interact with the children. For example, children who have become responsible members of the class community who can work and play independently by the end of the first two months of the school year can create three-dimensional paper-bag, paper-plate, or papier-mâché masks during an integrated study of the ways in which different cultures represent tricksters.

Some kindergarten teachers have created maps for treasure hunts that take place just beyond the classroom, outdoors, or within the school. Primary-age children can also produce mazes for one another. They can draw an aerial view of the classroom or the room in which they sleep at home. A treasure-hunt game within the classroom is also a source of delight.

Of course, woodworking and block constructions allow three-dimensional play representations. Children of primary age can plan their constructions with drawings, measurements, and written notes, and research their ideas by looking at photographs and reading.

And when these youngsters represent their imaginations by writing, they offer each other a valuable audience, much as they do in the oral playwriting of sociodramatic play. When children talk to one another during a writing activity, they may serve as an audience for voice as well. Unfortunately, some teachers insist on total silence when children are writing, coding conversation as "off-task" behavior. But in one case, seven-year-old children discussed with a child author the feasibility of his story; though the teacher assumed that the children were off-task, the children were really being supportive editors (Dyson, 1987).

Technology and Related Representations

Infants look at television, and toddlers take pleasure in the public-television program "Teletubbies," which features repetition, high predictability, simple visual presentations that clarify figure-ground relationships, and high-pitched voices that get youngsters' attention. These features contribute to early graphic reading just as they do to oral language. Indeed, the same principles apply to learning to understand and speak as well as read and write. To young children, these features feel playful because they let them construct their own connections at their own pace, assisted by the contrasting patterns; they can choose to ignore or pay attention. Although adults want to ensure that television does not substitute for real-world three-dimensional and human experiences, they need to take responsibility for monitoring children's television time and allowing space and time for play in the best ethical sense.

Interestingly, the use of a recipe to cook "Tubby custard," an offshoot of the television program, engaged working-class boys in writing (Marsh, 1999). In this way, television characters and themes can add to children's cultural and social "capital." In contrast, toddler twins who saw wrestlers on television, an unplanned occurrence in their home, began to engage in unwelcome rough-and-tumble play, an activity that their highly tolerant parents felt they had already been well equipped to represent (S. M. Hines, 1999).

The use of television games with a joystick and personal computers in the home can help preschoolers feel competent in making things happen. Again, we face the issue of relative time available for social and physical play. Computerized toys are also popular with preschoolers. Those children who have personal computers at home are likely to become comfortable with these toys. Still, an economic divide exists between those who can and cannot afford these costly playthings.

For kindergarten-age children, LOGO™ software helps them feel they can influence events. They can attempt to solve mazes individually or with a partner using the least number of pathways. To qualify as a plaything, software must conform to the principles of play: It should let children actively influence events, be self-motivated, and leave plenty of time to interact with other people and the three-dimensional world.

Some primary-age children might also enjoy virtual-reality games. These require players to wear or use sensors housed in helmets, gloves, or floor mats. As these forms of play expand, it is clear that there is a need for the creation of software and games that young children can control *and* that don't take up all of their time.

Children of primary age also can learn to use calculators. To play with calculators during activities such as estimation games, youngsters first need to develop an understanding of the functions that calculators serve.

Exposing children to these technologies builds their comfort with today's technological advances while helping them share social knowing with their contemporaries. Adults also need to devise ways for children to balance their time and maintain direct experiences with the world of the outdoors, objects, artifacts, and people.

Play with Many Forms of Knowing

Play is a condition for learning in early education that children control. Effective early childhood teachers respect the play process and value children's sense of empowerment and competence.

Quantitative knowing, physical knowing, social knowing, and representational knowing are curricular strands in early childhood education that help us to speak about what children do when they play. Although language describes these strands separately, representation and visual-spatial skills clearly overlap other ways of knowing. Given that the human brain works in connected and integrated ways, effective early childhood teachers attempt to integrate these ways of knowing. Chapter 12 extends the discussion in this chapter by focusing on the process of weaving the curricular strands into activities organized around dynamic themes.

12 Dynamic Themes

Weaving the Strands

This chapter weaves the quantitative, physical, social, and representational knowing strands outlined in the preceding chapter into experiences that teachers and young children can develop together. Activities are organized around five dynamic themes that cut across disciplines. A variety of activities that cluster around a dynamic theme offer children equivalent experiences because they represent the underlying imagery in more or less complex ways. This makes the activities interchangeable. This approach contrasts with one in which everybody does the same thing at the same time in the same way and then attests to the same result.

Teachers and Children Construct Dynamic Themes

Effective teachers can play a powerful role in deciding which activities are worthwhile for young children. They consider which activities offer children many opportunities for making connections, and they integrate conditions for learning. They know that young children are likely to devote their attention to ideas that have significance in their lives. They recognize that *emotional experiences often underlie and define the degree of significance of ideas.* For example, the emotional experiences that follow serve as entries into sample dynamic themes:

- A sense of rhythmic flow is part of the experience of *cyclical change.*
- A sense of struggle or challenge is part of the experience of *conflict or contrast (dialectical imagery).*
- Tentativeness and the psychological defense mechanism of sublimation (expressing socially unacceptable impulses in acceptable forms) are part of the experience of *indirect progress.*
- A sense of being flooded with emotion is part of the experience of *synergy (the whole is more than the sum of its parts).*

■ Emotional ambivalence and a sense of physically being in two places at once is part of the experience of *double bind*; for example, responding to love through clenched teeth or speaking confident-sounding words while quaking with the fear of rejection.

Table 12.1 summarizes the underlying emotional, perceptual, and sequential experiences that teachers consider among a sample of dynamic themes. The sequential rubric for each dynamic theme is a continuum that suggests ways to adapt to different children's developmental needs.

Sections that follow and resource appendices B through F provide examples of practical activities. The play-based activities are unified by each of five dynamic themes. To satisfy teachers' concern for "coverage" of school subjects, each appendix notes how sample activities represent predominant disciplines or strands of knowing. The purpose is not to focus on the particular disciplines or

TABLE 12.1   Emotional, Perceptual, and Sequential Experiences Underlying Dynamic Themes

	Cyclical Change	Conflict/Contract Dialectical Activity	Indirect Progress	Synergy	Double Bind
Underlying Emotional Experiences	Rhythmic flow	Struggle/challenge	Tentativeness, sublimation	Feeling of being flooded	Ambivalence
Underlying Perceptual Experiences	Duration, change through time	Polarities, contrasts	Sacrifice, postponement	Cooperation, transformation	Relationship between appearance and reality
Sequential Considerations	Acceptance of events	Impulsive negativity	Need for immediate results	Feeling of being submerged by results	Merging of representation and referent
	Receiving and sorting of events	Active resistance	Tentativeness; postponement	First stirrings of connecting with others	Increasing differentiation of representation from referent
	Anticipation of change	Passive resistance	Movement from more obvious to less apparent pathways	Increasing perception of connections between objects	Differentiation of referent from representation
	Creating of change over time	Increasingly subtle resistance	Influence over progress	Increasingly effective collaboration with others	Ability to deal with reality
		Increasingly influential resistance			

strands but to integrate relevant conditions for learning in early childhood education and multiple forms of representation. In the interest of reducing redundancy, each example offers samples of processes and representations that readers might generalize to other activities. The brief descriptions of five dynamic themes include cyclical change, dialectical activity (conflict/contrast), indirect progress, synergy (the whole is more than the sum of its parts), and double bind.

Cyclical-Change Dynamic Theme

Some representations of cyclical change include growth or life forms as diverse as plants, animals, and human beings. Other representations include changes of topography wrought by erosion or pollution, the migration of populations, or changes design or music styles. As is the case with other dynamic themes, cyclical change is extradisciplinary.

An underlying feature of experiences that represent cyclical change is the growing sense of duration and time. Figure 12.1 is one possible way to graphically represent cyclical change. Activities that represent human history or the life of a tree offer experiences with cyclical change. Thus not everyone needs to have the same set of experiences to understand cyclical change. Some components of Figure 12.1 appear in the sample activities of Appendix B. For instance, Appendix B lists ideas for an "Adopt a Tree" activity.

The examples below highlight the different ways in which teachers use the conditions for learning when working with preschool children as contrasted with kindergarten- or primary-age children.

- A preschool group engaged in more direct physical experiences with their adopted trees and fewer representational experiences. To illustrate, the children divided themselves into two groups, each of which selected one tree. They hugged "their" tree in different seasons, and noted the way their hands felt. They used a length of yarn to compare the diameters of the two trees. They compared photographs of themselves with their tree at different times during the year. They danced around their tree and sheltered in its shadow while listening to the teacher read stories during warm weather. In these ways, they engaged in the following conditions for learning: induction (comparing trees), cognitive dissonance (predicting and comparing), physical experience (touching and measuring), play (playing tag, dancing, climbing, and decorating), social experiences (sharing play with partners), revisiting (returning at different seasons), and feeling competent (establishing their own criteria and forms of representation). Children may experience all of these conditions for learning as playful.
- With their teacher's help, children recorded their predictions about possible changes and compared the results. Any activity that includes prediction and comparison lends itself to measurements. Activities might begin with nonstandard direct measures such as using a length of yarn to assess a plant's

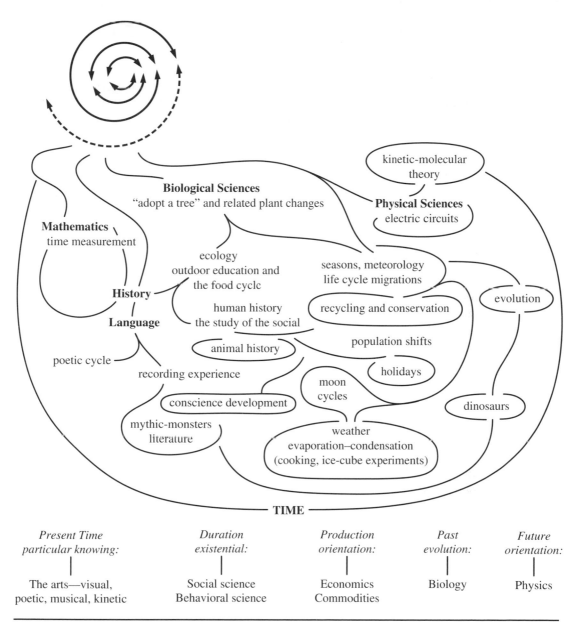

FIGURE 12.1 Cyclical-Change Dynamic Theme

sprouting and later growth. Children of kindergarten and primary age begin to use standard measures.

■ Preschool and kindergarten-age children traced the food cycle from economic and geographic perspectives. They started by visiting a supermarket or pumpkin farm as well as observing the school cafeteria's food delivery.

They also visited a local bakery when a truck was delivering flour and eggs. Real trips to a supermarket, pumpkin farm, or a school delivery entrance are relevant. Young children can plan the questions they might want to raise and discuss ways to find answers.

In all these activities, children made and recorded their predictions and compared their findings. They did so with photographs, drawings, dictated language, and writing.

Dialectical-Activity (Conflict/Contrast) Dynamic Theme

Some emotional, social, physical, and artistic forms of conflict/contrast follow:

- Young children experience sibling rivalry, getting lost, and resolving conflicts. They survive inconsistent treatment, hear disagreements, and participate in conflict. They experience negativity and polarities. They play at taking contrary positions. At first, young children may be active and outwardly expressive but, with experience, may later engage in passive forms of resistance. Holidays or celebrations of events that commemorate unlimited wants and limited resources (harvest festivals) or the overcoming of tyranny or injustice (Martin Luther King Day, Independence Day, or the Purim holiday) also represent the conflict/contrast theme.
- Children experience opposing forces in nature, such as air pressure, magnetism, gravitation, centrifugal and centripetal force, and a sneeze. They see rebounding action-reaction models, such as when balls bounce. The push and pull of waves at the seashore as well as the patterns in a painting by Picasso embody conflict/contrast in other forms.

All these experiences let children sample cognitive dissonance within active, playful activities that embody the dynamic theme of dialectical activity. They also have plenty of opportunities to encounter conflict and contrasts in their interactions with other children and with adults. Figure 12.2 is one possible way to graphically represent dialectical processes. Children who play with ramps or deal with issues of scarcity share an exposure to the conflict/contrast imagery. Some components of Figure 12.2 appear in the sample activities in Appendix C.

Indirect-Progress Dynamic Theme

The dynamic theme of indirect progress is a type of dialectical activity because it features a contrast between obvious and alternative ways to solve problems. For example, children use indirect progress when they

- play such games as checkers (*sacrificing* a piece for greater progress later on), knock hockey (hitting the puck against the side of the table in order to move

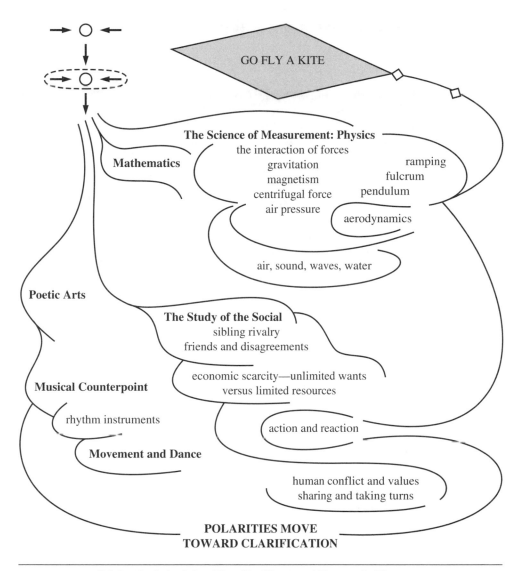

FIGURE 12.2   Dialectical-Activity (Conflict/Contrast) Dynamic Theme

it forward), jigsaw puzzles and Tangrams (reversing preconceptions and moving pieces), or when they use LOGO™ graphics to solve mazes on the computer.

■ postpone immediate gratification in favor of longer-term benefits, such as saving for a particular bicycle.

Some sample activities that represent the isomorphism of indirect progress appear in Appendix D.

Synergy (The Whole Exceeds the Sum of Its Parts)
Dynamic Theme

Some representations of synergy include

- the *relationship* between rubber bands and a ball made of rubber bands,
- the *relationship* between the elements of notes in a melody,
- the *transformation* of corn kernels into popcorn, and
- the *collaboration* of a group in the creation of a mural or a quilt.

To children, experiences of synergy feel like a delightful game. Youngsters find these experiences all the more satisfying when adults appreciate the children's self-organization.

An underlying feature of experiences that represent synergy is the growing sense of cooperation in various forms. The experiences share an underlying unity in the cooperative aspects that they represent. The experiences also lend themselves to representation in varied ways. Figure 12.3 is one possible way to graphically represent of synergy. Some examples of activities that represent synergy appear in Appendix E, with a slant toward identifying strands of knowing in order to satisfy a possible adult sense of the need to "cover" school subject-matter areas.

Double-Bind Dynamic Theme

Some representations of double bind include the following images that embody *ambivalence:*

- The push and pull of waves at the shore resembles a child's feeling of ambivalence at being separated from a significant adult on the first day of school.
- Conservation of quantity or the conservation of sound, when youngsters see both an upper case and a lower case letter at the same time, or the same letter representing multiple sounds (cat and face) create a double bind.
- Children often feel ambivalent about their siblings.
- The relationship of appearance and reality can conflict. For example, a person presents a smiling facade that masks hostility, yet others feel socially compelled to respond to the exterior smile while sensing the hostility. The surprise aspect of cognitive dissonance, the contrast between expectations and outcomes, can sometimes feel like a double bind. Appendix F includes sample activities that represent double bind.

Teachers Match Dynamic Themes,
Experiences, and Children

There are other dynamic themes that also offer different degrees of breadth; for example, "Differences Are Wonderful," "Many Families," "Friends and Loners,"

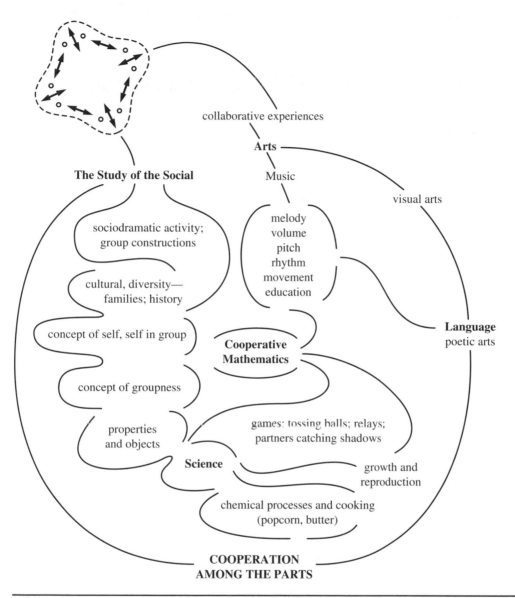

FIGURE 12.3   Synergy (The Whole Exceeds the Sum of Its Parts) Dynamic Theme

"Friends and Enemies," "Multicultural Immigration," "The Interaction of Forces in the Physical World," "The Interaction of Forces in the Living World," and "Beauty Across the World."

When planning activities and resources, *remember to think of the deeper dynamics underlying the themes.* For example, if children are excited about making popcorn, it is a trivial pursuit unless the teacher juxtaposes it with other synergistic experiences, such as those detailed above and in Appendix E. If children are interested in bears or wolves or dinosaurs, there are many dynamic connections to pursue with respect to comparing families, eating and survival strategies, habitats, and living conditions. Children will learn labels and information during the process of comparing, classifying, and reflecting on phenomena.

Teachers who plan with dynamic themes in mind choose activities that focus on *relationships*. Dynamic themes are perceptual models that emphasize the natural connectedness of different experiences. Teachers recognize that *dynamic themes are embedded in the interaction between the various surface forms and the underlying regularities (isomorphic images) of children's experiences. Children experience dynamic themes personally and intuitively through their capacity for imagery and imagination.*

How Nonlinear Theory Works (and Plays out) in Nonlinear Practice

The use of dynamic themes to construct curriculum helps to match teaching with the ways in which young children naturally develop meaning. Two powerful processes interact when teachers consider children's play and their development of meaning.

1. Young children demonstrate a grammar of experience that is the interaction of intuitive and logical thought, underlying imagery and surface metacommunication.
2. Phase transitions take place during the interaction of intuitive and logical thought. Early childhood teachers thoughtfully use phase transitions, a major process that bridges earlier familiar knowing with emerging meaning.

Young children's play reveals their grammar of experience. *The role of the early childhood teacher is to help construct phase transitions that children may perceive as meaningful.*

An Early-Childhood Grammar of Experience

Play is a window through which we can see how children develop and represent meaning. Children create mental models (assumptions about how the world works) as they share experiences, interact with others, and play. Dynamic themes are mental models of meaning. They are implicit, fluid, isomorphic imagery patterns. The underlying regularities of dynamic themes help children connect new meaning with their existing knowledge. The use of dynamic themes to construct curriculum should be based on the ways in which young children develop meaning.

Children use analogies to make connections and perceive the implicit meaning in different types of experiences. *Teachers support children's use of analogy by juxtaposing experiences that share an underlying dynamic theme, although the pattern may take various surface forms.*

Young children intuitively connect a surface experience in the physical world, for example, with a social experience when the experiences represent the same dynamic theme. In this way, they are making nonlinear (curved) connections between experiences. Young children's learning takes place in curved ways, not unlike the structure of European cities. If you make three right turns in a modern city that is laid out in a linear grid, you will return to your starting point; if you do the same in a European city, the shortest distance between two points often becomes a journey defined by curving paths. Dynamic themes more nearly match the nonlinear contours of young children's flow of meaningful learning than do boxes and grids.

Phase Transitions

Phase transitions, the moments during which children construct connections that define an underlying dynamic theme, can occur within the grammar of experience. (See Chapter 7.) These moments are the switch points at which children may perceive new directions and make new connections. During phase transitions, play and cognitive dissonance predominate among the conditions for learning.

Teachers can create cognitive dissonance and provide playful activities that support phase transitions. Indeed, phase transitions dovetail with a dynamic-themes curriculum because they highlight youngsters' perceptions and support transformational learning.

Oscillating Process. The same principles of learning—phase transitions and cognitive dissonance—define the process of youngsters' sociodramatic play. Children experience phase transitions when they make new connections and directly experience what they can do to influence events around them.

Phase transitions are the bridges between perceptions and concepts that children build as they interact with others. The movement across "bridges" (connections) may oscillate (two steps forward and one step backward or sideways) before the "crossing" (transformed meaning) is complete. Thus, the oscillation process may occur within both the child's personal revisiting or the teacher's provision of experiences over time.

Adapting to Development and Growth. Teachers who incorporate dynamic themes in curriculum engage with children in a playful, action-oriented way. (See Fromberg, 1993, 1995.) A dynamic-themes curriculum integrates play with other conditions for learning new meanings, including induction, cognitive dissonance, social interaction, physical experiences, revisiting, and competence. (See Figure 2.1 and Fromberg, 1995.) As children develop and grow, teachers can introduce additional variables, more complete examples of dynamic themes, and less physical and increasingly abstract forms of representational activities. Therefore,

teachers can add or reduce variables and complexity by placing different emphases on the seven conditions for learning.

A repertoire of alternative activities strengthens a teacher's decisions and
professional judgment about when to provide particular experiences. Alterna-
tives provide a scaffold for developing an interactive, dynamic, adaptable curriculum with children. A variety of experiences that cluster around a dynamic
theme offer children equivalent experiences because they represent the same underlying imagery in more or less complex ways.

A Variety of Tools.   *Teachers who use the dynamic-themes approach employ a variety
of inquiry methods to interpret concrete data.* In other words, they help learners find a
way to look beyond the cultural and political boundaries that adults impose on
knowledge. Children do not divide the world into history, geography, chemistry,
and art. Their flexibility is a potent force that early-childhood teachers can
nurture.

*Teachers soak the young child's environment with various surface experiences that
represent underlying regularities.* When young children have plenty of direct experiences and opportunities to play, they deepen their capacity for imagery and connection making. Effective teachers recognize that youngsters need immediate
personal involvement with materials rather than a lengthy introductory discussion. Talk and books come *after* the direct experiences.

Meanings exist in the linear and nonlinear experiences that social scientists,
scientists, and artists study. Children construct and represent meanings in many
forms by employing the same tools that scientists, social scientists, and artists use.
Play is among the many ways that children both develop and represent meaning.
The nonlinear processes of play and meaning, including thought, language, feelings, and emotions, all unfold together. Early-childhood teachers can match nonlinear learning with the nonlinear practice of a play-based, dynamic-themes
curriculum.

Integrating Meaning with
Dynamic Themes and Play

Dynamic themes are the mental models or isomorphic images that underlie the
meanings that children create. The same underlying dynamic theme or isomorphic image can appear transformed in a variety of direct experiences. *Dynamic
themes offer a way to connect young children's grammar of experience with the teacher's
capacity to create phase transitions.* This approach is not a magical pill. It is not a
wrapping that uniformly encloses different groups of children across the country.
However, it offers a way in which each teacher and group of children may construct together their own "fingerprint of experience." These fingerprints may differ on the surface from group to group but still share similar underlying
meanings. Play helps to integrate such interactive and emergent processes.

Play is lymphatic. Meaning is lymphatic. Reality is complex and nonlinear, and the "knowledge of reality or meaning does not lie in the Subject or the Object, but in the dynamic flow between them" (Bohm, cited in Udall, 1996). *Dynamic themes reflect this complex and nonlinear nature of reality.*

Direct experiences and imagination help young children to access dynamic themes. Teachers who plan, place, and sequence experiences consider the broad nature of dynamic themes such as cyclical change, conflict/contrast, indirect progress, synergy, and double bind. An effective teacher is conscious of the dynamic theme for the purpose of planning, estimating, and matching children's capacity to perceive. Youngsters implicitly experience the dynamic theme as a connection-making process.

Play integrates meaning and lets children represent their understanding of meaning. Young people engage enthusiastically in the meaning-building process when they have opportunities to *actively* construct meanings. Teachers who give children plenty of opportunities to play, thus contribute to youngsters' sense of success, power, and self-esteem. Such teachers truly care about children in the fullest professional sense.

SECTION FOUR

Dynamic Issues

The linear tradition in early childhood education has long predominated in the United States. But raising standards, expecting single correct answers, and introducing trivial content and skills out of context do not create educated citizens. Punishing schools whose students perform poorly on linear, standardized tests by reducing these schools' resources simply confounds assumptions about what constitutes worthwhile learning. It's also unfair to the children whose families already have few resources.

Dynamic theory and educational practice attempt to acknowledge the flow of children's experiences and perceptions. Dynamic curriculum depends on professional teachers who see youngsters' nonlinear, culturally specific play models and meaning as a basis for planning activities in the classroom.

In this section, Chapter 13, Present and Future Issues: The Power of Play, discusses the impact of play within cultural contexts, and explores present and future issues in early education. Chapter 14, Controversial Subject Matter, looks at what to play, how to play, when play occurs, and how play serves as an assessment tool. Chapter 15, Nonlinear Dynamic Theory and Practice in a Linear Context, discusses ways to advocate for children's play and to work with parents on stregthening play experiences. The book closes with a focus on the future of children's play and the paradigm shift in early education that a nonlinear dynamic theory of play and pedagogy suggests.

13 Present and Future Issues

The Power of Play

Play is an arena in which children exert power and make choices. Adults may have the power to restrict space and time, but children retain their capacity for fantasy and imagination.

Cultural Contexts

An agrarian or industrial society that supports itself with physical labor offers different play opportunities than does a technological and communication-based society. In agrarian and industrial societies, even today, very young children work. Play may be furtive or integrated with the work tasks.

For example young children in farm economies often work alongside adults. When they do so in settings that use hand tools, play often emerges within the work itself and includes adult participation (Whiting & Edwards, 1988). Anthropologists have noted how parents working in fields have attempted to engage children alongside the workplace in games, songs, or chants (Ibid.). In locations where parents are working outside the home, young people left at home often take care of even younger children. When they do, play can become an inter-age activity. Younger children observe older ones, sometimes imitating them and sometimes becoming props.

Children in subsistence economies often come to view themselves as disempowered and part of a larger, all-powerful system. However, Paolo Freire (1970), a revolutionary Brazilian adult literacy educator, documented a different, intriguing possibility. Freire envisioned reversing the perceptions of illiterate adults in an agrarian society so that they saw themselves as individually worthwhile and as capable of learning to read. Their fatalism had formed the context in which their children lived. When adults assume that they will never learn to read, and that they will always struggle to subsist, their children also learn not to have high expectations of themselves.

Teachers of preschool children from north African families also learned from adults how the family's oral folk tales perpetuated a sense of fatalism (Janiv,

1976). Some African American children (Ogbu, 1978) and other children of color in North America (Erickson & Mohatt, 1982) have concluded that there is no point in planning too far beyond the present. Anthropologists cite involuntary immigration and cultural discontinuities as contributing factors.

These examples support the notion that the underlying dynamics of children's play and thinking exist within the context of culture and the immediate environment. This context powerfully shapes some of the forms that play takes as it emerges as well as some of the spaces in which play may occur.

Teachers Appreciate Diversity

Not surprisingly, teachers from different cultural backgrounds have different expectations and work differently with children (Lubeck, 1985; Roopnarine, Johnson, & Hooper, 1994; Slaughter & Dombrowski, 1989; Tobin, Wu, & Davidson, 1989). On the one hand, play emerges within the context of each child's present cultural—and personal—event knowledge. On the other hand, each child functions within a structure of rules, the grammar of play, which helps him or her to transform the present and anticipate the future. At the same time, play is exquisitely centered in present-time experience, with a feeling that transcends the moment itself. In general, these situation-specific systems are steered by the implicit expectations of a child's family and community. In particular, power relationships influence the extent to which children can broaden their horizons within the scope of sociodramatic play.

However, early childhood teachers may serve children best when they try to appreciate each family's cultural values about work and play, their attitudes toward the present and the future, and their expectations regarding their children's possibilities. Teachers' sensitivity to families' perspectives may inform next steps for particular children. At the same time, teachers face the difficult ethical issue of becoming conscious of how their own cultural outlooks influence their expectations of children and how they interact within the school culture. This chapter focuses on related issues, with an awareness of the influence of historical, cultural, economic, and political contexts.

Work-Play Issues

In the United States, there appears to be an invisible time line that abruptly shifts adults' joy in playing with infants, toddlers, and preschoolers or doting on the play behaviors of young children. By the time children reach kindergarten and primary age, adults replace relatively unrestricted indulgence and time for play with an emphasis on the linear delivery of academic achievement. Concern arises over the "right time" or "right place" for children to play or not to play, the kind of play that is most appropriate, and the question of who should play with whom. Some of these adult concerns reflect cultural expectations concerning the role of childhood.

In school settings, including preschools and child-care centers, many teachers define play as separate from work or, as a sequel to or reward for work. This signals to children that play is less important than work. Actually, children will label an activity as work if an adult asks them to do it; and play if they choose the exact same activity for themselves (King, 1992). This dichotomy can reduce the sense of power that children feel within the school setting, a situation that may embitter children toward school in general and toward school-related subject matter in particular.

Nevertheless, there are "labors of love" in which a worker can feel empowered and self-motivated (Unger, 1998). The challenge for professional teachers is to create opportunities for young children to experience similar empowerment in most of what they do, and to offer a balance between work and play. Indeed, a significant way to evaluate children's learning would be to observe the attitudes that children display toward

- self-motivated reading,
- commitment to scholarly projects, and
- problem setting and solving

Teachers can also observe youngsters'

- use of knowledge,
- intellectual curiosity,
- the pursuit of intellectual ideas, and
- capacity to collaborate with others.

These methods for assessing children's broad learning touch on the relationships among why children play, where they may play, who may play, what kinds of play the culture may tolerate, and when to play.

Why Play?

The research findings discussed in Chapters 4 clearly point to the power of play as an influence on young children's development. In particular, play integrates social competence, language development, cognitive development, problem-solving skills, and creativity. Helping children exercise their power to play therefore deserves a significant focus in early childhood classes.

Ethical Considerations. There also are ethical reasons for enhancing children's opportunities to play. For one thing, play is the realm in which children can feel powerful. Moreover, as young children play, they use the syntax of play as well as the syntax of language, however silently, to plan and make judgments. "To some extent, this is done by talking silently to [them] selves, making narratives out of what might happen next, and then applying syntax-like rules of combination to rate. . . . "critical decisions, candidates, advertising, possible propaganda, and issues of danger or safety" (Calvin, 1996, p. 88). In addition, according to the

International Association for the Child's Right to Play and the United Nations Declaration of Rights of the Child (particularly Article 31), children have a human right to play. After all, play is valuable behavior in itself and part of the joy of being human.

Play and Imagination: Play, the Arts, and Related Experiences. *According to psychologist Lev Vygotsky (1962), play leads development, and imagination is a future-oriented phenomenon.* As children play, they imagine and project rules within which they then proceed to play. Their capacity to play reflects the use of concepts and skills that function in advance of their capacity to reflect on them. That is, their competence during play exceeds their performance outside the play framework. *Imagination is an implicit form of representation; play is an explicit form for representing imagination.* Imagination thus is an important part of learning and invention. It is one way in which humans compare the past with new experiences during learning. Imagination also lets us "[construct] images that are not found in completed form in reality. . . . Imagination is a necessary, integral aspect of realistic thinking" (Vygotsky, 1987, p. 349). As children play, they construct both images and products that simulate reality. Play therefore helps them move, in an oscillating fashion, along a continuum of representation that begins with physical and oral expression and continues into graphic representation.

Children represent their understandings in increasingly symbolic or abstract forms. If we consider that the brain develops in holistic ways by strengthening pathways and creating networks of connections, then it makes sense for teachers to provide an array of experiences that can infuse imaginative, representational, and play-related development. From this perspective, teachers would provide rich experiences in play and the arts, and encourage the use of imagery across the curriculum.

Through using our imagination, we try out new connections in the physical or social world before making a commitment in the course of discoveries and new creations. Adults list as their play the arts, sports, games, physical exertion, constructions, collecting, and gardening (Fromberg & Bergen, 1998). These experiences share the transcendent sense of involvement and satisfaction that children experience in their play. During these kinds of pastimes, people often have the opportunity to project their imaginations into planning or to fantasize.

Western cultures tend to elevate rational, linear processes to a more important status than imaginative, nonlinear processes. However,

> young children's classifications [are] no less complex, sophisticated, and orderly than the rational forms that are represented as correct. But we need to attend to the metaphoric connections that underlie young children's "confused" ordering schemes; these are often tied in with unsuspected qualities of the objects being classified (Egan, 1997, p. 214).

Professional teachers therefore appreciate children's imaginations when youngsters demonstrate alternative perspectives; such teachers can also appreciate children's metaphoric perspectives about ordinary events and objects.

Where to Play

Children play virtually anywhere, including indoors or outdoors at home, on the street, in a park, in a supermarket or department store, in a museum, in school, in a bomb shelter, or in a commercial play space. As pollution and the construction of roads and buildings increase, young people have fewer opportunities to use natural habitats in urban and suburban areas (Rivkin, 1998). Although urban centers have created rooftop playgrounds as well as "vest-pocket" parks for children, these spaces tend to be limiting when compared with suburban or rural outdoor play spaces; space plays a distinct role in the range and pace of imagination. The time available to play outdoors in the United States is further restricted by linear approaches in school that squeeze outdoor play and "recess" out of the curriculum (Sutton-Smith, 1988). Outdoor play, especially, offers opportunities for children to develop large-muscle skills, eye-hand coordination, and group-process skills. When children play outdoors through activities such as climbing, wheeling toys, digging, rolling, and building, they strengthen their sense of empowerment without the indoor constraints on noise and speed.

Adventure Playgrounds. "Adventure playgrounds," in which children can build shelters and other constructions from raw or recycled materials and engage in other creative activities, have been an urban response to shrinking natural habitats. The idea for adventure playgrounds started in Denmark and required the presence of a supervising adult to maintain a safe environment. "Adventure playgrounds never gained much popularity in the United States, largely because of their unsightliness, concerns with safety, and lack of well-trained play leaders" (Frost & Woods, 1998, p. 234). Nevertheless, a few public versions exist in the Sun Belt area of the United States.

Within school settings, it is relevant to consider the creative possibilities of some version of a construction-oriented playground. Teachers are present in such a setting, and a real construction option for children is a creative alternative to organized group games and sports, tag games, rough-and-tumble play, or milling around. At the same time, the addition of a construction option would not need to exclude the possibility for children to make other choices.

Caretaker-and-Child Playgrounds. In Great Britain, the One O'Clock Club, a public service, replicates a model preschool setting at one o'clock each weekday afternoon in an urban public park. Children are accompanied by an adult caretaker and participate indoors or outdoors in such activities as painting, art, construction activities, and water play. Caretakers are seated in the area and can observe preschool teachers interacting with children.

There is great value in having caretakers observe a professional's interaction with an unhappy or reticent child; the observer may learn about alternative ways in which to work with the child by seeing a professional model. This approach also lets adults share the responsibility of child care for a brief time. They can arrive and depart with their children at any time during the afternoon and stop for a cup of tea with other adults. Children are aware of their caretaker's presence and can begin learning the process of separation before they are old enough to enter a formal public-school setting.

In contrast, adults who take young children to outdoor play spaces in the United States often tend to miss both professional models as well as inter-generational support for their interactions with one another. However, in inclement weather, indoor commercial play spaces sometimes offer different degrees of play supervision.

Commercial Playgrounds.   Use of some commercial parks, both indoors and outdoors, is free to restaurant or shop users. Others require an admission fee. These kinds of facilities may offer children playground equipment or repetitive kinds of pastimes, such as bouncing in a pit full of plastic balls or sliding, spinning, and constructing activities. They also offer entertainments of various sorts, ranging from puppet shows, folk musicians, magicians, or videos. As with all settings that young children use, issues arise that include child empowerment, sensitive supervision, and healthfulness, such as the clean maintenance of surfaces that children use.

Computer Literacy and Interactive Technology.   Electronic games and video games are the mainstay of play for some children. Often, youngsters are solitary users of such technologies. Those who acquire computer literacy at an early age are privileged compared with those who do not have access to computers in the community or at school. At the same time, these technologies raise questions about what constitutes worthwhile electronic pastimes for young children.

We can evaluate commercial offerings by seeing whether they provide opportunities for imagination, personal choice, self-organization, and collaboration. For example, some toys are based on television programs. Children often use the toys to reproduce the television programs. If this reproduction is only replication and imitation, it may contradict meaningful play that represents self-organized imagination. Moreover, some programs are based on toys, constituting full-time toy advertisements (Kline, 1995). These examples typically do not fit the evaluative criteria.

With some commercial formats, the television, rather than the child, "scripts" the play (Provenzo, 1998, p. 515). Video games that require children to follow a set of rules or for which single outcomes exist are similar to workbook formats that also disempower children. More than a third of households in the United States have video games, many of which are sexist, racist, violent, and limiting (Ibid.). To qualify as self-organized, empowering play, these products must give youngsters opportunities to make choices, collaborate and negotiate with others, and use their imaginations.

When computer technologies, including virtual reality, offer children genuine opportunities to play, they become additional playground sites. For children who are physically challenged, computers may help them extend their power through the use of breath, voice, eye-movement, and finger control. Computers also can extend the playground for children of primary-school age by providing thoughtful access to the Internet and using many picture icons. The experience becomes especially integrative when teachers create their own home pages (Silvern, 1998).

As with all modalities, creating a balance of experiences is important. Sensitive teachers will see that word-processing and other computer software will take their place in a balanced way with sociodramatic play opportunities, games, and other play forms both indoors and outdoors.

There is a growing, multimillion-dollar industry of infant and toddler computer software. The software industry uses the term "lapwear" to describe the image of an adult who goes on line with a baby on his lap. Consider that a nine-month-old infant or a toddler may hit keys at random and begin to associate that action with some motion on the computer screen. We might wonder to what extent this play differs from hitting a button on a "busy box," turning a handle on a "jack-in-the-box," or swatting a mobile. And how might this play differ from a scenario in which an infant or toddler sits on a parent's lap as the two read a picture book together? To what extent does exposure to three- and two-dimensional experiences require balance in early life? There are currently no percentages or formulas to guide us. Therefore, we need to use common sense in deciding which experiences to offer. We must consider the broadest potential for meaningful experiences within which children can feel powerful, self-directed, and successful.

Who Will Play?

As adults play, it is interesting to see the impact on children's lives. Many shopping malls, for example, now feature virtual-reality playgrounds in which older children and adults put on helmets and sensory-wired clothing to experience such activities as a virtual high-speed chase, free fall, or boxing match. Adults have paid fees to enter jousting tournaments, climb urban "rock" faces, and don Velcro™ suits to leap (and stick!) against a Velcro™ wall.

At the same time, children, beginning in infancy, have been taught to swim, have engaged in gymnastics classes, and have taken lessons in another language. Toddlers, who have only recently learned to walk, have participated in similar activities as well as an assortment of sports and music instruction. Parents urge preschoolers to take part in similar activities as well as take dancing, science, puppetry, and computer classes. The activities increase in number and diversity with each year of a child's life, often leaving young children with little time for self-organized socialization and play.

The "right to play" has faced challenges in recent decades with the growth of extensive after-school and weekend instructional and adult-structured activities. Consider that 65 percent of women with children younger than six years of age work outside the home (Children's Defense Fund, 1999, p. 57). In the interest of safety and the enrichment of children's lives during their parents' absence, some adults have enrolled youngsters in after-school "instruction" that includes organized sports (such as gymnastics, swimming, tennis, soccer, and even preschool track), computer classes, group and individual music instruction, puppetry, and the arts. Children who remain at home with a family member or hired caretaker frequently spend time in front of a television set, either passively or while manipulating toys.

In particular, these chidren have little time for outdoor, self-organized play and thus lack opportunities to think, imagine, daydream, study the clouds, or create pretense with neighborhood children. There has been a plethora of literature about popular culture, children's addiction to television (Winn, 1977), and the "hurried child" (Elkind, 1981). Increasingly, adults are recognizing that children are style conscious at early ages. They seek to own, wear, and sport particular labels because they have seen advertising on television. Consumerism and the guidelines for defining play share little in common.

The Influence of Western Europe Traditions on Early Childhood Education

Despite a diverse population, the underlying culture of the United States derives mainly from the western European tradition that values work, individual effort, individual achievement, and competition. Most Westerners believe that knowledge is fixed within disciplines, and that young people's thinking needs to "conform" to these categories (Egan, 1997, p. 216). Many U.S. educational institutions only preserve this culture.

At the same time, schools have been the vehicle by which children of immigrant families have become acculturated and have achieved some economic independence. Theoretically, schools exist to develop a literate citizenry who can become thoughtful participants in the democratic process of voting and in the world of work. Indeed, work forms the cornerstone of this citizenship ideal.

However, within the framework of early-childhood education, play is not the antithesis of work. Rather, it's one way for youngsters to learn what society sanctions. Still, based on the appearance and forms of play, some lay people and teachers view play as insignificant for the development of citizenship and economic independence. In fact, educated school administrators and "the teacher next year" who have not learned about early-childhood education find the "look" of fine-quality early-childhood settings unacceptable. To the extent that play manifests part of early-childhood education, the "look" of such education can become a public-relations nightmare. The next chapter deals with controversial subject matter within the field of play, and offers some related ideas for teacher intervention.

14 Controversial Subject Matter

This chapter looks at controversial issues in play. It presents educational concerns about what to play, when to play, how to assess play, and how teachers might sensitively intervene.

What to Play?

Children's play themes grow out of their event knowledge. In the United States at this time, television is virtually universal. As part of contemporary development in varying degrees, young children play at being television superheroes and superheroines, enact teenage behavior, and explore violent themes or behavior.

Before the growth of television and film culture, children already imitated the behavior of teenagers, popular story characters from fairy tales, or fictional accounts. Children tested themes that involved argument and combat, and played out good and evil, angels and devils, threat and escape, love and hate, despair and hope, war and peace, win and loss, and mistakes and their consequences. In this respect, today's children connect with a long tradition; the underlying themes are similar, although the surface forms may look different. For example, the theme of "cops and robbers" in some urban neighborhoods now takes the form of "cops and teenagers" (D. Barnes, personal communication, 1994).

Gender Themes. Teachers of children see youngsters exploring questions about who can marry whom (Cahill & Theilheimer, 1999). They also witness children's acting out adolescent or adult sexual styles or behaviors. In Chapter 8, Kay and Ira's play included extensive "dating" behavior. Their teacher tried to steer them away from this theme by providing diversions and suggesting new planning sessions. Quite simply, there are no pills available in education for these borderline situations.

When children prove furtive or intrusive in their sex play, sensitive teachers can help them factually label body parts or define safe and appropriate behavior. Role play is another forum in which some teachers have worked out mutual respect and caring with children.

Beginning early, girls' and boys' play interests and toy choices tend to be gender-oriented. Most girls engage in more sedentary, small-muscle activities, homemaking, and fashion themes, while boys engage in more rough-and-tumble, construction, and outdoor-activity themes. Western culture sanctions girls', but not boys', broader interest in both boys' and girls' activities (Honig, 1998).

For example, when Eden and David were four years of age, for example, they played doctor and nurse. Eden reported to her mother that she was going to be a nurse when she grew up and that David was going to be a doctor like his father. Her mother asked her whether she preferred making decisions or following orders from somebody else. She thoughtfully acknowledged that she preferred making decisions and decided that, if doctors made decisions, she would prefer to be a doctor. She did indeed become a physician; David, a lawyer.

Labels, Toilet Talk, and Sexuality.   Teenage- or adult-sexuality elements in sociodramatic play typically make teachers feel uncomfortable. It is difficult to gauge: How much of the expression of such themes is imitation of television, neighborhood, or home? How much of it reflects distinctive family cultural mores such as nudity or the use of explicit adult labels? For example, a five-year-old mentioned the word *vagina* in a natural context during a carpool trip and was excluded by the parent driver from future participation in the carpool. This driver overreacted to a highly verbal child whose family used adult labels with comfort for all bodily functions.

Preschool children often play with toilet talk as part of their sense of humor and power (Bergen, 1998; Davidson, 1998). Teachers should assess how much of this behavior and vocabulary reflects childish imitation or testing and how much of it reveals child abuse. These are not easy questions, because they sometimes reflect conflicting cultural values.

Children are naturally curious about their own bodies, other people, and the world. This curiosity can be playful, spontaneous, occasional, and voluntary. This natural curiosity and sexual exploration differ from anxiety-based, obsessive, or aggressive behavior that involves contextually or personally inappropriate sexual behavior. Thoughtful educational researchers suggest that the following early-childhood behaviors indicate the need for family intervention by professionals:

- The child's interest in sex is out of proportion with his or her curiosity about other aspects of the world.
- Interest in sex is compulsive, to the exclusion of interest in other developmentally appropriate activities.
- The child is more knowledgeable about sexual behavior than other children of the same age, the same socioeconomic background, and from the same neighborhood. . . . [K]nowledge about sexuality does not have universal standards, but rather is affected by culture and context.
- The child approaches unfamiliar children, not friends, to engage in sexual behavior.
- The child bribes or forces another child to engage in sexual behavior.
- Other children often complain about the sexual behavior of the child.

■ When sexual matters are raised, the child becomes anxious, fearful, or angry (Johnson, cited in Essa & Murray, 1999, pp. 233–234).

Rough-and-Tumble Play. Rough-and-tumble play features aggression without aggressiveness, violence, or malevolent intent. For example, four-year-old Tim takes off his space helmet and uses it to hit the helmet that Eli is wearing:

TIM: [hitting Eli with his helmet] "Do you feel anything?"

ELI: "Ow! Ow!"

TIM: [giggles]

ELI: [giggles] "Boom! Boom!" [They hit each other back and forth several times, both giggling.] "Let's go get the commander."

TIM: "Blast off! Eli, how about we don't need helmets? This helmet is too big for me." [They switch helmets, then take them off.]

ELI: [places both helmets on his head; both continue developing their space-travel script]

This sort of play is not dangerous, although it may on rare occasions transmute into aggression (Pellegrini, 1998). Although rough-and-tumble play lets children explore aggression and hazards, teachers may remain uncomfortable with it even in the absence of physical danger.

Most early-education teachers are women who tend to feel uncomfortable with aggressive themes. However, learning to resolve aggression, engage in self-organization, build autonomy, fulfill responsibility, and achieve self-motivation are important goals in early-childhood education. Children need to build their own motives for ethical, fair, and peaceful resolution of differences and interpersonal problems. They need to learn alternative ways to deal with disagreements and conflicts. When teachers forbid aggressive behavior, children usually move their antisocial feelings underground. Later, these feelings may erupt in the absence of adult control. A recent survey suggests that overcontrolled, overscheduled, and pressured children are more prone to volatility and violence (Nickles & Ashcraft, cited in Doyle, 1999).

Some teachers and researchers who have observed war play (Carlsson-Paige & Levin, 1987) and extensive superhero play (Paley, 1984) saw these episodes as learning opportunities. They also role played and discussed alternative, mutually satisfying ways to resolve disagreements.

Teachers should encourage all children to particiate in adventurous, spatial activities as well as fine-motor and nurturing activities. Active kindergarten-block players who engaged regularly in superhero play needed at least half an hour before they were ready to engage in more sedentary art activities (Ibid.).

Competition and Cooperation. Many games end with a single winner. In games of two or more children, there are necessarily several (or many) losers. For the victor, winning itself is compensation. In team-based games, team members who lose together may feel some compensation in the experience of collective effort and camaraderie. Therefore, an emphasis on the fun of playing the game, the exercise of improved skills in completing increasingly difficult games, and the celebration of completion might provide young children with some balance when they lose a game. At such times, teachers can help take the sting out of losing by focusing attention on how sincerely, fairly, and skillfully, everyone played. The aim is to encourage youngsters' sense of competence and growth.

Some educators also recommend that teachers emphasize the value of differences. They suggest that noncompetitive games provide one way to reduce or eliminate teasing and bullying (Froschl & Sprung, 1999). (The survival mechanism of "closing down" learning potential in the face of bullying is consistent with what brain researchers have found.)

In addition to the pain of losing, many commercial games offer more variables than children may be able to juggle. However, it is probably unrealistic to expect children to play only cooperative games without single winners. Nevertheless, a balanced outlook toward competition and cooperation is a realistic goal. Teachers should plan as many such experiences as possible. They can also adapt games in ways that minimize winning and losing while increasing cooperation. A few examples follow.

- *Bingo or Lotto format*: Create all boards with the same photos, words, or puzzles but in a different order. In this format, all children complete the game at the same time. Five- and six-year-olds, for example, have happily played four separate boards in turn that had the same contents in a different order.
- *Board games*: Create a single moving piece that children take turns moving across the pathways to a goal, such as "Get E.T. Home," "The Elf Reaches the Pot of Gold at the End of the Rainbow," "The Children Find the Path out of the Forest." Some ways to organize board games include using a die or dice, a spinner, cards, and a mechanical or computer lottery.
- *Memory or Pairs or Concentration*: Feed the matched pair of cards to the Hungry Hippopotamus, Hungry Dog, or Munching Monkey.
- *Bowling*: Each week, the group keeps track of its combined scores with tallies or numerals and compares their scores across a month of Thursdays.
- *Physical games*: Individual skill games with changing individual goals, such as "jump over the rope," "crawl over a horizontal ladder," "limbo under a rope," and "play with mazes on paper or on the floor."
- *Puzzles*: Children of primary-school age enjoy word-find, crossword, and jigsaw puzzles that they can do alone, in pairs, or small groups. Jigsaw puzzles help youngsters learn about the relationships between parts and wholes.

  Size recommendations are as follows:

  - toddlers: a one-to-one match
  - three-year-olds: four to six pieces
  - four- to five-year-olds and older: up to twenty or thirty pieces

The cultural context defines the degree of tolerable competition and the expectations for different groups within the culture. "Most children in most cultural settings play both competitively and cooperatively, and often within the same game. In fact, in some societies group competition is encouraged precisely because it encourages cooperation and group loyalty" (Eifermann, cited in Hughes, 1999, p. 37).

Toy Selection. The question of which toys best fulfill the goals of early-childhood education has generated intense controversy. Many early-childhood educators deny the need to pander to popular culture when selecting toys for young children. For this group, blocks, sociodramatic play props, the arts, woodworking, and science and literacy materials need to be totally flexible in their use and classically generic. Most educators would want to see these kinds of playthings predominate in early-childhood education.

At the same time, we need to acknowledge that some children do not have access at home to the commercial playthings with which some children lace the imagery of their block constructions and other sociodramatic play. Such children are thus excluded from a body of event knowledge and might have limited potential to collaborate in sociodramatic play. One teacher, mindful that some children did not have a few popular toys, bought for the classroom a few popular toys, such as Cabbage Patch dolls (P. G. Ramsey, personal communication, 1998). The presence of these kinds of toys allowed all the children to communicate on a more level playing field, and facilitated "cross-group play" (Ramsey, 1998, p. 29).

Economic inequities are likely to continue, particularly as electronics technology augments toys. When toys have electronic enhancements, teachers should evaluate whether children can still interact with and influence the course of play. For example, children of primary-school age might create their own interactive toys by using computerized Lego™. Using a similar technology, children can program "smart" beads that transfer light across the beads, creating varied patterns. This kind of technology can transform day-to-day experience rather than duplicate the construction of bead patterns or Lego™ structures that children may collaboratively build. Psychologists have made the following observations about interactive and static toys:

> We have seen children play with elaborately constructed toys, motorized toys, wind-up objects, and even Transformer™ cars for a short while because the familiarity of the toy matches their preestablished schemas and evokes the affect of joy. But these toys often end up at the bottom of the toy chest, their batteries dead. Children choose large blocks, Legos, miniature people, and makeshift objects for longer periods of sustained play (Singer, 1994, p. 21).

A major criterion for selecting toys is that children can use the toy for more than one purpose. The sociodramatic and construction equipment mentioned above, as well as water, sand, climbing equipment, and cardboard cartons, all have more than one purpose. Additional criteria include the following:

- The toys help children feel comfortable with ambiguity and complexity while retaining a sense of competence. Children can interpret and use equipment that offers ambiguity, opportunity for complexity, and representational variety; they can freely use their imaginations.
- The toys may be used by one or more children, mainly independent of adult support (but within an adult's oversight, for the sake of safety).
- The toys are gender-neutral and avoid stereotypes of gender, ethnicity, age, or ability.
- The toys give children opportunities to solve problems of different degrees of difficulty.
- The toys are sturdy and safe.

With Whom to Play?

Unspoken cultural values often influence the way adults interact with children. The discussion that follows deals with equity issues that may influence children's play.

Cultural Equity.   An anthropologist (Heath, 1983) who studied black and white working-class and middle-class families in rural and urban settings found that the urban, middle-class, black and white children arrived at school with similar ways of working and playing. In contrast, the working-class black and white children arrived at school with different ways of working and playing.

The working-class black children were able to create narratives, use powerful metaphors, and integrate humor into their conversations. They had participated in more inter-age and intergenerational activities, and demonstrated creative uses of time and space. The primary-grade teachers typically did not appreciate these perspectives, preferring to hear single, "correct" answers. By the time the children arrived in the intermediate grades, where teachers required them to use interpretive and fluid skills, many had become discouraged and alienated from school life. In chaos theory language, the children and the teachers were focused on different "attractors."

In contrast, young working-class white children were taught to provide single correct answers to questions, to use toys in a single correct way, and to keep things in the same space. Their primary-grade teachers appreciated these perspectives. However, these children typically did not flourish in the intermediate grades, where teachers expected them to apply comprehension skills and make connections between ideas. These dramatic contrasts between cultural experiences point to the need for teachers to be sensitive to such influences in the lives of children.

"Those teachers who appreciate the strengths that children bring to school, who welcome alternative solutions to problems, who ask questions for which more than one response is expected—in short, who adapt to children—provision classrooms for play" (Fromberg, 1998, p. 200). Failing to notice or discounting children's distinctive cultural and personal ways of thinking and learning is to engage in culturally irrelevant teaching, thereby withholding learning opportunities and perpetuating racism (Ladson-Billings, 1995) and classism.

In many school districts, children who have been identified as gifted, most often on the basis of IQ scores, receive from their special teachers liberal doses of imaginative play, creative construction activities, and rich exposure to a range of art forms and computer literacy in a nonlinear way. Many children who have been defined as slower, low-income, bilingual, or culturally different have been offered liberal doses of drill in fragmented skills and memorization of isolated information in a linear way. Yet, all children prosper by having opportunities to use their imaginations, represent their ideas through a variety of art forms, and play in their own ways.

Gender Equity.   Gender equity is a distinct outgrowth of cultural equity. Some parents might discourage children from playing gender-associated activities through toy selection, the degree of closeness or freedom that they permit, and the degree of physical involvement that they tolerate. They may ask children to stop an activity, or pointedly substitute another direction. Parents usually encourage girls to remain close, play with domestic types of toys, and move more quietly and sedately than boys.

Children integrate their culture's gender-role expectations beginning in their toddlerhood. For example, a three-year-old boy who was trying to walk in women's high heels in the classroom faced the ridicule of older children. Boys in many classrooms dominate block play. When teachers provide equivalent access or double the amount of available blocks, boys *and* girls use the blocks, often in same-gendered dyads (Rogers, 1985). Anthropologists have found that, beginning with four-year-olds, many children select chums of the same gender (Whiting, Edwards et al., 1988).

Special Learning Needs.   For development to progress, children need to be safe and feel that adults accept their play. Some children with physical disabilities may not experience some forms of play as enjoyable because they cannot control the process. Their parents, perhaps feeling overly protective, may have discouraged such self-motivated play (Mindes, 1998). Children who have language delays communicate with difficulty in sociodramatic play and "may develop defensive, aggressive, or passive actions to mask the pain. . . . If other play activity choices are not available, they may engage in disruptive behavior" (Ibid., p. 210).

Youngsters' social competence follows metarepresentation, because they can consider situations "as if" they were thinking from the perspective of other people. Children from large families typically gain metacognition and self-reflection readily, perhaps owing to the rich feedback they get from more people at an early age.

Other researchers have observed that autistic children have difficulty with the "as-if" aspect of play, the capacity to engage in metarepresentation, which is part of the young child's developing theory of mind (Leslie & Frith, 1988). However, autistic children do engage in play activities with constructions, objects, and computer games. Some teachers of preschool-age autistic children have found that weighted vests help the children to feel more comfortable in the potentially overstimulating environment of an inclusive classroom. They have also found that providing sufficient uninterrupted wait-time gives such children an opportunity to sort out comments and responses to other people.

Moreover, evidence suggests that the play of children with autism increases when teachers and more capable child players have supported their play and imagination in socially constructed ways (Wolfberg, 1999). "Mastering the skills necessary for peer group entry is of critical importance for children with autism and others who frequently encounter peer rejection" (Ibid., p. 38). Autistic children benefit when teachers provide a consistent and predictable (Ibid., p. 48) sequence that includes parallel play, activities that engage children in a common focus, and activities in which children collaborate toward a common goal (Ibid., p. 49). When teachers recognize the autistic children's echolalia (echoing another's comments) and repetitive comments (repeating their own statements) as initial signals of meaningful communication, they can respond and build on the comments. The typically developing children can then observe the teacher's modeling and gradually include the autistic children in accepting ways (Ibid., passim). *The most effective interventions take place when teachers use phase-transition opportunities to interpret and model for both novice and experienced players.*

Just as phase transitions reflect an oscillation between states of being, feeling, and understanding, so does attention reflect an oscillation between stimulation, focus, and absorption. Research suggests that the brains of children who have attention-deficit disorders are wired to seek novelty; thus they appear to be "paying attention to everything" (Jensen, 1998, p. 49). Teachers can modify the pace of stimulation to allow reactivity time and balance individual and group time, engagement and reflection, familiarity and novelty.

Teachers also need to consider reactivity time in relation to individual children with different approaches to play. Children with Down syndrome may need additional time to change the focus of their attention. They may respond better to visual than auditory phenomena. Teachers can offer a narrow range of challenges and take an active role in interaction, while anticipating a slower reaction time (Appl, 1998). Asking a question such as, "Would you . . . ?" when there is no real choice only creates ambiguity for a child with Down syndrome. Instead, a direct comment such as, "It is time now to . . ." clarifies the situation (Ibid.).

During sociodramatic play, in which children frequently change the focus of their attention, a child with Down syndrome may be particularly slow to shift attention. His expressive language delays are related to muscle control. His receptive language delays are related to the pace with which he integrates new concepts. Sensitive teachers model pausing to listen carefully. They also display an attentive body posture and eye contact with increased wait-time.

Typically developing preschool children within inclusive settings learn to follow the lead of a teacher who models a small range of challenges along with respect and caring for each child. Teachers who show respect, caring, and support for physically challenged children can serve children with Down syndrome, autistic children, and children with other developmental needs. Such teachers can serve in this way while modeling for typically developing children how they might include all children in play. Teachers have other ways as well to adapt to individual learning needs of children in inclusive settings. For example, for children who have a hearing disability, teachers can place mirrors in different locations to help children see what is happening behind them (Kieff & Casbergue, 2000, p. 73).

Effective teachers remain conscious of the principles that define play. They are particularly sensitive to the issue of a child's activity choice. They provide challenges that include both an informed choice and a possible chance for success. This means that the teacher may need to adapt play provisions in some of the following ways:

- *Physical setting:* additional railings, height of equipment, clipboards with additional fasteners to hold down paper or board games, card stands, Velcro™ closings, and textured materials
- *Material:* fist-accessible hand grips on housekeeping play materials, frames for holding blocks, and left-handed and four-fingered scissors
- *Amount of time available for participation:* stagger the time available for different children to engage in centers
- *Clear contrasts:* focus a single, clear figure against a familiar background, and provide an environment that is relatively free of unnecessary visual or auditory distractions
- *Pacing:* provide sufficient advance notice for closing down, cleanup, and transition to another activity; in general, minimize and reduce the number of transitions during the day

Teachers can also adjust definitions of what play means from each child's perspective and what represents progress for an individual child. A child may be "frozen" on a material or piece of play equipment for weeks at a time. For example, four-year-old Carl entered the outdoor playground each day and took possession of a red wagon, dragging it along to block play and indoor hospital play. The wagon's bulk impeded his mobility in sociodramatic play settings and table activities. Yet he attached himself to it in much the same way that younger children hold onto a blanket or washcloth from home. After a few weeks, the teacher was able to increase his involvement with other children and playthings by integrating other play activities with the wagon play. After several more weeks, the teacher removed the red-wagon option for everybody before the school day began, so that Carl could continue to build a sense of security in using other playthings.

Play Therapy. Play therapy as a "remedial" field highlights the value of play for all children. One benefit of ordinary play, outside a formal therapeutic situation, is that it lets children explore their concerns, fears, and wishes in a safe environment and develop a sense of mastery. Professional play therapists focus attention on children's feelings. They encourage children to freely use pretend play and role play in a permissive environment outside the classroom. Such therapists also vary the relationship between play structure and therapeutic intervention to support a child's sense of control, imagination, creativity, realistic self-image, and sense of success (Leland, 1983). Play therapists use specialized strategies, usually with individual children on a regular schedule, under conditions that are not possible for classroom teachers. (See Gitlin-Weiner, 1998, and Schaefer & O'Connor, 1983.) Nevertheless, play therapists appreciate what educators of young children can see: "A major function of play is the changing of what may be unmanageable in reality to manageable situations through symbolic representation that provides children with opportunities for learning to cope by engaging in self-directed exploration" (Landreth, 1993, p. 51).

Teachers may also find some insights by looking at children's play within hospital settings. In hospital settings, role play and ritualized play are particularly evident. Rituals, which may include rhythm as well as repetition, help children gain control over seemingly uncontrollable discomforts, separations, and threats (Gaynard, 1998). Young children in hospital settings comfort themselves through these forms of play. Adult-guided play that can prepare young children for uncomfortable experiences is really a cross between role playing and storytelling; the possibility of knowing what to expect may increase the child's sense of control over his or her environment. The imagery in such preparation parallels in part the notion of script building in sociodramatic play. Merely playing with a hospital-based child-life professional can provide comfort (Ibid.). Some of these patterns of play may follow the recovering child into the classroom.

Celebrating Inclusion.   Early-childhood teachers committed to adapting curriculum to the needs of individual children create a classroom climate of inclusion. A recent study of the notion that "you can't say, you can't play," a practice developed by Vivian Paley (1992), found that young children collaborate adeptly to implement this shared policy (Sapon-Shevin, Dobbelaere, Corrigan, Goodman, & Mastin, 1998). In those classrooms where children invite one another home for birthday parties, this inclusionary policy may be undermined. Some teachers of kindergarten- and primary-age children have anticipated this problem and have encouraged consensus among the children and their parents about invitations. In the interest of party size, one primary-age class agreed that any birthday party for a boy would include all boys in the class and for a girl would include all girls. Another teacher and class agreed that there would be no invitations distributed at school. Still another teacher and class agreed that the entire class would celebrate all birthdays only in school.

Building a sense of competence and inclusion entails making each child the temporary center of attention. One teacher led a group of six-year-olds as they took turns being the highlighted child at a daily meeting. Group members would each state something nice about that child. One day, a child said, with a shy grin, that another was "bad." When the teacher challenged the speaker's adherence to the "nice" rule, the speaker explained to the teacher that "ba-a-a-d" meant "foxy-y-y," both terms of admiration among local adolescents.

In another strategy, a different seven-year-old child each week was featured on a classroom bulletin board. Parents provided photographs and biographical data ranging from birth weight to illnesses, family trips, and special events. Other children in the class wrote brief "something nice about . . ." comments and posted them. The focus child wrote about his or her favorite activities, heroes and heroines, career aspirations, and a wish that could make the world a better place. When the teacher asked children for a "wish," they often mentioned material goods or a trip to Disney World; when she asked them to make a "wish to make the world better and help people," the children's contributions become more meaningful.

When to Play?

The idea of choosing to play or not to play alone or with others deserves consideration when children engage in after-school activities. Some writers have warned about the need to compensate children for the lack of opportunities for "recess" (Sutton-Smith, 1988) during the school day. Others have urged educators to provide for time for children to choose to be passive, alone, or "inactive" (Mulligan, 1996, pp. 112–113), chase around with others (Corsaro, 1985), or to simply observe.

In any case, nobody questions tiny children's right to play. It is when children enter the kindergarten and primary grades that a seismic shift occurs in adults' expectations. And the work now assigned to youngsters often takes the shape of adult-directed linear activity that is goal-oriented rather than episodic, and narrowly defined as correct or incorrect. A recent compilation of anecdotal data indicates that play continues to exist into adults' professional life, enriches it, and contributes to self-motivation in the disciplines and professional life. Successful archaeologists, artists, biologists, business people, chemists, dancers, journalists, lawyers, mathematicians, physicians, sociologists, and theologians continue to play in their work. (See Fromberg & Bergen, 1998, Section VI.) Therefore, educators must provide opportunities for all young children to self-organize their play if society expects them to become self-directed citizens.

Play as an Assessment Tool

Children at play reveal a great deal about what they understand. Their coordination, social competence, language and problem-solving skills, emotional tone and control, and fluency and flexibility all provide a living, open book to the educated professional. At any time, no single form of assessment can accurately represent the accomplishments of young children, because young people grow at different rates. Each child also develops at a different pace at different times in his or her development, and in relation to different skills and capacities. For example, the vocalizations of an eleven-month-old who understands some language may become less evident as she begins to take steps by holding on and then walking. Life balances out.

Teachers need to be alert to the fact that assessment signals their priorities. For example, if only reading and writing is the subject of individual teacher conferences, children learn the message. From time to time, effective educators should reflect with children about their creative dramatics, their problem solving in sociodramatic play situations, and their collected art projects.

As teachers observe children at play, they notice the development of youngsters' abilities to adapt their play to different audiences.[14.1] This oral ability is a foundation for authors' ability to write in different "voices" that communicate with different audiences. The thematic content of young children's play reveals their developing category systems and understanding of events. If assessment focuses on children's development of meanings, then it would make sense to value different forms and products. Thoughtful teachers recognize that the distinctive and different profile of strengths for some children will be apparent in their representational competencies.

As children play with objects, they progress from more literal to more imaginary and symbolic use of objects; for example, pretending to eat with a spoon as compared with pretending to feed a pretend doll with an imaginary spoon. Block constructions become increasingly more complex, representative, and the place where children create their own imaginary environments that they then inhabit. A broad periodic review of children's drawings and photographs of their constructions, as well as records of their participation in various centers, can help teachers see areas in which individual children may need to spend more time.

Play and Controversial Subject Matter: Some Final Thoughts

This chapter's review of controversial subject matter in children's play includes consideration of issues of gender, socioeconomic, and ability equity. In the United States, the cultural context generates controversial issues and devalues play. Therefore, early-education policy needs to foster an understanding of the significance of young children's play. The next chapter includes an executive summary to help address some of these issues with parents. It also elaborates on the paradigm shift from linear to nonlinear early education.

[14.1]Teachers who work with young children across a school year can accurately assess learning needs and accomplishments (Shepard & Smith, 1988; Teale, 1988). Young children are more likely to express their understandings in the context of familiar people and settings. Standardized test programs typically do not fulfill the criteria of in-depth observations and familiar context.

15 Nonlinear Dynamic Theory and Practice in a Linear Context

This chapter discusses how and why nonlinear dynamic theory and practice might flourish in a linear cultural context. The discussion includes ways to advocate for young children's play by communicating the benefits of play and dynamic curriculum to educators, policy makers, and parents. The chapter concludes by providing a rationale for a nonlinear theory of play and meaning with implications for early education.

Advocating for Children's Play: Some Questions and Answers for Parents and Other Policy Makers

It is especially difficult in a linear culture to communicate the power of play as a nonlinear, dynamic, powerful network of relationships to learning. It is much easier for some adults to check off a list of boxes on standardized tests.

Parents and policy makers need labels for playful-looking activities that they can understand as significant, in their terms. It may be politic to advertise continuously what children *are* learning when they play and to interpret children's play, without calling it play. Alternative language such as "integrated learning experiences," "learning activities," "active study projects," "science experiments," "center time," "activity periods," and "work periods" may help. Parents and policy makers may also need more information about the power of play and "active learning" in early childhood. Below is an executive summary about play and a variety of other formats to use when communicating with parents about youngsters' learning.

An Executive Summary:
The Power of Play in Early Education

QUESTION: What is my child learning in school?

ANSWER: Your child is having important experiences with the sciences, the social sciences, mathematics, literacy, and the arts. Many of the activities look like play and feel like play because he is an active learner.

QUESTION: If children play, then how will you cover the curriculum?

ANSWER: Play is one powerful way in which children learn. Research tells us that play helps youngsters to improve their thinking skills, social skills, language skills, and problem-solving skills. We plan events in school that integrate the full range of school learning, and include play as well as other ways that children learn. For example, our curriculum emphasizes playful activities in the sciences and the social sciences. Each part of the program builds in literacy and number skills that make sense to the children because they need to draw, read, write, and measure in order to solve real problems that have meaning to them. We usually do much more than the minimal state curriculum expectations.

QUESTION: How are you preparing my child for the rigors of the teacher next year?

ANSWER: Your child has educational choices that can both challenge her and offer her a chance to feel successful in school. When she feels successful, she tries harder. It is easier for her to learn more concepts when she feels confident. We work toward making this the richest year possible, knowing that this is the best way to prepare her for the future.

QUESTION: How do you keep control of the class if the children have choices?

ANSWER: The choices are educationally important. Different children may be doing different things at different times and have equivalent experiences in which they can feel successful. When they make a choice, they feel more responsible for their activity and work harder in playful ways.

QUESTION: What can we do at home to help?

ANSWER: Research suggests that children who have strong imaginations can concentrate on ideas and make connections between ideas better than those who do not have strong imaginations. Research also tells us that parents who play at pretending with their children at home influence their children's imaginations, their intelligence, and their language skills (Levenstein, 1992; Singer & Singer, 1998). Finally, research indicates that imagination helps children to think like scientists (Jensen, 1998, p. 38) as well as writers and artists. Here are some things that other parents have done at home, which you might have done or might be thinking about doing:

- Build with blocks if you have them, as well as with safe items from kitchen cabinets. Building with objects helps your child build images of objects in space.
- When you buy toys, buy the kinds that your child can use in more than one way, such as blocks and play dough. It is also useful to play games that build patterns, such as with foods or buttons. Make collections of things, such as jar covers, rocks, and leaves; egg cartons can hold some of your collections.
- It is useful to play games that involve rolling, tossing, and throwing bean-bags and balls. These activities help children develop eye and hand coordination. In addition, board games and card games help children develop flexible strategies. *Children need visual images of space in order to imagine mathematical, scientific, and geographic concepts.*
- Play pretend games, such as peek-a-boo: make believe you're feeding pretend animals; play at costume dress-up. Let your child play with pots and spoons near you when you are cooking, or hammer materials when you are fixing things. Offer her a toy telephone when you are talking on the telephone. Pretend to talk on the phone together.
- When you have differences, tell her what she needs to do rather than what you do not prefer her to do.
- Frequently tell your child what he is seeing when he is at home, outdoors, or in a shop. Role play: "What do I [parent] do if I lose sight of you in a department store?"
- Begin reading sturdy books with a single picture on each page during the first months of your child's life; read to him or her every day. It helps when your child sees you reading newspapers, magazines, and books. Tell her what you are writing when you make up shopping lists, pay bills, and write letters. Give him paper and pencils to write when you do. *Children will increase their language skills when they hear a lot of talk about everyday things, see pictures, look at books, and see you write and read*
- Play naming games with infants, using body parts and magazine pictures (Honig & Brophy, 1996).

QUESTION: Will my child get into an Ivy League college?

ANSWER: It helps if your family went there first; the rest remains for us to imagine.

Because you asked what you could do to help your child, it is important

to schedule more time in which children might choose to look at clouds; observe ants, construction crews, and older children at play; spend time with a friend; and choose or not choose to play (Fromberg, 1998, p. 205).

Feeling powerful, cared for, and listened to, feels like love.

Ways to Communicate
Children's Progress to Parents

There is a variety of other ways to communicate with parents. Parents need to feel that their child's teacher respects them and their child. When you communicate with parents, remember:

1. Different arrangements define the family unit.
2. Parents know their children.
3. Parents can tell you their priorities, beliefs, and category systems.
4. Adults who feel empowered and see themselves as capable are more likely to try to learn new things (Freire, 1970). Each parent needs courtesy, respect, and empathy.
5. Parents are busy and have multiple tasks to perform.
6. Parents are sharing their child with you.

What Is Worth Communicating?

Academic achievement is a goal of education, but early education is not just about academic achievement. Early education is also about what is worthwhile in young children's lives and what is a valuable use of time. Early education for young children is also about having meaningful experiences, becoming more human, maintaining great expectations, and moving toward becoming responsible and caring parents and citizens. Here are a few messages to send parents that support the presence of exploration and play in early childhood:

- How children use their knowledge: Merely knowing how to read is a limited accomplishment unless children choose to use the skill. Photographs and written material show how children choose to use reading and writing as part of playful activities.
- How children's choices develop sophistication: Children increasingly select more complex and meaningful pastimes.
- How children's play shows increasing complexity and use of language skills: Children play for longer periods of time with more elaborate content and appropriate, expanded vocabulary and syntax.
- How children increase their interest in stories and how their sociodramatic play scripts represent their expanding event knowledge: Children self-select literature as an activity choice. The content of their socio-dramatic play reflects their everyday experiences as well as the contents of literature.
- How children's social competence develops: Children learn how to enter into and negotiate play and other social situations.
- How children approach solving problems and how they solve them: Children attempt more than one way to solve a problem and are comfortable collaborating with others.
- How children ask increasingly complex questions: Children are able to risk asking questions as they identify disparities in the world. (See Harris, 2000.)

- Which events and experiences children share in the classroom: Particular anecdotes demonstrate that the teacher is aware of each child's contribution to the class.
- How the teacher appreciates the unique qualities of the children: There are distinctive ways in which the teacher plans for each child's participation in a rich array of experiences. The teacher speaks of each child with specificity and warmth.

Through What Forms?

Curriculum Highlights.   Prepare children at the end of each day to review what they have done that day; this will help them answer the parents' welcoming question, "What did you do in school today?"

Place a poster on the classroom door that summarizes special events of the day or week and lists the stories the group has heard. Add photographs of and informative captions about children engaged in play. In addition, place photos of in-class activities in the hallway and in the classroom.

For preverbal children, prepare a parent-teacher loose-leaf book in which both parents and teachers can share information about the child's day.

In kindergarten, send homework activities in zippered bags that children and parents can share, such as "How many brothers and sisters did parents and grandparents have?"

In primary-school groups, circulate backpacks each week that contain books for parents and children to read together; an article for parents; some science, social science, or arts projects; some games that they can do together; and a notebook in which to record reactions to the backpack experience (Quinn, 1996). With families for whom English is a second language, schools can provide a translator.

Label areas in the room in ways that communicate to other adults the significance of the activities.

Beginning in kindergarten, correspond daily with each child through his or her journal; begin in late autumn for some children as they become ready to participate.

Post the photograph of an author whose books the children have enjoyed. If the youngsters have written to the author and he or she has responded, post the response.

Post language-experience charts that document children's reactions to trips, visitors, and other classroom events.

Save samples or photographs of children's products, such as drawings, paintings, writings, block constructions, and costumed occasions. Create a portfolio for each child and invite children to suggest items for inclusion. (See Nilsen, 1997; Wiener & Cohen, 1997.)

Beginning in kindergarten, save the mathematics notebooks and writing journals that the children create.

Meetings and Other Communication.   Prepare slides and videotapes for sharing at evening or breakfast parent meetings.

Meet individual parents for conferences at school, at home, and on the telephone, with email as a supplement. Prepare anecdotes about each child to share with parents. Informal parent contacts take place when parents drop off or pick up their children. Keep in mind that parents typically feel rushed when they drop off children and teachers feel rushed at the end of the day (Endsley & Minish, 1991).

Home visiting has been an early-childhood tradition that seems to be fading. A home visit is valuable, however, and helps the teacher to understand the child's cultural context and available playthings. It provides an opportunity to share play with the family and child together. It can also help parents and teachers to build a sense of partnership and community.

Written communications sent home to parents can take several formats:

- A one-line note home to each of four (pick a number that suits you) children each day that tells about one thing that the child enjoyed doing in school that day
- A twice-a-year, two-letter reporting form to kindergarten and primary-grade parents. (One letter documents events that the class shared and is the same for all children. The other letter is an individual statement concerning the distinctive participation and accomplishments of each child.)
- A Web page on which each class may provide information about what children have done. (In the future, this practice is likely to spread. This communication method is accessible at some public libraries as well as at home.)
- A periodic newsletter that includes information about print resources and Internet sites that focus on families and children.

Group parent meetings can take place over breakfast, in the evening, and at special occasions. One special occasion in which parents of children in kindergarten and primary grades can participate is in the "immigration museum." In this format, on the same day, parents bring family documents, photographs, keepsakes, and artifacts. These items are labeled, displayed, and enjoyed by all the participants. A family-immigration time line, including the placement of flags on a map of the globe, also provides a rich opportunity to share and learn together.

When parents serve as classroom volunteers teachers can model effective ways to work with children and interpret the significance of play activities. Effective inclusion of parents is likely to be more successful after the parents have had some orientation to parents' participation and contributions.

What Is the Role of Play in Early Education for the Future?

Particularly now, when opportunities for young children to play are eroding or under attack, we must consider the power of play in early education. Educators and child-development specialists have criticized the linear, uniform, workbook-oriented, and trivial informational curriculum that policy makers have been pressuring teachers to follow with increasingly younger children (Bredekamp & Copple, 1997; Egan, 1999; Elkind, 1981; Kohn, 2000; Sigel, 1987).

Politicians, seeking simple linear solutions, tell us that we need well-prepared, capable, and effective teachers and that early education is important to society and the economy. Their solutions are to raise standardized test scores by having teachers transmit only a narrow range of uniform information and isolated skills. The question of how to educate young children is a complex problem that cannot be solved by simple solutions. Early-childhood teachers face particularly complex challenges. They must simultaneously interpret the learning needs of usually preliterate, sometimes preverbal, children and then translate adult understandings into experiences that young children may perceive as meaningful.

Research confirms that play and meaning are connected and indeed central to the education of young children. As one integrated condition for learning, play serves to unify many aspects of development that include social competence, language and cognitive development, and, to some extent, creative fluency.

This book has looked at nonlinear theories—script theory, chaos theory, and theory of mind—that confirm the nonlinear dynamics that underlie human experience and early learning through play. The nonlinear dynamic theory of play and meaning matches the nonlinear ways children develop meaning, and it makes sense to match teaching with the ways in which youngsters learn. The nonlinear, dynamic-themes model of teaching helps teachers to flexibly achieve that match. This model of early education is an intellectual orientation. It differs from a linear academic orientation, which centers on isolated skills. The linear academic approach that has predominated in the United States has been tried, and has failed.

A dynamic-themes curriculum advocates that educators focus on relationships and ideas that recognize the world as complex and education as transformational rather than only additive. It is an adaptable model, because it offers different entry points for different teachers and groups of children.

From Academic to Intellectual Early Education

This book has discussed the place of play within a paradigm shift in early education that is guided by nonlinear dynamic systems theory. *The issue is not whether to take either an academic or an intellectual approach to early education, but how to make a meaningful connection between them.* The intent is not to say that only nonlinear meaning is significant but that educators need to emphasize meaningful learning and integrate linear knowledge and skills in supportive ways. It means that children spend most of their time in school focused on significant integrated content rather than isolated skills and arbitrary information.

It is helpful to consider these relative emphases when looking at Figure 15.1, A Paradigm Shift in Early Education: Implications of Nonlinear Dynamic Systems Theory. The paradigm shift includes play as one condition for learning within the broader processes and context of early education. The focus of content is meanings, connections, and imagery that teachers define in a variety of experiences

FIGURE 15.1   A Paradigm Shift in Early Education: Implications of Nonlinear Dynamic Systems Theory

. . . . **continuum** . . . .

Philosophy

Behaviorism	Social construction/post-modern

Process

Linear	Non-linear
Deterministic	Emergent
Academic	Intellectual
Play as relief from work	Play as a condition for learning
Predictable behavior	Unpredictable patterns
Small input: small output	Sensitive Dependence on Initial Conditions

Content

Focus on information	Focus on meaning and connections
Facts and memory	Vivid imagery and meaning
Focus on teaching content	Focus on ways of student learning
Knowledge as transmitted (closed loop)	Knowing as self-organizing (dynamic systems)
Play as subsidiary action	Play as transformational focus
Single correct method and answer	Multiple models and interpretations
Workbooks	Active projects/experiences

Product

Information (additive)	Isomorphic imagery (integrated)
Uniform representations, two-dimensional	Multiple representations, including play

Communication

Transmission	Transactional (Rosenblatt, 1969)

Teacher's Roles

Major planner	Flexible negotiator
Teacher responsibility	Shared responsibility
Culturally transparent	Culturally relevant pedagogy
Technical/Interpretive reflection	Interpretive/Ethical reflection (Van Manen, 1977)
External rewards and punishment	Social construction of self-organized knowing

Student's Roles

Information gleaner	Connection maker
Respondent	Problem setter and solver; oral playwright
Individual competitor	Collaborative community member

Time

Mostly short blocks	Short and long blocks

Grouping

Mostly whole group, individual tasks	Mostly smaller groups, cooperative and individual

Assessment

Uniform, standardized	Multiple forms
For closure	For ongoing planning
	Seeking knowledge
	Using knowledge

that cut across disciplines. The products or outcomes of children's dynamic learning includes information that is part of the isomorphic imagery that they experience. The teacher negotiates experiences flexibly, with sensitivity to children's cultural event knowledge; teachers and children construct learning together. Thus, children have opportunities to function as connection makers, problem setters as well as solvers, and oral playwrights. They spend most of their time in small groups, although they also participate in some whole-group and individual activities. In turn, teachers evaluate children's learning in many ways in order to make relevant future plans with children; they value knowing how children use and pursue knowledge as well as what children know and can do.

The dynamic-themes curriculum model outlined in Figure 15.1 (and Chapter 12) replaces demands with influence and replaces external reward and punishment with children's personal motives for the social construction of knowing. To plan early education with a dynamic-themes outlook is to help young children look forward to great expectations in their lives, to prepare for the unpredictable futures that they face, and to savor the aesthetic and personal joys of the present. *Within the dynamic-themes, nonlinear conception of early curriculum, play is a central, significant, empowering, representational, and integrated condition for learning.*

A Balanced Future: The Future in Balance

Play in school takes place in a social environment that children experience as meaningful. Meaning comes out of the particular contexts (Nelson, 1985) of particular children and their teacher. A teacher who is committed to meaning does not focus only on a single "correct" answer, but on the processes that children use to develop deeper understandings and make connections. A nonlinear teacher helps young children prepare for the future described in the following image: "We are drowning in information, while starving for wisdom. The world henceforth, will be run by people who are synthesizers, people able to put together the right information at the right time, think critically about it, and make important choices wisely" (Wilson, 1998, p. 269). The study of separate subjects does not foster synthesizing. Teachers who want to "cover" separate subjects feel that they do not have enough time to teach. The use of dynamic themes that cut across separate subject areas unifies the isomorphic images that represent different disciplines. Teachers and children who become comfortable with isomorphic imagery are able to serve the current and future need for deeper creative understanding.

When deeper understandings take root, they cannot be blown away by a passing breeze. Roots transmit real nourishment, not contrived connections. A teacher committed to respecting and supporting young children's meanings and play welcomes unexpected events and varied forms of cooperation. A teacher who respects and recognizes complexity in learning does not solve complex educational problems with simplistic solutions. A nonlinear teacher keeps in balance order and wholesome chaos; control and freedom; and play and work. Such a teacher recognizes the importance of the play- (or "learning") -ground as well as the new "figure" that emerges from the familiar background, and the value of play as the domain of children's power.

Neither caring nor isolated knowledge is enough for the twenty-first century early-childhood teacher. Youngsters need to experience the power to think, act, and feel, possibilities that an effective teacher supports by creating phase-transition happenings. Phase transitions give children the potential to feel successful *as they extend both their nonlinear and linear learning during exploration and play.*

Harmony in Particular Times and Places.   The diverse experiences that represent any dynamic theme grow out of the interactions of particular children and their teacher at a particular time and place. Teachers who provide such diverse experiences recognize that different children doing different things at different times may have equivalent experiences. Teachers show caring by respecting the ways that young children construct meaning and make available experiences that are rich in action and meaning for children. Among integrated conditions for learning, teachers include the lymphatic power of play in early childhood to merge linear and nonlinear, logical and intuitive meanings. When the "attractors" of teaching and learning harmonize, children are less likely to feel alienated and will self-organize into other attractors (Nakkula, 1999).

A harmonious tradition among Native American potters was to return seed grain to the earth in exchange for clay. They recognized the connectedness of all things in the world and the importance of maintaining a balance in nature. We would do well to learn from this perspective as we work with young children. Whatever strengths, powers, or personal resources we ask children to diminish in a school setting need appropriate compensation; play offers children the opportunity to create a balanced experience. Young children bring many strengths to the future:

- They know how to explore and play in the world.
- They are at the zenith of flexibility for thinking and ordering the world; they are intuitive thinkers.
- They can live with ambiguity.
- They take risks.
- They are able to express authentic emotions.
- They experience the aesthetic mode of knowing as a powerful force.
- They want to be friends.

Because young children possess these distinctive strengths, early-childhood education is not a stepping-stone to more important concerns but a time that is valuable and critical.

Enriching Future Early Education.   What, then, should we do to enrich the future education of young children?

- Educators need to preserve young children's strengths as they celebrate the present. Scheduling and provisioning for play and playful experiences empowers children to develop meaning and skills that they will use later.

- Educators must advocate for play in early-childhood education. Reaching out to and involving policy makers and parents will help to deepen understanding of the power of play and meaning.
- Educators need to use dynamic themes to develop alternative experiences and strategies that flexibly match teaching and learning. Educators who can accomplish this matching create phase transitions, the bridges between familiar and emerging meanings.

If play is the lymphatic system of meaning, then the dynamic-themes curriculum is the heartbeat that pumps challenges through that system, as children learn to construct fresh meaning. In the new century, school play takes place in diverse social and cultural environments that need hearts, hands, heads, and help.

Play Themes

Sociodramatic Play Themes of Four-Year-Olds with House, Hospital, and Blocks

The following list summarizes the play of four-year-olds during an average of three morning center times of one hour duration each week for six months. The observations took place at the Hofstra University Lindner-Goldberg Child Care Institute. One-third of the children's families received Department of Social Services support; 5 percent received scholarships; and the remainder came from tuition-paying university employees, students, and other families. Approximately 40 percent are children of color.

	Areas:		
Themes:	**House**	**Hospital**	**Blocks**
Baby-doll care	X	X	
Being a baby	X	X	
Grooming (curling iron)	X		
Construction of enclosure/herding	X	X	X
Date, mother's preparation for	X		
Destruction of enclosure			X
Cooking	X		
Preparation of medications		X	
Medical diagnosis, dressing of wounds		X	
Dress-up (adult, fantasy/medical)	X	X	
Eating	X	X	
Fire	X	X	X
Tornado	X		
Moving	X		
Parade/obstacle course/promenade	X		X
Picnic	X	X	
Rough-and-tumble	X	X	X
Sleepover	X	X	X
Physician	X	X	
Telephone	X	X	
Medical examinations		X	
Mending of wounds		X	
Eye chart (literacy)		X	
Seeking of medical help		X	
Waiting room		X	
Boyfriend-girlfriend		X	X
Transportation			X

Themes:	House	Hospital	Blocks
Gunplay			x
Monsters			x
Superheroes	x		x
Being a dog			x
Building a dog house			x
Swimming and rescue			x
Death		x	x
Wedding			x
TV, role-play watching			x
Vacation plans			x

Sample Sociodramatic Play Themes of Two- to Six-Year-Olds

The following list reveals the variety of sociodramatic play themes in which four hundred children between two and six years of age engaged. During a four-year period, early-childhood graduate students collected anecdotes that described the play of children from diverse ethnic and economic backgrounds in the New York City metropolitan region.

Themes: Age:	2	3	4	5–6
Baby-doll care		x	x	x
Being a baby		x	x	
Baby care		x	x	
Construction of enclosure/herding		x	x	
Destruction of enclosure		x	x	
Cooking	x	x	x	x
TV-show chef				x
Preparation of medications			x	
Dress-up (adult, fantasy/medical)	x	x		x
Grooming		x		
Divorce		x		
Mother's domination of father			x	
Siblings		x	x	
New-baby jealousy			x	
Parental discipline			x	
Parental nurturance			x	
Eating		x	x	
Mother's going to work		x		
Mother's preparation for a date			x	
Babysitter		x	x	
Housekeeper			x	
Food shopping		x		x
Fire (fear and flight)		x	x	x
Firefighter		x	x	x
Parade/obstacle course/promenade		x	x	
Mazes			x	

Themes:	Age:	2	3	4	5–6
Doll-stroller promenade			x		
Promenade of dogs, role play			x		
Dog's toilet functions			x		
Picnic		x	x	x	
Rough-and-tumble/herding		x	x	x	x
Wrestling dolls			x		
Sleeping rituals		x	x	x	x
Sleepover			x	x	
Telephone		x	x	x	x
Telephone 911				x	
Medical examinations				x	
Mending of wounds				x	
Eye chart (literacy)				x	
Seeking of medical help				x	
Waiting room				x	
Boyfriend-girlfriend				x	
Transportation		x	x	x	
Driving with CB radio				x	
Racing autos and crashing				x	
Gunplay				x	x
Good/bad guys, hidden weapons		x	x		
Monsters			x	x	
Dinosaurs			x		
Being a dog		x		x	
Building a dog house				x	
Swimming and rescue				x	
Death				x	x
Wedding party				x	x
Wedding; bride makes dinner					x
TV, role-play watching				x	
Batman and Robin role play		x	x		
Sleeping Beauty roles		x	x		
Big Bird			x		
Teenage Ninja Turtles			x	x	
Power Rangers				x	x
Turbo Rangers				x	
Dinoman (tornado)				x	
Robin Hood, good and evil				x	x
Peter Pan, capture and saving				x	x
Three Little Pigs			x		
Addams family, TV mimicry				x	
Cowboys and Indians				x	
Snow White				x	
Pocohontas				x	
TV samurai					x
Columbus Day, binoculars					x
Outer space, aliens, and forts				x	
Mock battles				x	x

Themes:	Age:	2	3	4	5–6
Olympics				x	x
Going to movies		x	x		
Hunt and chase fantasy		x	x		
Microphone, role play				x	
TV-show production				x	
Commercial production				x	
Peace sign, shaking hands			x		
Beauty parlor (boys and girls)			x		
Beauty parlor (literacy)					x
Birthday party/tea party			x		
Supermarket consumer			x	x	
Supermarket workers (literacy)					x
Pizza shop		x	x	x	x
Bakery		x	x		
Restaurant (literacy)			x		x
Auto mechanic/gas station			x	x	
Negotiation with "head" mechanic			x	x	
Police				x	x
Police and shooting of dolls			x		
Police and robbers/teenagers					x
Garbage collection					x
Teacher role play				x	x
Playing school, trickster				x	
Physician				x	
Dentist					x
Submarine captain					x
Barber shop					x
Pet store					x
Credit cards					x
Bus driver				x	
Race-car driver				x	
Bank (literacy)				x	x
Chasing			x		
Camera play			x		x
Vacations				x	
Packing, moving				x	
Farm			x	x	
Jungle					x
Shark and rescue					x
Zoo, role play young adults					x
Surprise party, young adult					x
Circus					x
Chinese New Year dragon					x
New neighbors, welcoming					x
Driving to McDonald's					x
Barbie auto party					x
Concert, setting up of show					x
Church/temple trip and worship					x

Cyclical Change

Dynamic-Theme Experiences

Adopt a Tree and Related Plant Changes
(biology and history included)

A kindergarten class adopted a tree in the schoolyard. They visited their tree at different seasons throughout the year and viewed photographs of their tree during each season. These are some of the things they did with their tree:

- They made observational drawings, choosing from among colored pencils, crayons, charcoal, and colored chalks.
- They made bark rubbings.
- They compared bark rubbings from older and younger trees.
- They compared their tree with the tree adopted by another class.
- They marked the shadows of the tree at different times during the day and year, and played with catching each other's shadows in relation to the tree's shadow.
- They dictated cinquains (five-line stanzas) about their tree in different seasons.
- They collected leaves in the fall, and compared the leaves of their tree with the shapes of leaves from other trees.
- They used their tree as a snowball target, as a maypole around which to play games and dance, and as a shady spot for story time and singing.
- They dictated ideas and engaged in inventive spelling, writing about what they might see and wondering "what if" they were a tree at different seasons or in different locations.
- They measured the circumference of the trunk with hand spans, cubit spans (elbow to middle finger in length), yarn, and, late in the school year, with tape measures marked by both inches and centimeters.
- They kept comparison charts of their findings. They shared their findings with other classes.

The Food Cycle and Gardening
(biology, economics, geography, and history included)

Adults refer to activities such as gardening and collecting as play. Planting and gardening offer opportunities to perceive cyclical change. For young children, the point of such activities is the experience of any change over time, not necessarily a full cycle. *Young children's learning is legitimately episodic.*

Planting seeds demonstrates cyclical change, especially if the seeds scooped out of a pumpkin in the autumn are dried and saved for spring planting. Some teachers have had preschool or kindergarten children plant their own pumpkin seeds in individual, used milk containers to provide a beribboned presentation for Mother's Day. In the interest of good feelings, teachers sometimes surreptitiously plant "replacement" containers for those children whose seeds do not sprout. One teacher who did this had the following revelation provided by Daniel when he received his "replacement" container instead of the original container that did not sprout:

DANIEL: "Teacher, this is a miracle."

TEACHER: "What do you mean, Daniel?"

DANIEL: "My seeds grew even though I had eaten them."

(J. Koch, Personal communication, 1996)

Teachers can control *one variable at a time* within the process of cognitive dissonance in the pursuit of children's construction of learning. With the children, they have done the following:

- Predicted how many days it might take the pumpkin seeds, lima beans, or mung beans to sprout in plastic bags containing wet towels
- Placed some class plants in the dark and others on the sunny window sill
- Given some plants more or less water, food or no food
- Compared the sprouting and growth of fresh green peas that they have removed from the pods and planted in both soil and towel-soaked plastic bags, with that of planted frozen green peas
- Labeled each variable with the date
- Photographed their activities and compared the starting points with the results

Other types of plants that change rapidly include bean and alfalfa sprouts, carrot tops, avocado pits, sweet potato plants, and green peas. Bulbs, flowers from seeds, and vegetable seeds can grow in a window box or outdoor garden.

With any of these plants, it is important to vary elements such as water, heat, light, and plant food, *one at a time*. It is also relevant, for example, to predict what might happen if you add water alone or water and plant food, with all other variables remaining the same.

Human History
(biology, history, geography, sociology, and economics included)

Photographic time lines are playful when they feature each child's photographic history as well as the teacher's photographic time line from infancy to the present.

Teachers also have invited a grandparent or community elder who can bring photographs and offer *oral histories* to the children. It is important to prepare visitors to discuss such issues as "how things used to be" before television or when they lived on a farm. Children can plan questions to ask visitors.

Whether they create a photographic time line of themselves, class pets, or a school trip, children might have equivalent experiences in cyclical change. After all, different children doing different things at different times may have equivalent experiences.

It is also greatly exciting to bring in a baby who can be the subject of observation and measurement at different times throughout the school year. Again, recordings include photographs, yarn strips *to measure the length and girth of the baby*, drawings, and language experience. Some families might have a newborn's footprint that children can compare with the later outline of the baby's foot. Families that have saved preschoolers' or primary-school children's baby shoes or other clothing have shared some samples for comparison with current clothing items. Audiotapes of vocalizations at different times might also be relevant.

Children enjoy *marking their height* at different times during the school year, using nonstandard direct (an equivalent single length of yarn) or nonstandard discontinuous (numbers of blocks) measures and then standard measures. Each kindergarten-age child might have a personal notebook in which to record his or her weight and height early and then later in the year.

Population Shifts
(geography, economics, and history included)

Teachers and children of kindergarten and primary age *surveyed their current family sizes* and compared them with the family sizes of their parents' and grandparents' generations. They mapped immigration travels with family involvement during an *immigration and multicultural museum breakfast*. They *compared family sizes across generations*, and compared family sizes across city and country life. A culminating book such as Virginia Lee Burton's *The Little House* lends itself to opportunities for dramatic play and may also stimulate local trips.

Animal History
(biology and history incuded)

Gerbils and guinea pigs have lent themselves to the study of change in similar ways. Some groups weighed their gerbils using balance scales, predicted weights, and recorded them. Children compared their predictions and findings over time. These sorts of activities lend themselves to multiple forms of representation that include drawing, writing, and photography.

Land snails offer another form of study that can extend to habitat comparisons. The terrarium of the land snail begs comparison with an aquarium, pond, or desert habitat. For example, land snails began their visit to a classroom (children of preschool, kindergarten, and primary-school age) with each child receiving a transparent "salad bar" container with added holes for air. Each container included wet paper towels, twigs, pebbles, and two snails.

Children observed the snails with lenses, flashlights, and offerings of unsalted and unprocessed foods. Some teachers and their children *created surveys* of what snails eat based on their study. They had the following experiences when they engaged in the following activities:

- They observed the snails' interactions within their physical environments and with one another.
- They saw new generations of snails appear.
- They saw snails die.
- They explored and played with their snails.
- They represented their activities in a variety of symbolic forms that included drawing, surveys, language experience, inventive spelling, and imaginative stories.
- They recorded proposed names for class snails and voted on a name.
- Along the way, they inductively learned about cyclical change.

The following format encourages powerful learning: first observing, then sharing observations; raising questions; sharing likenesses and possible findings; asking new questions; then considering "What might happen if . . . ?"

Teachers and children can also read books about snails. However, the class would use books only *after* observing and talking about actual events. Nonfiction books serve best as part of cognitive dissonance *after* children have had experiences and talked about them. *When used after real experiences, books enrich the brain connections that children have made during the multisensory experience of handling, seeing, smelling, and listening.* There are books about snails that are useful for primary-age children (Johnson, 1982) and preschool or kindergarten-age children (Ryder, 1982). Beware: Some toddlers might be tempted to eat the snails!

Tadpoles. In the kindergarten and primary grades at one school, young children and their teachers raised tadpoles from eggs and fed them crumbs and fish food in an aquarium. The tadpoles came from a local pond in the springtime. When the peeper frogs developed, the class removed them from the water to a terrarium. The publication *Eggs and Tadpoles* (Elementary Science Study, 1974) offers an array of interesting ideas for teachers and children to pursue. These activities provided experiences that represent cyclical change.

Chicks. Equivalent experiences with cyclical change are possible in such activities as hatching chicks from an incubator. Local 4H clubs can supply a school with the eggs and an incubator.

Mealworm study for primary-age children is another exciting activity that exemplifies cyclical change. Mealworms are available at local pet shops.

Butterfly gardens have been used successfully with preschool children and are commercially available.

Dinosaur study involves some degree of controversy in early childhood be-cause dinosaurs lived long ago and are now extinct. Nevertheless, dinosaurs appeal to young children's imaginations because of their multisyllabic, prestigious names. They may also help children come to terms with issues of their own development of conscience and their personal monsters. Children have also seen museum replicas of dinosaurs.

Teachers and youngsters can classify vegetarian and carnivorous dinosaurs by comparing their limbs, tails, and footprints. Children have also classified other animals' tails, paws, ears, size, teeth, skin textures, mobility, and adaptation patterns. In the spirit of a guessing game, some teachers have used small models of dinosaurs to encourage children to play at estimating how many Unifix™ cubes taller or shorter different dinosaurs were. Then, the class members built cube towers to compare their estimations.

Teachers can make the concept of a *fossil* accessible with plaster-of-paris hand or footprints. Printing with sponges, vegetables, and later with words adds to the fossil concept. Feeling the soil during different seasons, making predictions, attempting to create footprints, and then comparing the attempts can add to the study. For preschool children and toddlers, exploring different densities builds toward later understandings.

The following activities related to absorption and desiccation have offered preschool children opportunities to create cognitive dissonance: Which objects might absorb more or less water? How long might it take for grapes to dry into raisins?

For children of primary-school age, fossil study might lead to the study of rock formations and the roles of heat and pressure. For example, kindergarten- and primary-age children have recommended various ways in which they might sort the rocks that they collected.

Time
(biology, physics, chemistry, and history included)

Related activities that represent cyclical change might include some of the following:

- Children measured the number of birds at a *bird feeder* at different times during the school day by moving pegs from one box to another (preschool, kindergarten).
- They surveyed *heartbeat rates* before and after running for one minute (primary).
- They created the concept of a *sun dial* by marking the passage of shadows on oaktag outdoors in relation to clock time (primary).

Children of preschool age played with creating a *shadow* in front or in back of themselves. They tried to hide their shadow, jumped on it, and chased it. Play with shadows helped children of primary-school age grasp the concept of time in relation to the sun. Here are some playful suggestions:

> Play with light from the sun to make shadows.
> Make funny-shaped shadows. . . .
> Who can make the longest shadow?
> Who can make the shortest shadow?
> Can you hide your shadow?
> Can you jump on your shadow?
> Stand upside down and make a shadow.
> Can you make a shadow with four arms and four legs?
> Can you move without your shadow moving?
> Can you stand with your shadow in front of you?
> Can you stand with your shadow behind you?
>
> (Richards, 1992, p. 15)

Youngsters may attempt to imagine their growth and have difficulty sorting out the concept of time. However, they do notice plants and animals that die, food that decays, and metal that rusts. They hear about the death of elderly and sometimes younger people. They also engage in sociodramatic and pretend play concerning the related themes of age and death; the pretend play also may involve solitary use of toy figures or dramatizing a drawing.

Weather
(chemistry, economics, geography, history, and the arts included)

Attention to the weather can integrate the study of sciences and social sciences in ways that do not necessarily involve a daily ritual but that do extend possibilities for learning. It is worthwhile to take the weather more seriously than the usual preoccupation with, "Today is Monday. It is cloudy and raining. We will have indoor lunch." It is relevant to take a different approach to weather beyond what's always been done.

Schools typically have studied weather as part of science study. The rain and snow cycle are relevant to the study of cyclical change. Bird migrations are seasonal. Children of primary-school age enjoy creating and stocking *bird feeders*, identifying birds, observing their behavior, and imagining the theme of flight.

Children learn about *temperature* through direct daily experiences. Teachers can offer contrasts when children play with melting and freezing water, with and without salt. They can vary conditions such as ice cubes in the mouth, in a closet, on a windowsill in the sun, and on the radiator or a heated cooking surface. Children can predict and compare the rate of melting ice cubes that are wrapped in newspapers, nylon, or wool, as well as other materials.

They've created the rain cycle in a terrarium or after laundering doll clothes by inverting a transparent container over the garments drying on the radiator. Children can also see examples of the *evaporation and condensation cycle* by observing cooking activities.

Teachers have helped children to become conscious of the *temperature* by using comparisons:

- "Which object is warmer or cooler?" (comparing objects in the classroom)
- "Which glass of water is warmer?" (comparing water poured from the same source and then placed in the sun or in a shaded corner of the classroom)
- "Which materials seem warmer?" (comparing woolen mitten, wooden ruler, and steel fork)
- "Whose hands are warmer/colder?"
- "How can we warm up the cooler hands?"
- "Which materials absorbed/shed water?" (Children can survey and sort the materials into separate containers.)
- "Which materials might dry more quickly/slowly indoors and outdoors?"
- "Which materials did dry more quickly/slowly indoors and outdoors?"

Young children enjoy the prestige and sheer fun of sucking ice cubes. Kindergarten-age children can predict whether big or small ice cubes take more time to melt. Their teacher provides one new variable at a time, such as melting a large and small ice cube in the air, ice cubes of equal size in the air or cool water, and cubes in cool or warm tap water. Children make predictions, monitor the ice cubes, and compare their findings.

In one school, kindergarten- and primary-school children created coverings and containers to slow down the melting process and then made coverings to speed up the melting process. They predicted and compared how water would look when frozen into plastic ziplock bags, and in cylindrical and square-edged transparent plastic containers. They discussed the dramatic bursting of the plastic cover on a container that they had filled to the top with water before freezing. The children represented their predictions and experiences in survey charts, drawings, and writing, according to their skills. Their teachers photographed events along the way to document the experience and provide a basis for discussion.

Aesthetic experiences can also help children grasp the impact of temperature. Children have viewed a snowfall through the window, danced the fall of snowflakes, and taken a walk around the school on crunching snow.

Holidays
(history, economics, geography, sociology, and chemistry included)

Many schools don't explore holidays' relevance to the weather and cyclical change. However, we know that celebrations mark the harvest of food or the commemoration of survival after famine across cultures. For example, kindergarten-age children have celebrated Kwanzaa (Africa) to commemorate a plentiful harvest, St. Patrick's Day (Ireland) to memorialize the potato famine, Trung Thu (Vietnam) and N'cwala (Zambia) to mark the harvest, Divali (India) to acknowledge prosperity, and Thanksgiving Day (United States) to commemorate the survival and peaceful strivings of the Iroquois. A social scientist (Donna Barnes) has designed playful activities around the Thanksgiving theme that reflect the important role of colonial women. On the surface, "holidays differ from outdoor education or the weather. On the deeper level, they represent cyclical changes of passing-through struggles in human lives" (Fromberg, 1982, p. 195). A source book of seasonal holidays attributes the themes of new life, energy, growth, and celebration to the spring season; plentiful food to the summer; harvest and remembrance to the autumn; and brightening the world with light and warmth to the winter (Kindersley, 1997).

Recycling and Conservation (geography and political science included)

Children can trace the process of garbage recycling and the water cycle. Everyday events, rather than highlighted artificial or trivial "units," can help them experience the dynamic theme of cyclical change. For example, one kindergarten class collected water drips in the sink and marked containers with dates and times to provide evidence to the school custodian of the need for faucet repair. They added drawings and notes with inventive spelling. Their sense of political influence and a strong research attitude gave them a sense of pride in effecting change.

Electrical Circuits (chemistry included)

Kindergarten-age children have created electrical circuits with clamps and a battery that power a light bulb, buzzer, or bell in their sociodramatic play centers. They have used protected wires of varying lengths to play with the construction and then use of the circuits. (Most adults find that a light bulb is the least disruptive form for classroom use.) The electric circuit is another form in which young children can directly experience cyclical change.

Moon Cycles

Primary-age children can participate in checking the cycles of the moon and representing them in a journal. They can take care always to view the moon from the same position. They can then compare the night sky and the morning sky when both the sun and the moon are present, and experience some cognitive dissonance.

There are many children's books that represent cyclical change in a variety of implicit ways through nonfiction (Berger, 1995; Carle, 1970, 1986; de Paola, 1975; Helldorfer, 1994; Onyefulu, 1998; Rohman, 1994; Schlein, 1953; Selsam, 1980; Wood, 1998). Fiction opportunities abound as well (Brown, 1946, 1965; Burton, 1988; Garland, 1998; Gilman, 1992; Hall, 1997; Heide & Gilliland, 1990; Heine, 1983; Heller, 1987; Jonas, 1982, 1983, 1986; Krauss, 1945, 1947; Lundgren, 1972; McCloskey, 1952; McKissack, 1997; Miles, 1971; Schlein, 1960; Trottier, 1998; Yashima, 1970).

APPENDIX C

Dialectical Activity

Dynamic-Theme Experiences

Magnets
(physics included)

Toddlers have used magnets to collect spilled paper clips and other objects. Children of preschool age predicted which objects a magnet is likely to attract. For these youngsters, teachers provided sorting baskets for the predictions and comparisons. Cognitive dissonance emerged when children predicted that the magnet would attract all shiny, smooth, and hard materials but found that some materials that looked similar, such as copper, were not attracted.

As a next step, four-year-olds predicted whether a large magnet or a small magnet would attract more paper clips. Teachers provided a strong bar magnet and a weaker but larger horseshoe magnet to create an opportunity for cognitive dissonance. The kids found great drama in predicting, then adding paper clips one by one to each magnet. Kindergarten-age children enjoyed predicting, repeating their various approaches to "trick" the magnets, and comparing their results.

Children of kindergarten and primary age magnetized blunt-tipped embroidery needles by moving a magnet along them in a single direction while holding the eye of the needle. They then observed the attraction of opposing ends and attempted to "trick" their magnetized needles. These early images of attraction and repulsion establish a thread that later connects to the imagery underlying electromagnets and the behavior of subatomic particles. *The underlying dynamic themes become the basis for building connections among images over time.*

Waves: Play with Water, Air, and Sound
(physics, geography, chemistry, and the arts included)

Following a cognitive-dissonance format, teachers have provided resources to help children explore and play with the properties of water. Toddlers observed objects that float and sink, tried to sink objects by holding them down, and poured water through openings of different shapes. Preschool-age children predicted which objects would likely float or sink, and their teachers provided containers for their predictions and comparisons. Cognitive dissonance occurred when children predicted that the large object would sink and the small object would float. They wondered whether a penny would still sink even if it were blown up in a balloon that they had seen floating. Children of kindergarten and primary age can also figure out how to float objects that would otherwise sink, a form of construction play and design technology.

Kindergarten- and primary-age children have played at blowing directly on the water and through straws into the water to make waves. Children of preschool age played with water wheels and poured higher or lower streams of water to create different degrees of force.

Children enjoy filling containers to the point at which they overflow. Some children of preschool and kindergarten age have played with adding a spoonful at a time to a nearly full container.

Children of primary age can also control an eyedropper. They add one drop of water at a time to a container that looks full, to test whether it has reached its capacity. They enjoy making predictions and watching the water molecules mount. Surprise is an important component of phase transitions.

The City Museum of St. Louis, Missouri, offers delight to people of all ages with a huge, suspended boiler that shifts its center of gravity as it fills with water. Eventually, the entire bulk dumps into a causeway rimmed with stone escape ledges. Shrieks of delight punctuate each dumping as children attempt to anticipate the flood, run out of the water chute, or leap onto a ledge. Professional sources offer additional examples of water play (Elementary Science Study, 1971; Richards, Collis, & Kincaid, 1995/1987).

Air Play (physics, chemistry, and geography included).   Preschoolers actively sort those things that are easier or more difficult to blow with their own breath or with a drinking straw. They delight in blowing the paper covers off drinking straws—a way of learning about air that most adults don't appreciate!

One kindergarten teacher encouraged children to predict and compare the relative ease with which they might blow different objects by puffing through a drinking straw:

- The youngsters marked floor squares and attempted to predict which objects they could propel beyond one, two, or more squares.
- They blew up balloons with their own breath and with manual balloon pumps.
- They played with air- and water-propelled rocket launchers outdoors.
- They blew marbles through mazes.
- They used straws to create sand art and air-propelled paintings.
- They placed a small book, doll, or block on top of a zippered plastic bag from which a straw protruded. They then blew air through the straw to move the objects.

Additional ideas for activities involving balloons and inflatable toys have been published for teachers who have used them with kindergarten- and primary-age children. (See Zubrowski, 1990.)

Bubbles provide another focus for play, beginning with toddlers and soapsuds in their bath water. Young children enjoy blowing bubbles in their glass of milk, feeling bubbles in carbonated water, and seeing bubbles appear in their water play. Teachers of preschool-age children who can blow out rather than suck in liquids can add detergents to water and encourage bubble play with various objects such as whisks and eggbeaters. Children can also use straws, wands of different shapes, plastic mesh, and plastic berry containers. They predict and discover the effect of color added to the bubble solution. Kindergarten- and primary-age children can discover how to make bigger or multiple bubbles, and how to collapse or sustain bubbles by using a wet or dry finger. (See Zubrowski, 1979.)

Young children also imagine themselves contained within a bubble, "become" a bubble, dance as if they are bubbles, and walk as if bubbles are on the ground. This use of personal analogy lets children play with ideas and represent their understanding of concepts in ways that the teacher can assess.

Colloquial language has mocked the notion of somebody "merely blowing bubbles." However, advanced mathematicians in recent years have studied the subject of bubbles, trying to understand their geometry and their role in helping us understand aspects of the universe itself.

Wind and Erosion (geography, physics, economics, and sociology included).
Preschool-age children see commercial kites and play with those they have made themselves. Kindergarten- and primary-age children play with the different aerodynamic properties of kites, including the following:

- They vary the shapes of materials and the direction of propulsion.
- They build on their play with the propulsion of paper straws and paper planes.
- They try to propel their constructions farther by varying the size of the straw, the opening of the straw, the length of the string, and the shape of the constructions.
- They add a paper clip or two to different places on their constructions.
- They vary the type of materials used, including paper, cloth, and plastic.
- They consider the angles of construction. They wondered why heavy airplanes can fly. (See Atkinson, 1995.)

Movement Education and Angular Momentum. When children spin as they dance, they explore moving faster when they bring in their arms, which conserves angular momentum. Teachers can explain to kids that a star spins also more rapidly after it contracts. Children intuitively learn to spin in dances and games, and they compare streamlined vehicles with their kites. Their play includes the following activities:

- Kindergarten-age children blow up balloons and let the air out, feeling the flow on their skin and hearing the sound of the exiting air.
- They use a balloon pump and see that a smaller balloon containing the same amount of air as a larger balloon travels farther because the air exits more forcefully.

- They compare the propulsion of a balloon filled with air and one filled with water.
- They see a toy boat propelled by the air escaping from an attached balloon; they create racing games with boats and make predictions about the speed of different boats; they wonder whether the location of the balloon makes a difference and then see what happens.
- They draw pictures on the balloons before blowing them up and then compare the pictures afterward, learning about topology while taking delight in the contrasted transformations.
- Outdoors and in the gymnasium, groups of kindergarten- and primary-school children play with gigantic parachutes in various ways, such as running under the parachute before the other children lower it.

Sound.   Infants and toddlers play with sound as a matter of course. They imitate animal sounds as well as the sounds of people in their lives. They begin to sing and play with pitch, dynamics, and volume. Preschoolers intentionally alter how loudly they shriek, sometimes to the point of throat strain. They enjoy pounding on their chests as they speak in order to hear the vibration. They put their ears on the chest of a speaking adult, and giggle at the tickle of vibrations.

From playing with rattles, banging on pans, and then using rhythm instruments, children directly experience sound. They play with various informal noise-making materials and more formal rhythm instruments. They shout in each other's ears and speak on the telephone. They construct their own listening devices that include paper cups and strings, tubes, and funnels. They rub a fingertip around the rims of glasses, and tap a spoon on glasses filled with varying amounts of water—often in restaurants, often to the limits of adult tolerance. In addition, kindergarten- and primary-school children enjoy part singing; they create rhythmic clapping to chanted jingles and rap messages. Some youngsters at this age begin to play formal musical instruments. In short, they play with sound by using objects as well as their own bodies and voices. Schools typically offer group singing and group playing of rhythm instruments.

Ramps and Related Activities
(physics, chemistry, and mathematics included)

Children in one first-grade class engaged in ramp activities with blocks set at different heights. Here are some of their play activities:

- They predicted which objects would roll farther along the path, based on the angle of the ramp.
- They played with different loads.
- They placed white masking tape at their predicted stopping place and tan masking tape at the actual end of the roll.
- They measured the prediction and the result using a meter stick, wrote their findings in personal notebooks, and later combined their findings on a class chart.

- They discussed which variables contributed to the distance that objects rolled, such as the height of the ramp, nature of the object, and degree of thrust.
- They enjoyed the activity so much that they decided to combine their electrical circuit activity with the ramping. They created a series of ramps and boxes by predicting the distances that the ball would roll into a basket. They embellished this concept by having their ball roll over a switch that would close an electric circuit in order to turn on a light. They also added transparent plastic cylinders as well as cardboard cylinders.
- They used nylon fabric and sandpaper to vary the ramp surfaces.
- Different groups of children compared their strategies and observations.
- Kindergarten-age children used boxes with elastic or string to pull blocks and toys up a ramp. Children of primary-school age measured the different lengths of stretch that the elastic required in order to drag down different contents in the box.

Kindergarten-age and younger children experience the nature of resistance by propelling objects and themselves across surfaces as varied as an inclined plane while holding an adult's hand or a slide in the park. They attempt to pull a wagon uphill or down an inclined plane with more or less load. They build wooden-block structures and figure out by trial and error how to align blocks for their preferred angle or inclined interfaces. These direct, physical experiences help them achieve more complex physical learnings. Materials in the kindergarten and primary grades, such as the Marble Railway (Childcraft) and K'Nex Arch Bridge Technology construction materials, elaborate on the generic block play of preschool children.

Youngsters also represent their play in various ways. For example, a group of four-year-olds made predictions and collected objects in the classroom that rolled or did not roll, and placed them in smiling-face or frowning-face containers. They contrasted the textures and angles of the objects before and after trying to roll them down ramps of various heights. They varied one height at a time. Some children used a chart with a smiling and a frowning face and placed a copy of their own photograph under the prediction that they made.

Kindergarten and primary-grade children have played at bowling and at using a pendulum, varying the direction of the bob as well as the length of the string. They varied the force and became aware of the degree of arc that they needed to bring down their targets. They considered how heavier or lighter twine and how longer or shorter twine influenced their aim. Children of primary age measured and surveyed the heights of the bob before and after the arc, while the youngest children simply played with their aim and made intuitive adjustments.

Kids can also have many experiences by dropping and bouncing balls of various sizes and densities as well as objects such as empty containers, aluminum foil, and other objects of different sizes and shapes. Teachers can encourage them to observe first, predict distances of rebound, compare their findings, seriate the propelled objects, and record their findings. Kindergarten and primary-grade children have measured the distance of rebound using yardsticks, measuring wheels, and folding rulers.

Another form of "rebounding" relates to density and solubility of liquids. Toddlers and preschoolers have explored mixing oil and water, ketchup and milk, juice and syrup, soap liquid and poster paint. Preschoolers predicted, played with, and compared the propulsion of such things as a penny, marble, key, sponge, and wooden bead through oil, water, shampoo, and syrup. They learned about the resistance of objects traveling through liquids of different densities. Kindergarten- and primary-age children have predicted and seriated the densities and progression of objects through liquids of various densities. Their teachers used various graphic representations to record their predictions and their findings.

Fulcrum Play
(physics, music, and economics included)

Using a seesaw, young children have explored balancing with different points of the fulcrum as they (a) walked along while an adult held their hand and (b) experimented with different objects to see how to create a balance or tip the balance. Toddlers and preschoolers used rocking boats with gusto; they also created their own balance scales.

One kindergarten teacher sat with a small group of children who were blindfolded and asked them to judge the relative weight of objects. The kids then looked at the objects without the blindfolds on, then tested their predictions by using a standard balance scale. Another kindergarten group predicted how many pennies and then, in turn, how many other objects could balance the weight of their guinea pig. Kindergarten-age children also predicted the relative weight of dry to wet sand and compared their findings after using a balance scale. Using containers of different shape, they employed the balance scale to test their guesses about which contained the same amount of water. Kindergarten children, using a suspended wire hanger, have created mobiles and explored ways to balance the parts.

When youngsters compare their predictions with their findings, cognitive dissonance takes place. Teachers who provide more opportunities for cognitive dissonance afford young children more opportunities for transformational and constructive learning. Teachers who support transformational learning are teaching in nonlinear ways. Young children, in turn, experience such learning as play when they can control an open-ended process.

Interaction of Forces
(physics, mathematics, and the arts included)

Gravitation can contrast with air pressure, magnetism, and centrifugal force. There are many activities in which children directly feel these contrasts.

Infants and toddlers experience the dialectical model in such early experiences as sucking and blowing. They appreciate their own power in keeping objects submerged in the bath water. They experience conflict in the disparity between what they want and how others comply. They enjoy the predictability of seeing objects fall to the ground.

Preschoolers and kindergarten children have played with dropping objects such as a shuttlecock, feather, wooden bead, card, piece of paper, marble, and rubber ball. They discussed their observations, and the teacher inverted reality by asking, "Why doesn't it fall up?"

Preschool children have also listened to counterpoint in music. Kindergarten children have seen dialectical images in visual arts such as Picasso paintings, compared painters who use different styles to represent similar themes, and created rhythmic-movement activities that involved syncopation and opposites. They have heard the same music interpreted by different performers and heard folk tales retold with different interpretations; they have discussed the differences and voted for their favorite versions. Kindergarten and primary-grade children have engaged in choral speaking and round singing that creates a dialectical experience.

Primary-grade children have heard, read, and compared biographies of the same person written by different authors. They enjoy the multiple viewpoints and argue about the nature of truth.

Scarcity
(economics, sociology, and sciences included)

The issues of supply and demand pull in social, economic, and scientific threads. For example, children want to use equipment that other children are using. Infants and toddlers experience the dissonance between what they want and what they have or can acquire on their own or with the help of others. Teachers repeatedly encourage children to wait their turn and to share materials with others. All human beings experience the contrast between what they want and what they might have or are able to do. Each person can jump only so high or run so fast or reach so many targets with a ball.

Through social feedback, human beings learn to work through many of the differences between wants and resources. Preschool teachers use puppets to play with some of these issues. Teachers of kindergarten and primary-grade children role play to represent conflicts and alternative ways to resolve them; for example, "What are some other ways he could have solved the problem without lying?" They read stories that deal with sibling rivalry and acceptance or rejection by others. They discuss with children how these stories relate to the children's lives.

Voting
(political science, sociology, multicultural education)

Voting is one way that children can experience the contrasts of viewpoints. Through many varied experiences, in which teachers respect the children's choices, kids come to appreciate differences and the value of taking turns. Some examples of play with voting follow.

During a *national election*, a public early-childhood center that served children between three and seven years of age prepared voting centers in the school lobby. The centers contained blue or red markings to denote the Republican and Democratic parties. Outside the voting booths were tables with ballots to mark under a picture and word poster of choices. There was a curtain and a ballot box. Each child had a chance to vote. The results were announced and compared with the national election as well as with the local community's results. It was interesting, if not surprising, to notice that the children's choices were the same as their local community.

Another school offered classes an opportunity to match *photographs of teachers* from their early childhood years with contemporary photographs of teachers. Each class submitted their votes. All classes received some form of recognition, such as new library books, colored pencils, and board games.

Beginning in preschool classes, teachers and children can *survey children's preferences*. Selecting a colored sticker, four-year-olds placed on a grid their favorite color, compared the longest row, and saw the teacher record the outcomes, such as, "8 children like red; 6 children like blue; 5 children like yellow; red is the favorite color." Similar surveys were done using red, yellow, and green apples, with accompanying colored stickers.

Some teachers placed photographs depicting television programs, covers of books by the same author, or types of pets on the survey chart. During the activity period, children then placed photocopies of their photograph on the grid to vote for their favorite choice; later on, the entire group met to discuss results.

Some children's books that share the dialectical model are fictional works by Alexander, 1971; de Regniers, 1953; Flack, 1989; Jonell & Mathers, 1999; Keats, 1967; Lorbiecki, 1998; McCloskey, 1968; Polacco, 1998; Rosenberg, 1986; Sendak, 1963; and Yezerski, 1998. Nonfiction includes work by Kent, 1998.

APPENDIX D

Indirect Progress

Dynamic-Theme Experiences

Puzzles and Mazes (biology and physics)

Three-dimensional puzzles and hedgerow mazes are a particularly delightful play form for kindergarten children as well as adults. A potato maze permits sprouts to grow out through a small hole at one end of a box that lets in minimal light: "Make a potato maze from an old shoe box. Put a freshly sprouting potato at one end of your maze box. . . . Keep the lid on except for an occasional peek" (Richards, 1989, p. 27).

Preschool-age children have successfully used obstacle courses in outdoor playgrounds with such items as balance boards, ramps, hoops, and boxes. Geographic concepts that build toward a sense of space are inherent in such "indirectly direct" physical experiences. Primary-age children appreciate the nonfiction book *Hoists, Cranes, and Derricks* (Zim & Skelly, 1969).

Leverage and Other Indirect
Physical and Social Knowing Activities
(physics, economics, political science, and chemistry
included)

A child who wants to enter a play situation may use the indirect statement, "Would you like to hold my key chain?" as a form of social leverage. "I'll be your friend if you give me that truck now" may be an indirect way to acquire an object. Teachers have used role playing with kindergarten- and primary-age children to influence their capacity to identify with other children's perspectives.

Beginning in preschool, children learn to remove carpentry nails by holding the hammer claw to pull "backwards," applying leverage. Children explore centrifugal force together by twirling together and then spinning away from each other.

The pulley as a wheel and rope that changes the direction of force is an indirect means to lift weights and move objects. Children see pulleys at construction sites, harbors, quarries, pumping sites, and outdoor clotheslines in some areas. Kindergarten children have used pulleys to lift blocks and send messages and toys across the room in a basket. Children in primary grades identified substances by indirect means. They compared how baking soda and sugar dissolve in water and observed the impact of salt and sugar on melting ice cubes. Children have used other indirect ways to classify materials. They have identified salt or sugar in water by seeing what happened after the water evaporated. They have identified metals using magnets.

Kindergarten children can indirectly identify bacteria by comparing apple slices that they placed in two Petrie dishes before and after they washed their hands. Children in primary classes have indirectly identified the oxidation of metal by noticing rust, and the decay of foods by observing mold formation.

When children dance and jump, their muscles learn to bend and stretch in the opposite direction in order to propel their jump or help them turn faster. Kids learn to pull their arms back to pitch a ball farther. Through trial and error, they solve the problem of pushing a mat further into a closet in order to pull it out.

Kindergarten children have used an air pump to blow up a balloon, and have played with pumping air and water to launch toy rockets outdoors.

Children's literature that deals with tricksters and folklore also demonstrates indirect progress. (See fictional works by Brown, 1947; Cohen, 1998; Credle, 1934; Flack, 1958; Hogrogian, 1971; Joosse, 1991; MacDonald with Vathanaprida, 1998; Slobodkina, 1989; Tworkov, 1989.)

APPENDIX E

Synergy

Dynamic-Theme Experiences

Physical and Social Knowing

Experiences that emphasize physical knowing are presented first, followed by experiences that emphasize social knowing.

- Comparing surprises and explosive events, such as volcanoes, tornados, and stampedes (sciences, social science)
- Shadow-catching games outdoors (physical knowing)
- Chasing and tag games (physical knowing)
- Partners or small-group ball toss; or assembly of simple machines together (physical knowing)
- Cooking food products that dramatically change form, such as eggs, butter, home-made ice cream, yeast dough, and popcorn. Children in kindergarten and primary grades have measured changes in volume, shape, and weight after they cooked the foods. Four-year-olds observed the drying of such foods as apples and green peas; they estimated how long it might take for a grape to become a raisin and then compared their findings with actual events. Their experience was similar to playing a guessing game (chemistry).
- Melting wax and old crayons in primary grades to create candles and fresh recycled crayons (chemistry)
- Dissolving substances and observing what happens when a drop of colored water enters a transparent container of clear water
- Filling a cup and counting the number of drops deposited by an eye dropper before overflow occurs (physical knowing)
- Creating shadows that are thin, wide, long, short, sharp, fuzzy, moving, still, with small and large objects. Friends make their shadows shake hands, enclose an object on the ground within a shadow, draw around a shadow, and create a shadow with six arms. They create shadows with four feet, lie or sit on their shadow, and sit on their shadow while moving without making the shadow move (Richards, Collis, & Kincaid, 1995/1987).
- Reproduction of plants through seeds, cuttings, and sprouts, as well as reproduction of animals such as tadpoles in an aquarium and on land, fish in an aquarium, land snails in a terrarium, and dipsosaurus doralis in a desert. (The dynamic theme of synergy is represented from an ecological standpoint of the habitats.)

- Comparing variables for plants and animals, such as light, water, and nutrients (biology)
- Understanding the interdependence of the environment, animals, plants, and seeds. Some primary-grade children studied pollution, recycling waste, and the rain forest. A book that focuses on ongoing change in the world of objects and living things as a synergistic collaboration is Douglas Wood's (1998) *Making the World* (physical and social knowing).

Social and Multicultural Knowing

Many synergy experiences support social knowing and multicultural education. Examples of activities follow:

- Sociodramatic play is a powerful collaboration (social knowing).
- Children of primary-school age in some locales have created family trees with family involvement (social knowing).
- Teachers can encourage meaningful projects that look at holidays across cultures. For example, classes might celebrate harvests and the avoidance of famine (see Chapter 7); safety from oppression, such as the United States' Independence Day and Martin Luther King Day, the Jewish holidays of Passover and Hannukah, and Mexico's Cinquo de Mayo; success, such as Japan's Kodomono-hi; and filial support, such as India's Raksha Banahan (social, multicultural knowing).
- Kindergarten and primary-grade children can make masks together for play productions (social, multicultural knowing).
- Classes can display photographs, posters, and books depicting human beings around the world engaging in similar pastimes, such as nurturing, cooking, working together, playing games together, and driving and traveling in trucks, automobiles and boats together (social science).
- Kids might make cooperative products, such as a mural tablecloth for a family breakfast (economics).
- Teachers can help youngsters organize a buddy system of pairs or groups of four, beginning in preschool. This strategy both encourages collaboration and respects children's capacity for independence. Other forms include playing with partners and small groups as well as reading in the primary grades with pair-share and then pairs-share (social knowing).
- Kindergarten children can run relay races (social knowing).
- Preschoolers and some toddlers can share a rocking boat (social and physical knowing).
- Class members may play collaborative, noncompetitive games such as "Stand Up," in which a group tries to stand up together in a circle as they hold one another's hands with their backs facing the center of the circle (Fleuegelman, 1976, p. 65).
- Kindergarten children have adopted a construction site and documented the events unfolding there with photographs, drawings, and invented spelling.

They noted the multiple roles of construction participants by interviewing the workers (for example, one electrician was also a father, husband, brother, son, and bowling-league member), created a time line, made drawings, wrote, and read about collaboration (sociology, history).

- Kindergarten children and their parents created an immigration map, time line, and museum of family artifacts, and engaged in multicultural festivals (history, geography, multicultural knowing). (This activity represents both the dynamic themes of synergy and cyclical change.)
- An "author's theater," in which primary-grade children collaborated to dramatize one another's written pieces (Dyson, 1997) dignified children's ideas.

Quantitative and Spatial Knowing Activities

Collaboration continues to be the underlying feature in experiences that emphasize quantitative and spatial knowing. Examples follow.

- Surveys by two or more children. For example, pairs of three-year-olds asked, "How many trucks/cars pass our classroom window?" They used a three-minute egg timer and took turns moving pegs to keep tallies (quantitative knowing).
- Cooperative mathematical games, such as board and card games; pairs of children measuring with a measuring wheel; youngsters making nonstandard measures of a partner's height and limbs (quantitative knowing)
- Planning with others and building structures together with wooden floor blocks (quantitative knowing).
- Collaboratively hiding objects in games that move from simple hide-and-seek in preschool to treasure maps in kindergarten and primary grades (spatial knowing, geography).
- Using large paper to outline a partner's body for "mapping," and then completing the project by drawing or making a collage (spatial knowing, geography).

Representational Knowing and Arts

Young children express themselves physically through a variety of art forms. Play activities, in themselves, reveal children's theory of mind as well as their event knowledge. In addition, children draw, build, paint, sculpt, dance, pantomime, dramatize, speak, and write in order to represent their experiences. The broadly drawn examples that follow share the cooperative aspect of the dynamic theme of synergy.

- Children, seated back-to-back, take turns placing and instructing a partner to place objects. They might use a farm diorama, beads and laces, geoboards, blocks aligned in a box, sets of shapes or colors, or small blocks (representational knowing).

- String figures, such as Cat's Cradle, require collaboration. Although one person holds the figure while another manipulates it, more than two children can play by taking turns around a circle of three or four individuals. Several players together can serve as a support system for one another (social and representational knowing).

Collaborative arts activities encompass a variety of forms, including the following:

- Movement education (collaborative dance development in preschool, such as partner "mirrors" and group "frozen" sculptures for photographs; creative dramatics and folk dances that are collaborative and synergistic in kindergarten; and square or circle dances in the primary grades, where pairs group, regroup, and then reconstitute structures (physical and representational knowing).
- Music (group creation of melodies, poetic song development, and part singing).
- Exposure to orchestras or children participating in rhythm-band activity.
- Other collaborative experiences (role playing, drawing, writing, or graphing).
- Artistic products that represent collaboration (creations of quilts, tablecloths, or murals to commemorate events throughout the year) (representational arts).
- Working together at the computer with graphics software (representational and social knowing).
- Combining colors with food dye, paint, and overlaid plastic discs (physical and representational knowing).
- Viewing reproductions of a visual artist's body of work and considering the distinctive "whole" of that artist's style along with the holistic styles of other artists' work. Kindergarten children have successfully grasped the underlying visual analogies across a body of work represented by different artists, such as Renoir, Dali, Matisse, and Picasso, as well as illustrators of children's books, such as Eric Carle and Gerald McDermott (arts).
- Pairs of children taking turns and collaborating to stretch lengths of knitted or plastic bands into different shapes, accompanied by music (arts).
- Kindergarten and primary-grade games involving a parachute in a gymnasium or outdoors. (This activity represents the two themes of synergy and dialectical processes (social and physical knowing).
- Creating class books with shared topics, such as family differences, changes in the school yard, friends and fights, giving and taking, wishes and dreams, science splendors, artists' studio, and so forth (representational knowing).
- Preparing audiotapes of youngsters' stories or retelling stories for others to hear (representational knowing).
- Children in primary grades planning together, creating puppets, and presenting puppet shows (social and representational knowing).

Children's books, whose underlying structure is synergistic, include folk tales (Southgate, 1970; Young, 1992), realistic fiction (Havill, 1986, 1989; Jonas, 1984; Rylant, 1985; Whelan, 1992; Wilkins, 1992; Williams, 1982; Wyeth, 1998), and nonfiction (Bang, 1983; Coerr, 1977; Morris, 1992). Young children take delight in hearing their teacher read these books aloud.

Double Bind

Dynamic-Theme Experiences

Quantitative and Physical Knowing

Children enjoy many opportunities to explore and play with the conservation of liquids as well as with letter shapes and their sounds in words. For example, preschool-age children find it difficult to understand that a larger nickel is worth less than a smaller dime. Preschool and kindergarten children also often predict that a larger object is likely to be heavier than a smaller object. They experience cognitive dissonance when they make predictions that are contrary to their observations after playing with a balance scale. They might similarly predict that larger objects are more likely to sink than smaller objects are, and that large magnets will be stronger than smaller magnets. Only after they have had many chances to play with the balance scale, the magnet, and the water will they attain conservation. (See earlier section on dialectical themes for activities that let children experience cognitive dissonance and influence their environment through design technology.)

For example, when a four-year-old asked for ice-cream money, her father usually gave her a dollar bill. One hot day, he gave her a handful of quarters. She pleaded with him to give her a dollar bill because she thought the storekeeper would not give her an ice cream. The father insisted that the two forms of money represented the same value. However, she insisted otherwise, and eventually fell to the sidewalk weeping. He became so angry because she did not trust his word that he didn't let her have any ice cream that day. Rather than an insight into the equivalence of four quarters and a dollar, the main lesson this child learned was that her father's anger was a prelude to deprivation.

The above incident represents the double-bind theme and would inform the child's future approaches to extracting favors from her father (quantitative and social knowing). Playing with symmetry in mirrors and the notion of reflections as reversals of images becomes another double-bind experience (physical knowing). Finally, the thorn and the rose offer an aesthetic and metaphoric image of the double-bind theme (physical and representational knowing).

Social Knowing

Children experience a double bind before their theory of mind develops; for example, when trying to play out another's perspective or imagine what somebody else might be seeing from a different location than their own. A few notes on double bind and social knowing:

- Group consensus is difficult to absorb at any age when your opinion differs from the group and you are obliged to go along with the group.
- Cleanup is a double bind because it is difficult for young children. It's especially challenging for children who may have a disability; they might struggle to change what they are doing even though they might be looking forward to the next activity.
- Sarcasm is a double bind for the aggressor as well as the victim.
- In political life, adults as well as young children often have difficulty separating appearance and reality. For example, they attribute to an office holder the patina of his or her institution. However, it was a young child in one folk story who said that "the emperor had no clothes."

There are some imaginative children's books that represent the underlying image of double bind (Bauer, 1981; Joosse, 1991; Say, 1993; Vavra, 1968).

GLOSSARY

analogue   Two phenomena that have some elements in common and others not in common

chaos theory   A body of thought that attempts to understand the processes underlying dynamic systems

cognitive dissonance   The result of a perceived discrepancy between an expectation and reality

complexity theory   A body of thought that studies the phase transitions between states

construction play   Building with three-dimensional materials

dynamic   In motion

dynamic theme   An underlying image that becomes apparent in a variety of surface forms; a way to organize curriculum

early childhood   Birth through eight years of age

event knowledge   Understanding gathered through experiences, which human beings can use to interpret later experiences

exploration   The attempt to find out how things or people function

functional play   *See* exploration

fractal   A form that replicates itself on different scales

intuitive thought   Directly experienced meaning

isomorph   A similar, underlying image that takes different surface forms

linear   Narrow, convergent, uniform, and finite

lymphatic system   The biological system that brings nutrients to and removes waste from a living body

meaning   Directly experienced understanding; the result of making sense of an experience

metaphor   A figure of speech that refers to one thing as if it were something else

model   An image, construction, or system that represents experience

nonlinear   Having multiple and divergent directions

phase transition   The bridge or change from one state to another, such as from ignorance to knowing

play   Self-motivated suspension of reality; treating of one thing as if it were another

referent   Something referred to

representation   Depiction of something in another medium, such as a play episode, drama, or art form

scaffold   A figurative learning platform provided by a person, object, or situation; scaffolding helps move the learning process from the unknown toward the knowable

script theory   The rule-bound interaction between players that generates pretense

sensitive dependence on initial conditions   The phenomenon by which small input may yield a disproportionate output

social knowledge   Information that is transmitted, such as dates, places, labels, and procedures

sociodramatic play   Pretense engaged in together by two or more individuals

tangent   The edge of an idea, shape, or object

theory of mind   An awareness of one's own thoughts, feelings, beliefs, intentions, and wishes, and those of other people

theory   A projection or model that infers a system of interactions

transformational knowledge   Knowledge that is generated from one form into another

REFERENCES

Adler, A. (1923). *The practice and theory of individual psychology* (P. Radin, Trans.). London: Routledge & Kegan Paul.

Aldis, D. (1975). *Play fighting.* New York: Academic Press.

Alexander, M. (1971). *Nobody asked me if I wanted a baby sister.* New York: Dial.

Allport, F. (1955). *Theories of perception and the concept of structure.* New York: Wiley.

Allport, G. (1958). The functional autonomy of motives. In C. L. Stacey & M. F. DeMartino (Eds.), *Understanding human motives* (pp. 68–81). Cleveland: Howard Allen.

Almy, M., Monighan-Nourot, P., Scales, B., & Van Hoorn, J. (1984). Recent research on play: The teacher's perspective. In L. G. Katz (Ed.), *Current topics in early childhood education* (Vol. 5) (pp. 1–25). Norwood, NJ: Ablex.

Appl, D. J. (1998). Children with Down syndrome: Implications for adult-child interactions in inclusive settings. *Childhood Education, 75*(1), 39–43.

Astington, J. W. (1993). *The child's discovery of mind.* Cambridge, MA: Harvard University Press.

Astington, J. W., & Pelletier, J. (1999). *Theory of mind and representational understanding in early childhood education.* Presentation at annual meeting of the American Educational Research Association, Montreal, Canada.

Atkinson, S. (1995). Children making paper planes. In S. Atkinson & M. Fleer (Eds.), *Science with reason* (pp. 26–31). Portsmouth, NH: Heinemann.

Bagley, D. M., & Klass, P. H. (1997). Comparison of the quality of preschoolers' play in housekeeping and thematic sociodramatic play centers. *Journal of Research in Childhood Education, 12*(1), 71–77.

Bang, M. (1983). *Ten, nine, eight.* New York: Mulberry.

Barnes, D. (1994). Personal communication.

Bartsch, K., & Wellman, H. M. (1995). *Children talk about the mind.* New York: Oxford University Press.

Bateson, G. (1971). The message 'this is play.' In R. E. Herron & B. Sutton-Smith (Eds.), *Child's play* (pp. 261–266). New York: Wiley.

Bateson, G. (1972). *Steps to an ecology of mind.* New York: Ballantine.

Bateson, G. (1976). A theory of play and fantasy. In J. S. Bruner, A. Jolly, & K. Sylva (Eds.), *Play—Its role in development and evolution.* New York: Basic Books.

Bateson, G. (1979). *Mind and nature.* New York: E. P. Dutton.

Bauer, C. F. (1981). *My mom travels a lot* (N. W. Parker, Illus.). New York: Frederick Warne.

Belth, M. (1970). *The new world of education.* Boston: Allyn & Bacon.

Belth, M. (1993). *Metaphor and thinking* (F.T. Johansen, Ed.). Lanham, MD: University Press of America.

Benson, M. S. (1997). Psychological causation and goal-based episodes: Low income children's emerging narrative skills. *Early Childhood Research Quarterly, 12*(4), 439–457.

Bergen, D. (1998). Play as a context for humor development. In D. P. Fromberg & D. Bergen (Eds.), *Play from birth to twelve and beyond: Contexts, perspectives, and meanings* (pp. 324–337). New York: Garland.

Berger, M. (1995). *Who cares about the weather?* New York: Newbridge Communications.

Black, H. (1989). Interactive pretense: Social and symbolic skills in preschool play groups. *Merrill-Palmer Quarterly, 35*(4), 379–397.

Blurton Jones, N. (1976). Rough-and-tumble play among nursery school children. In J. S. Bruner, A. Jolly, & K. Sylva (Eds.), *Play—Its role in development and evolution* (pp. 352–362). New York: Basic Books.

Bredekamp, S., & Copple, C. (1997). *Developmentally appropriate practice in early childhood programs.* Washington, DC: National Association for the Education of Young Children.

Bretherton, I. (1985). Pretense: Practicing and playing with social understanding. In C. C. Brown & A. W. Gottfried (Eds.), *Play interactions* (pp. 69–79). Skillman, NJ: Johnson & Johnson.

Bretherton, I., O'Connell, B., Shore, C., & Bates, E. (1984). The effect of contextual variation on symbolic play development from 20 to 28 months. In I. Bretherton (Ed.), *Symbolic play: The development of social understanding* (pp. 271–298). New York: Academic Press.

Briscoe, M. G. (1984, November 1). Tides, solutions and nutrients. *Nature,* 15.

Brown, M. (1947). *Stone soup: An old tale.* New York: Charles Scribner's Sons.

Brown, M. W. (1946). *The little island* (L. Weisgard, Illus.). Garden City, NY: Doubleday.

Brown, M. W. (1965). *The dead bird* (R. Charlip, Illus.). New York: Harper Collins. (Original work published 1938.)

Brown, R., & Bellugi, U. (1964). Three processes in the child's acquisition of syntax. In E. H. Lenneberg (Ed.), *New directions in the study of language* (pp. 131–161). Cambridge, MA: MIT Press.

Bruner, J. S. (1966). *Toward a theory of instruction.* Cambridge, MA: Harvard University Press.

Bruner, J. S. (1980). *Under five in Britain.* Ypsilanti, MI: High/Scope.

Bruner, J. S., Jolly, A., & Sylva, K. (Eds.). (1976). *Play—Its role in development and evolution.* New York: Basic Books.

Buchsbaum, H. K., & Emde, R. N. (1990). Play narratives in 36-month-old children. *The Psychoanalytic Study of the Child, 45,* 129–155.

Burton, V. L. (1988). *The little house.* Boston: Houghton Mifflin. (Original work published 1942.)

Cahill, B. J., & Theilheimer, R. (1999). "Can Tommy and Sam get married?" Questions about gender, sexuality, and young children. *Young Children, 54*(1), 27–31.

Calvin, W. H. (1996). *How brains think: Evolving intelligence, then and now.* New York: Basic Books.

Carle, E. (1970). *The very hungry caterpillar.* New York: G. P. Putnam's Sons.

Carle, E. (1986). *Papa, please get the moon for me.* New York: Scholastic.

Carlsson-Paige, N., & Levin, D. E. (1987). *The war play dilemma: Balancing needs and values in the early childhood classroom.* New York: Teachers College Press.

Casti, J. L. (1994). *Complexification: Explaining a paradoxical world through the science of surprise.* New York: Harper Collins.

Cazden, C. (1971). Language programs for young children: Notes from England and Wales. In C. S. Lavatelli (Ed.), *Language training in early childhood education* (pp. 119–153). Urbana: University of Illinois Press.

Children's Defense Fund (1999). Citing U.S. Department of Labor, Bureau of Labor Statistics, 1998. In *The state of America's children yearbook.* Washington, DC: Author.

Christie, J. F. (Ed.) (1991). *Play and early literacy development.* Albany: State University of New York Press.

Christie, J. F., Johnsen, E. P., & Peckover, R. B. (1988). The effects of play period duration on children's play patterns. *Journal of Research in Childhood Education, 3*(2), 123–131.

Chukovsky, K. (1963). *From two to five* (M. Morton, Trans. & Ed.). Berkeley: University of California Press.

Clark, K., & Clark, M. (1939). The development of consciousness of self and the emergence of racial identity in Negro preschool children. *Journal of Social Psychology, 10,* 591–599.

Clark, P. M., Griffing, P. S., & Johnson, L. G. (1989). Symbolic play and ideational fluency as aspects of the evolving divergent cognitive style in young children. *Early Child Development and Care, 51,* 77–88.

Coerr, E. (1977). *Sadako and the thousand paper cranes.* New York: Bantam Doubleday Dell.

Cohen, B. (1998). *Molly's pilgrim* (rev. ed.) (D. M. Duffy, Illus.). New York: Lothrop, Lee & Shepard. (Original text copyright 1983.)

Cole, D., & LaVoie, J. C. (1985). Fantasy play and related cognitive development in 2- to 16-year-olds. *Developmental Psychology, 21*(1), 233–240.

Collard, R. R. (1979). Exploration and play. In B. Sutton-Smith (Ed.), *Play and learning* (pp. 45–68). New York: Gardner Press.

Connolly, J. A., & Doyle, A. (1984). Relation of social fantasy play to social competence in preschoolers. *Developmental Psychology, 20*(5), 797–806.

Cook, D. (1996). Mathematical sense making and role playing in the nursery. *Early Child Development and Care, 121,* 56–66.

Cooper, P. (1993). *When stories come to school.* New York: Teachers and Writers Collaborative.

Coplan, R. J., & Rubin, K. H. (1998). Social play. In D. P Fromberg & D. Bergen (Eds.), *Play from birth to twelve and beyond: Contexts, perspectives, and meanings* (pp. 368–377). New York: Garland.

Copple, C. C., Cocking, R. R., & Matthews, W. S. (1984). Objects, symbols, and substitutions: The nature of the cognitive activity during symbolic play. In T. D. Yawkey & A. D. Pellegrini (Eds.), *Child's play: Developmental and applied* (pp. 105–123). Hillsdale, NJ: Erlbaum.

Corsaro, W. A. (1985). Friendship and social integration in peer culture. In W. A. Corsaro (Ed.), *Friendship and peer culture in the early years* (pp. 121–170). Norwood, NJ: Aplex.

Corsaro, W. A. (1990). The underlife of the nursery school: Young children's social representations of adult rules. In G. Duveen & B. Lloyd (Eds.), *Social representations and the development of knowledge* (pp. 11–26). New York: Cambridge University Press.

Credle, E. (1934). *Down down the mountain* (E. Credle, Illus.). Nashville, TN: Thomas Nelson.

Csikszentmihalyi, M. (1976). The Americanization of rock-climbing. In J. S. Bruner, A. Jolly, & K. Sylva (Eds.), *Play—Its role in development and evolution* (pp. 484–488). New York: Basic Books.

Csikszentmihalyi, M. (1988). Introduction: The flow of experience and its significance for human psychology. In M. Csikszentmihalyi & I. S. Csikszentmihalyi (Eds.), *Optimal experience: Psychological studies in flow consciousness* (pp. 3–14; 15–35; 364–383). New York: Cambridge University Press.

Csikszentmihalyi, M., & Csikszentmihalyi, I. S. (1988). *Optimal experience: Psychological studies in flow consciousness.* New York: Cambridge University Press.

Dansky, J. L. (1985). Questioning "A paradigm questioned": A commentary on Simon and Smith. *Merrill-Palmer Quarterly, 31,* 279–284.

Dansky, J. L. (1986). Play and creativity in young children. In K. Blanchard, W. W. Anderson, G. E. Chick, & E. P. Johnsen (Eds.), *The many faces of play* (pp. 69–79). Champaign, IL: Human Kinetics.

Davidson, J. I. F. (1998). Language and play: Natural partners. In D. P. Fromberg & D. Bergen (Eds.), *Play from birth to twelve and beyond: Contexts, perspectives, and meanings* (pp. 175–183.). New York: Garland.

Davidson, P. S. (1977). *Idea book for Cuisenaire rods at the primary level.* New Rochelle, NY: Cuisenaire Co. of America.

De Gaetano, Y., Williams, L. R., & Volk, D. (1998). *Kaleidoscope: A multicultural approach for the primary school classroom.* Upper Saddle River, NJ: Merrill.

De Paola, T. (1975). *The cloud book.* New York: Scholastic.

De Regniers, B. S. (1953). *The giant story* (M. Sendak, Illus.). New York: Harper & Row.

Dewey, J. (1933). *How we think.* Boston: D. C. Heath.

Dodge, M. K., & Frost, J. L. (1986). Children's dramatic play: Influence of thematic and nonthematic settings. *Childhood Education, 62*(1), 166–170.

Doyle, L. (1999, August 22). Killers among us. *The New York Times Magazine,* 13–14.

Dunn, J., & Dale, H. (1984). I a daddy: 2-year-olds' collaboration in joint pretend with sibling and mother. In I. Bretherton (Eds.), *Symbolic play: The development of social understanding* (pp. 131–157). New York: Academic Press.

Dunn, S., & Larson, R. (1990). *Design technology: Children's engineering.* Bristol, PA: Falmer.

Dyson, A. H. (1987). The value of "time off-task": Young children's spontaneous talk and deliberate text. *Harvard Educational Review, 57*(4), 396–420.

Dyson, A. H. (1997). *Writing superheroes: Contemporary childhood, popular culture, and classroom literacy.* New York: Teachers College Press.

Eckerman, C. P., & Didow, S. M. (1989). Toddlers' social coordinations: Changing responses to another's invitation to play. *Developmental Psychology, 25*(5), 794–804.

Edwards, C., Gandini, L., & Forman, G. (1998). *The hundred languages of children,* 2nd ed. Norwood, NJ: Ablex.

Egan, K. (1997). *The educated mind: How cognitive tools shape our understanding.* Chicago: University of Chicago Press.

Egan, K. (1999). *Children's minds talking rabbits & clockwork oranges.* New York: Teacher College Press.

Eifermann, R. (1971). Social play in childhood. In R. E. Herron & B. Sutton-Smith (Eds.), *Child's play* (pp. 270–297). New York: Wiley.

Eisen, G. (1988). *Children and play in the Holocaust: Games among the shadows.* Amherst: University of Massachusetts Press.

Eisner, E. W. (1990). The role of art and play in children's cognitive development. In E. Klugman & S. Smilansky (Eds.), *Children's play and learning: Perspectives and policy implications* (pp. 43–56). New York: Teachers College Press.

Elementary Science Study Teachers' Guides (1971). *Drops, streams, and containers.* New York: McGraw-Hill.

Elementary Science Study Teachers' Guide (1974). *Eggs and tadpoles.* New York: McGraw-Hill.

Elkind, D. (1981). *The hurried child.* Reading, MA: Addison-Wesley.

Ellul, J. (1965). *The technological society* (J. Wilkinson, Trans.). New York: Knopf.

Endsley, R. C., & Minish, P. A. (1991). Parent-staff communication in day care centers during morning and afternoon transitions. *Early Childhood Research Quarterly, 6*(2), 119–135.

Erickson, F., & Mohatt, G. (1982). Cultural organization or participation structures in two classrooms of Indian students. In G. Spindler (Ed.), *Doing the ethnography of schooling: Educational anthropology in action* (pp. 132–174). New York: Holt, Rinehart & Winston.

Essa, E. L., & Murray, D. I (1999). Sexual play: When should you be concerned? *Childhood Education, 75*(4), 231–234. [citing Johnson, T.D. (1991, August, September). Understanding the sexual behaviors of young children. *SIECUS Report,* pp. 8–15]

Fagot, B. (1997). Attachment, parenting, and peer interactions of toddler children. *Developmental Psychology, 33*(3), 489–499.

Fagot, B., & Leve, L. (1998). Gender identity and play. In D. P. Fromberg & D. Bergen (Eds.), *Play from birth to twelve and beyond: Contexts, perspectives, and meanings* (pp. 187–192). New York: Garland.

Farver, J. (1996). Aggressive behavior in preschoolers' social networks. *Early Childhood Research Quarterly, 11*(3), 333–350.

Farver, J., & Wimbarti, S. (1995). Indonesian children's play with their mothers and other siblings. *Child Development, 66*(5), 1493–1503.

Fein, G. G. (1975). A transformational analysis of pretending. *Developmental Psychology, 11*(3), 291–296.

Fein, G. G. (1985). The affective psychology of play. In C. C. Brown & A. W. Gottfried (Eds.), *Play interactions* (pp. 19–28). Skillman, NJ: Johnson & Johnson.

Feitelson, D., & Ross, G. S. (1973). The neglected actor—Play. *Human Development, 16*(3), 202–223.

Fenson, L. (1984). Developmental trends for action and speech in pretend play. In I. Bretherton (Ed.), *Symbolic play: The development of social understanding* (pp. 249–270). New York: Academic Press.

Fenson, L. (1985). The developmental progression of exploration and play. In C. C. Brown & A. W. Gottfried (Eds.), *Play interactions* (pp. 31–36). Skillman, NJ: Johnson & Johnson.

Flack, M. (1958). *Ask Mr. Bear*. New York: Simon & Schuster.

Flack, M. (1989). *Angus lost*. Garden City, NY: Doubleday.

Fleuegelman, A. (1976). *The new games book*. Garden City, NY: Doubleday.

Forbes, D., & Yablick, G. (1984). The organization of dramatic content in children's fantasy play. In F. Kessel & A. Goncu (Eds.), *Analyzing children's play dialogues* (pp. 230–236). San Francisco, CA: Jossey-Bass.

Fowles, J. (1969). *The French lieutenant's woman*. Boston: Little Brown.

Freire, P. (1970, August). Cultural action and conscientization. *Harvard Educational Review, 40*(2), 452–477.

Freud, S. (1959). Beyond the pleasure principle (J. Strachey, Trans.). New York: Bantam. (Original work published in 1928.)

Freud, S. (1960). *Jokes and their relation to the unconscious* (J. Strachey, Trans.). New York: Norton. (Original work published 1916.)

Freyberg, J. T. (1973). Increasing the imaginative play of urban disadvantaged children through systematic training. In J. L. Singer (Ed.), *The child's world of make-believe: Experimental studies of imaginative play* (pp. 129–154). New York: Academic Press.

Fromberg, D. P. (1976). Syntax model games and language in early education. *Journal of Psycholinguistic Research, 5*(6), 245–260.

Fromberg, D. P. (1977). *Early childhood education: A perceptual models curriculum*. New York: Wiley.

Fromberg, D. (1982). Transformational knowledge: Perceptual models as a cooperative content base for the early education of children. In S. Hill & B. J. Barnes (Eds.), *Young children and their families* (pp. 191–206). Lexington, MA: Lexington Books.

Fromberg, D. P. (1993). The content of integrated early childhood education. In Kraus International (Eds.), *Early childhood education: A curriculum resource book* (pp. 66–79). Millwood, NY: Kraus International.

Fromberg, D. P. (1995). *The full-day kindergarten: Planning and practicing a dynamic themes curriculum* (2nd ed.). New York: Teachers College Press.

Fromberg, D. P. (1998). Play issues in early childhood education. In C. Seefeldt & A. Galper (Eds.), *Continuing issues in early childhood education* (2nd ed.) (pp. 190–212). New York: Teachers College Press.

Fromberg, D. P. (1999). A review of research on play. In C. Seefeldt (Ed.), *The early childhood curriculum: Current findings in theory and practice,* (3rd ed.) (pp. 27–53). New York: Teachers College Press.

Fromberg, D. P., & Bergen, D. (Eds.) (1998). *Play from birth to twelve and beyond: Contexts, perspectives, and meanings.* New York: Garland.

Froschl, M., & Sprung, B. (1999). On purpose: Addressing teaching and bullying in early childhood. *Young Children, 54*(2), 70–72.

Frost, J. L., & Woods, I. C. (1998). Perspectives on play in playgrounds. In D. P. Fromberg & D. Bergen (Eds.), *Play from birth to twelve and beyond: Contexts, perspectives, and meanings* (pp. 232–240). New York: Garland.

Galda, L., Pellegrini, A. D., & Cox, S. (1989). The short-term, longitudinal study of preschoolers' emergent literacy. *Research in the Teaching of English, 23*(3), 292–309.

Gardner, H. (1982). *Art, mind, and brain: A cognitive approach to creativity.* New York: Basic Books.

Garland, S. (1998). *My father's boat* (T. Rand, Illus.). New York: Scholastic.

Garvey, C. (1979). Communicational controls in social play. In B. Sutton-Smith (Ed.), *Play and learning* (pp. 109–125). New York: Gardner Press.

Garvey, C. (1993). Diversity in the conversational repertoire: The case of conflicts and social pretending. *Cognition and Instruction, 11*(3&4), 251–264.

Gaynard, L. (1998). Play as ritual in health care settings. In D. P. Fromberg & D. Bergen (Eds.), *Play from birth to twelve and beyond: Contexts, perspectives, and meanings* (pp. 248–256). New York: Garland.

Geertz, C. (1976). Deep play: A description of the Balinese cockfight. In J. S. Bruner, A. Jolly, & K. Sylva (Eds.), *Play—Its role in development and evolution* (pp. 656–674). New York: Basic Books.

Gilman, P. (1992). *Something from nothing.* New York: Scholastic.

Gitlin-Weiner, K. (1998). Clinical perspectives on play. In D. P. Fromberg & D. Bergen (Eds.), *Play from birth to twelve and beyond: Contexts, perspectives, and meanings* (pp. 77–92). New York: Garland.

Gleick, J. (1987). *Chaos.* New York: Viking.

Gleick, J. (1998). *Genius: The life and science of Richard Feynman.* New York: Pantheon.

Goldstein, L. (1999). The relational zone: The role of caring relationships in the co-construction of mind. *American Educational Research Journal, 36*(3), 647–673.

Goleman, D. (1995). *Emotional intelligence.* New York: Bantam.

Goode, E. (2000, August 8). How culture molds habits of thought. *New York Times,* F1, F4.

Goodman, M. E. (1964). *Race awareness in young children.* New York: Collier.

Haberman, M. (1995). *Star teachers of children in poverty.* West Lafayette, IN: Phi Delta Kappa.

Haight, W., & Miller, P. J. (1992). The development of everyday pretend play: A longitudinal study of mothers' participation. *Merrill-Palmer Research Quarterly, 38*(3), 331–349.

Hall, D. (1997). *Ox-cart man* (B. Cooney, Illus.). New York: Viking.

Harris, P. L. (2000). On not falling down to earth: Children's metaphysical questions. In K. S. Rosengren, C. N. Johnson, & P. L. Harris (Eds.), *Imagining the impossible: Magical, scientific, and religious thinking in children* (pp. 157–178). Cambridge: Cambridge University Press.

Harris, P. L., & Kavanaugh, R. D. (1993). Young children's understanding of pretense. *Monographs of the Society for Research in Child Development No. 231, 58*(1).

Hart, B., & Risley, T. R. (1975). Incidental teaching of language in the preschool. *Journal of Applied Behavior Analysis, 8*(4), 411–420.

Hart, B., & Risley, T. R. (1995). *Meaningful differences in the everyday experience of young American children.* Baltimore: Paul H. Brookes.

Havill, J. (1986). *Jamaica's find* (A. S. O'Brien, Illus.). Boston: Houghton Mifflin.

Havill, J. (1989). *Jamaica tag-along* (A. S. O'Brien, Illus.). Boston: Houghton Mifflin.

Heath, S. B. (1983). *Ways with words: Language, life, and work in communities and classrooms.* New York: Cambridge University Press.

Heide, F. P., & Gilliland, J. H. (1990). *The day of Ahmed's secret* (T. Lewis, Illus.). New York: Lothrop, Lee & Shepard.

Heine, H. (1983). *The most wonderful egg in the world.* New York: Atheneum.

Helldorfer, M. C. (1994). *Gather up, gather in: A book of seasons* (V. Pedersen, Illus.). New York: Viking.

Heller, R. (1987). *Chickens aren't the only ones.* New York: Grosset & Dunlap.

Hines, S. M. (1999). Personal communication.

Hogrogian, N. (1971). *One fine day.* London: Collier-Macmillan.

Holte, J. (Ed.) (1990). *Chaos: The new science.* St. Peter, MN: Gustavus Adolphus College.

Honig, A. S. (1998). Sociocultural influences on gender-role behaviors in children's play. In D. P. Fromberg & D. Bergen (Eds.), *Play from birth to twelve and beyond: Contexts, perspectives and meanings* (pp. 338–347). New York: Garland.

Honig, A. S., & Brophy, H. E. (1996). *Talking with your baby: Family as the first school.* Syracuse: University of Syracuse Press.

Howes, C., with Unger, O., & Matheson, C. C. (1992). *The collaborative construction of pretend: Social pretend play functions.* Albany: State University of New York Press.

Hughes, F. P. (1999). *Children, play, and development* (3rd ed.). Boston: Allyn & Bacon.

Huizinga, J. (1955). *Homo ludens: A study of the play elements in culture.* Boston: Beacon.

Hutt, C. (1976). Exploration and play in children. In J. S. Bruner, A. Jolly, & K. Sylva (Eds.), *Play—Its role in development and evolution* (pp. 202–215). New York: Basic Books.

Jana, R. (1998). Toying with science. *The New York Times Magazine, 22*, 26, 56.

Janiv, N. (1976, April). Kedmah. Paper presented at the Bicentennial Conference on Early Childhood Education, Coral Gables, FL.

Jensen, E. (1998). *Teaching with the brain in mind.* Alexandria, VA: Association for Supervision and Curriculum Development.

Johnson, J. E. (1998). Play development from ages four to eight. In D.P. Fromberg & D. Bergen (Eds.), *Play from birth to twelve and beyond: Contexts, perspectives, and meanings* (pp. 146–153). New York: Garland.

Johnson, S. A. (1982). *Snails.* Minneapolis, MN: Lerner.

Jonas, A. (1982). *When you were a baby.* New York: Greenwillow.

Jonas, A. (1983). *Round trip* (p. 232). New York: Greenwillow.

Jonas, A. (1984). *The quilt.* New York: Greenwillow.

Jonas, A. (1986). *Now we can go.* New York: Greenwillow.

Jonell, L., & Mathers, P. (1999). *It's my birthday, too.* New York: G. P. Putnam's Sons.

Jones, E., & Reynolds, G. (1997). *Master players: Learning from children at play.* New York: Teachers College Press.

Joosse, B. M. (1991). *Mama, do you love me?* (B. Lavelle, Illus.). San Francisco, CA: Chronicle Books.

Kaku, M. (1997). *Visions: Science revolution for the twenty-first century.* New York: Basic Books.

Kamii, C., & DeVries, R. (1980). *Group games in early education.* Washington, DC: National Association for the Education of Young Children.

Kamii, C., & DeVries, R. (1993). *Physical knowledge in preschool education*. New York: Teachers College Press.

Karp, K. (1988). *The teaching of elementary school mathematics: The relationship between how math is taught and teachers' attitudes*. Unpublished Ed.D. dissertation, Hofstra University.

Kean, E. (1998). Chemists and play. In D. P. Fromberg & D. Bergen (Eds.), *Play from birth to twelve and beyond: Contexts, perspectives, and meanings* (pp. 468–472). New York: Garland.

Keats, E. J. (1967). *Peter's chair*. New York: Harper & Row.

Kent, P. (1998). *Hidden under the ground: The world beneath your feet*. New York: Dutton.

Kieff, J. E., & Casbergue, R. M. (2000). *Playful learning and teaching: Integrating play into preschool and primary programs*. Boston: Allyn & Bacon.

Kindersley, A. (1997). *Children just like me: Celebrations* (B. Kindersley, Photos.). New York: DK Publishing.

King, N. (1992). The impact of context on the play of young children. In S. Kessler & B. Swadener (Eds.), *Reconceptualizing the early childhood curriculum* (pp. 42–61). New York: Teachers College Press.

Kirschenblatt-Gimblett, B. (1979). Speech play and the verbal art. In B. Sutton-Smith (Ed.), *Play and learning* (pp. 219–238). New York: Gardner.

Kline, S. (1995). The promotion and marketing of toys: Time to rethink the paradox? In A.D. Pellegrini (Ed.), *The future of play theory* (pp. 165–185). Albany: State University of New York Press.

Klugman, E., & Fasoli, L. (1995). Taking the high road toward a definition of play. In E. Klugman (Ed.), *Play, policy and practice* (pp. 195–201). St. Paul, MN: Redleaf Press.

Koch, J. (1996). Personal communication.

Kohn, A. (1996). *Beyond discipline: From compliance to community*. Alexandria, VA: Association for Supervision and Curriculum Development.

Kohn, A. (1999). The deadly effects of tougher standards. Presentation at the Association for Supervision and Curriculum Development, San Francisco.

Kohn, A. (2000). Burnt at the high stakes. *Journal of Teacher Education, 51*(4), 315–327.

Krauss, R. (1945). *The carrot seed*. New York: Harper & Row.

Krauss, R. (1947). *The growing story* (P. Rowand, Illus.). New York: Harper & Row.

Ladson-Billings, G. (1995). *The dreamkeepers: Successful teachers of African American children*. San Francisco: Jossey-Bass.

Lancy, D. F. (1984). Play in anthropological perspective. In P. K. Smith (Ed.), *Play in animals and humans* (pp. 293–303). New York: Basil Blackwell.

Landeck, B. (1950). *Songs to grow on*. New York: William Sloane Associates.

Landreth, G. (1993). Self-expressive communication. In C. E. Schaeffer (Ed.), *The therapeutic powers of play* (pp. 41–63). Northvale, NJ: Jason Aronson.

Langer, S. (1948). *Philosophy in a new key*. New York: Mentor. (Original work published in 1942.)

Leland, H. (1983). Play therapy for mentally retarded and developmentally disabled children. In C. E. Schaefer & K. J. O'Connor (Eds.). *Handbook of play therapy* (pp. 436–454). New York: Wiley.

Leslie, A. M. (1995). Pretending and believing: Issues in the theory of ToMM. In J. Mehler & S. Franck (Eds.), *COGNITION on cognition* (pp. 193–220). Cambridge, MA: MIT Press.

Leslie, A. M., & Frith, U. (1988). Autistic children's understanding of seeing, knowing, and believing. *British Journal of Developmental Psychology, 6*(4), 315–324.

Levenstein, P. (1992). Mother-child home program ("Toy Demonstrators"). In L. R. Williams & D. P. Fromberg (Eds.), *The encyclopedia of early childhood education* (pp. 481–482). New York: Garland.

Levy, A. K., Schaefer, L., & Phelps, P. C. (1986). Increased preschool effectiveness: Enhancing the language abilities of 3- and 4-year-old children through planned sociodramatic play. *Early Childhood Research Quarterly, 1,* 133–140.

Lorbiecki, M. (1998). *Sister Anne's hands* (K. W. Popp, Illus.). New York: Dial.

Lubeck, S. (1985). *Sandbox society: Early education in black and white America—A comparative ethnography.* London: Falmer.

Lundgren, M. (1972). *Matt's grandfather* (F. Hald, Illus.). New York: Putnam.

Maccoby, E. E., & Jacklin, C. T. (1974). *The psychology of sex differences.* Stanford, CA: Stanford University Press.

MacDonald, M. R. with Vathanaprida, S. (1998). *The girl who wore too much* (Y. L. Davis, Illus.). Little Rock, AR: August House Little Folks.

Malaguzzi, L. et al. (1996). *Catalog of the exhibit: The hundred languages of children.* Reggio Emilia, Italy: Reggio Children.

Mall, P. D. (1995). Early modeling of drinking behavior by Native American elementary school children. *The International Journal of the Addictions, 30*(9), 1187–1197.

Mardell, B. (2000). *From basketball to the Beatles: In search of compelling early childhood curriculum.* Portsmouth, NH: Heinemann.

Marsh, A. J. (1999). Teletubby tales: Popular culture in the early years language and literacy curriculum. Presentation at the annual meeting of the American Educational Research Association, Montreal, Canada.

McCartney, K. (1984). Effect of quality of day care environment on children's language development. *Developmental Psychology, 20*(2), 244–260.

McCloskey, R. (1952). *One morning in Maine.* New York: Viking.

McCloskey, R. (1968). *Blueberries for Sal.* New York: Viking. (Original work published 1948.)

McGhee, P. E., Etheridge, L., & Berg, N.A. (1984). Effect of toy structure on preschool children's pretend play. *Journal of Catholic Education, 144,* 209–217.

McKissack, P. C. (1997). *Ma dear's aprons* (F. Cooper, Illus.). New York: Atheneum.

McLoyd, V. (1983). The effects of the structure of play objects on the pretend play of low-income preschool children. *Child Development, 54*(3), 626–635.

McLuhan, M. (1963). We need a new picture of knowledge. In A. Frazier (Ed.), *New insights and the curriculum* (pp. 57–70). Washington, DC: Association for Supervision and Curriculum Development.

Miles, M. (1971). *Annie and the old one.* Boston: Little Brown.

Mindes, G. (1998). "Can I play too?" In D. P. Fromberg & D. Bergen (Eds.), *Play from birth to twelve and beyond: Contexts, perspectives, and meanings* (pp. 208–214). New York: Garland.

Moran, J. D., II, Sawyers, J. K., Fu, V. R., & Milgram, R. M. (1984). Predicting imaginative play in preschool children. *Gifted Child Quarterly, 28*(2), 92–94.

Morgan, R. (1982). *The anatomy of freedom: Physics and global politics.* Garden City, NY: Anchor.

Morris, A. (1992). *Houses and houses* (K. Heyman, Photos). New York: Lothrop, Lee & Shepard.

Morrow, L. M. (1997). *The literacy center.* York, ME: Stenhouse.

Mulligan, V. (1996). *Children's play*. Ontario, Canada: Addison-Wesley.

Nakkula, M. (1999). Hermeneutics, chaos/complexity theory and constructivist learning in children and adults who work with them. Presentation at the annual meeting of the American Educational Research Association, Montreal, Canada.

Nelson, K. (1985). *Making sense: The acquisition of shared meaning*. Orlando, FL: Academic Press.

Nelson, K. et al. (1986). *Event knowledge: Structure and function in development*. Mahwah, NJ: Lawrence Erlbaum.

Nilsen, B. A. (1997). *Week by week: Plans for observing and recording young children*. Albany, NY: Delmar.

O'Brien, M., & Bi, X. (1995). Language learning in context: Teacher and toddler speech in three classroom play areas. *Topics in Early Childhood Special Education, 15*(2), 148–163.

Ogbu, J. U. (1978). *Minority education and caste*. New York: Academic Press.

Onyefulu, I. (1998). *Grandfather's work: A traditional healer in Nigeria*. Brookfield, CT: Millbrook Press.

Opie, I., & Opie, P. (1976). Street games: Counting-out and chasing. In J. S. Bruner, A. Jolly, & K. Sylva (Eds.), *Play—Its role in development and evolution* (pp. 394–412). New York: Basic Books.

Owocki, G. (1999). *Literacy through play*. Portsmouth, NH: Heinemann.

Paley, V. G. (1981). *Wally's stories*. Cambridge: Harvard University Press.

Paley, V. G. (1984). *Boys and girls: Superheroes in the doll corner*. Chicago: University of Chicago Press.

Paley, V. G. (1992). *You can't say that you can't play*. Chicago: University of Chicago Press.

Peitgen, H. (1990). The causality principle, deterministic laws and chaos. In J. Holte (Ed.), *Chaos: The new science* (pp. 34–43). St. Peter, MN: Gustavus Adolphus College.

Pellegrini, A. D. (1987). Rough-and-tumble play and social problem solving flexibility. *Creativity Research Journal, 5*(1), 12–26.

Pellegrini, A. D. (1998). Rough-and-tumble play from childhood to adolescence. In D. P. Fromberg & D. Bergen (Eds.), *Play from birth to twelve and beyond: Contexts, perspectives, and meanings* (pp. 401–408). New York: Garland.

Pellegrini, A. D., & Galda, L. (1982). The effects of thematic-fantasy play training on the development of children's story comprehension. *American Educational Research Journal, 19*(3), 443–452.

Pellegrini, A. D., & Perlmutter, J. C. (1989). Classroom effects on children's play. *Developmental Psychology, 25*(2), 289–296.

Peller, L. E. (1971). Models of children's play. In R. E. Herron & B. Sutton-Smith (Eds.), *Child's play* (pp. 110–125). New York: Wiley.

Perner, J. (1991). *Understanding and the representational world*. Cambridge, MA: MIT Press.

Phenix, P. (1964). *Realms of meaning*. New York: McGraw-Hill.

Piaget, J. (1962). *Play, dreams, and imitation in childhood* (C. Gattegno & F. M. Hodgson, Trans.). New York: W.W. Norton. (Original work published 1951.)

Piaget, J. (1966). Response to Brian Sutton-Smith. *Psychological Review, 73*(2), 111–112.

Piaget, J. (1976). *The grasp of consciousness*. Cambridge, MA: Harvard University Press.

Piaget, J., & Inhelder, B. (1969). *The psychology of the child* (H. Weaver, Trans.). New York: Basic Books.

Piaget, J., & Inhelder, B. (1973). *Memory and intelligence*. New York: Basic Books.

Piaget, J. et al. (1965). *The moral judgment of the child* (M. Gabain, Trans.). New York: Free Press.

Polacco, P. (1998). *Thank you, Mr. Falker*. New York: Philomel.

Porter, J. D. R. (1971). *Black child, white child*. Cambridge, MA: Harvard University Press.

Prawat, R. S. (1999). Dewey, Peirce, and the learning process. *American Educational Research Journal, 36*(1), 47–76.

Provenzo, E. F., Jr. (1998). Electronically mediated playscapes. In D. P. Fromberg & D. Bergen (Eds.), *Play from birth to twelve and beyond: Contexts, perspectives, and meanings* (pp. 513–518). New York: Garland.

Pulaski, M. A. (1973). Toys and imaginative play. In J. S. Singer (Ed.), *The child's world of make-believe: Experimental studies of imaginative play* (pp. 73–103). New York: Academic Press.

Quinn, M. (1996). *Take home literacy backpacks*. New York: Scholastic.

Ramsey, P. G. (1998). Personal communication.

Ramsey, P. G. (1998). Diversity and play: Influences of race, culture, class, and gender. In D. P. Fromberg & D. Bergen (Eds.), *Play from birth to twelve and beyond: Contexts, perspectives, and meanings* (pp. 23–33). New York: Garland.

Reiber, R. W., & Carton, A. S. (Eds.) (1987). *The collected works of L. S. Vygotsky* (Vol. 1). *Problems of general psychology* (N. Minick, Trans.). New York: Plenum.

Richards, R. (1989). *Early start to nature*. Hemel Hempstead, Herts, England: Simon & Schuster, and Brattleboro, VT: Teachers' Laboratory.

Richards, R., (1992). *An early start to energy and its effects*. Hemel Hempstead, Herts, England: Simon & Schuster, and Brattleboro, VT: Teachers' Laboratory.

Richards, R., Collis, M., & Kincaid, D. (1995/1987). *An early start to science*. Cheltenham, England: Stanley Thorne, and Brattleboro, VT: Teachers' Laboratory.

Rivkin, M. S. (1998). Children's outdoor play: An endangered activity. In D. P. Fromberg & D. Bergen (Eds.), *Play from birth to twelve and beyond: Contexts, perspectives, and meanings* (pp. 225–231). New York: Garland.

Robertson, R., & Combs, A. (Eds.) (1995). *Chaos theory in psychology and the life sciences*. Mahwah, NJ: Lawrence Erlbaum.

Rogers, D. L. (1985). Relationships between block play and the social development of children. *Early Child Development and Care, 20*, 245–261.

Rohman, E. (1994). *Time flies*. New York: Scholastic.

Roopnarine, J. L., Johnson, J. E., & Hooper, F. H. (Eds.) (1994). *Children's play in diverse cultures*. Albany: State University of New York Press.

Rosenberg, M. B. (1986). *Living in two worlds* (G. Ancona, Photo.). New York: Lothrop, Lee & Shepard.

Rosenblatt, L. (1969). Towards a transactional theory of reading. *Journal of Reading Behavior, 10*(1), 31–34.

Rosengren, K. S., Johnson, C. N., & Harris, P. L. (2000). *Imagining the impossible: Magical, scientific, and religious thinking in children*. Cambridge: Cambridge University Press.

Ryder, J. (1982). *The snail's spell* (L. Cherry, Illus.). New York: Puffin.

Rylant, C. (1985). *The relatives came* (S. Gammell, Illus.). New York: Bradbury Press.

Sapon-Shevin, M., with Dobbelaere, A., Corrigan, C., Goodman, K., & Mastin, M. (1998). Everyone here can play. *Educational Leadership, 56*(1), 42–45.

Say, A. (1993). *Grandfather's journey*. New York: Houghton Mifflin.

Scales, B., Almy, M., Nicolopoulou, A., & Ervin-Tripp, S. (Eds.) (1991). *Play and the social context of development*. New York: Teachers College Press.

Schaefer, C. E., & O'Connor, K. J. (1983). *Handbook of play therapy*. New York: Wiley.

Schank, R., & Abelson, R. (1977). *Scripts, plans, goals and understanding: An inquiry into human knowledge structures*. Hillsdale, NJ: Lawrence Erlbaum.

Schlein, M. (1953). *Fast is not a ladybug* (L. Kessler, Illus.). New York: Scott.

Schlein, M. (1960). *My family* (H. Weiss, Illus.). New York: Abelard-Schuman.

Schrader, D. E. (2000). Theology and physical science: A story of developmental influences at the boundaries. In K. S. Rosengren, C. N. Johnson, & P.L. Harris (Eds.), *Imagining the impossible: Magical, scientific, and religious thinking in children* (pp. 372–404). Cambridge: Cambridge University Press.

Schwartzman, H. B. (1978). *Transformations: The anthropology of children's play*. New York: Plenum.

Selsam, M. (1980). *All about eggs* (S. Fleischer, Illus.). Reading, MA: Addison-Wesley.

Sendak, M. (1963). *Where the wild things are*. New York: Harper & Row.

Serbin, L. (1978). Teachers, peers, and play preferences: An environmental approach to sex typing in the preschool. In B. Sprung (Ed.), *Perspectives on nonsexist early childhood education* (pp. 79–93). New York: Teachers College Press.

Sheldon, A. (1992). Conflict talk: Sociolinguistic challenges to self-assertion and how young girls meet them. *Merrill-Palmer Quarterly, 38*(1), 95–117.

Shepard, L. A., & Smith, M. L. (1988, November). Escalating academic demand in kindergarten: Counterproductive policies. *Elementary School Journal, 89*(2), 135–145.

Shore, C. (1990). Combinatorial play, conceptual development, and early multi-word speech. *Developmental Psychology, 22*(2), 184–190.

Shore, R. (1997). *Rethinking the brain: New insights into early development*. New York: Families and Work Institute.

Sigel, I. E. (1987). Does hothousing rob children of their childhood? *Early Childhood Research Quarterly, 2*(3), 211–226.

Silvern, S. B. (1998). Educational implications of play with computers. In D. P. Fromberg & D. Bergen (Eds.), *Play from birth to twelve and beyond: Contexts, perspectives, and meanings* (pp. 530–536). New York: Garland.

Simon, T., & Smith, P. K. (1985a). A role for play in children's problem-solving: Time to think again. In J. L. Frost & Sunderlin (Eds.), When children play. *Proceedings of the International Conference on Play and Play Environments* (pp. 55–59). Wheaton, MD: Association for Childhood Education International.

Simon, T., & Smith, P. K. (1985b). Play and problem solving: A paradigm questioned. *Merrill-Palmer Quarterly, 31*(3), 265–277.

Simon, T., & Smith, P. K. (1985c). Problems with a play paradigm: A reply to Dansky. *Merrill-Palmer Quarterly, 32*(2), 205–209.

Singer, D. G., & Singer, J. L. (1998). Fantasy and imagination. In D. P. Fromberg & D. Bergen (Eds.), *Play from birth to twelve and beyond: Contexts, perspectives, and meanings* (pp. 313–318). New York: Garland.

Singer, J. L. (1973). *The child's world of make-believe: Experimental studies of imaginative play*. New York: Academic Press.

Singer, J. L. (1994). Imaginative play and adaptive development. In J. H. Goldstein (Eds.), *Toys, play and child development* (pp. 6–26). New York: Cambridge University Press.

Singer, J., & Singer, D. (1979). The values of imagination. In B. Sutton-Smith (Ed.), *Play and learning* (pp. 195–218). New York: Gardner.

Slaughter, V. T., & Dombrowski, J. (1989). Cultural continuities and discontinuities: Impact on social and pretend play. In M. N. Bloch & A. D. Pellegrini (Eds.), *The ecological context of children's play* (pp. 282–310). Norwood, NJ: Ablex.

Slobodkina, E. (1989). *Caps for sale*. New York: Scholastic. (Original work published 1947.)

Smilansky, S. (1968). *The effects of sociodramatic play on disadvantaged preschool children*. New York: Wiley.

Smith, P. K. (Ed.). (1984). *Play in animals and humans*. New York: Basil Blackwell.

Smith, P. K., & Whitney, S. (1987). Play and associative fluency: Experimenter effect may be responsible for previous positive findings. *Developmental Psychology, 23*(1), 49–53.

Southgate, V. (Retold) (1970). *The enormous turnip*. Loughborough, England: Wills & Hepworth.

Sullivan, W. (1985, January 8). Strange, scroll-like wave is linked to biological processes. *The New York Times*, C3.

Sutton-Smith, B. (1988). Radicalizing childhood: The multivocal voice. In L. R. Williams & D. P. Fromberg (Eds.), *Defining the field of early childhood education* (pp. 77–140). Charlottesville, VA: W. Alton Jones Foundation.

Sylwester, R. (1995). *A celebration of neurons: An educator's guide to the human brain*. Alexandria, VA: Association for Supervision and Curriculum Development.

Taylor, M., & Carlson, S. M. (1997). The relation between individual differences in fantasy and theory of mind. *Child Development, 68*(3), 436–455.

Teale, W. H. (1988, November). Developmentally appropriate assessment of reading and writing in the early childhood classroom. *Elementary School Journal, 89*(2), 173–183.

Tobin, J. J., Wu, D. Y. H., & Davidson, D. H. (1989). *Preschool in three cultures: Japan, China, and the United States*. New Haven, CT: Yale University Press.

Trawick-Smith, J. (1994). *Interactions in the classroom: Facilitating play in the early years*. New York: Merrill Macmillan.

Trottier, M. (1998). *Prairie willow* (L. Fernandez & R. Jacobson, Illus.). New York: Stoddart Kids.

Tworkov, J. (1989). *The camel who took a walk* (R. Duvoisin, Illus.). New York: Dutton. (Original work published 1974.)

Udall, N. (1996). Creative transformation: A design perspective. *Journal of Creative Behavior, 30*(1), 39–51.

Unger, L. (1998). Mixing business with pleasure. In D. P. Fromberg & D. Bergen (Eds.), *Play from birth to twelve and beyond: Contexts, perspectives, and meanings* (pp. 485–492). New York: Garland.

VanderVen, K. (1998). Play, Proteus, and paradox: Education for a chaotic and super-symmetric world. In D. P. Fromberg & D. Bergen (Eds.), *Play from birth to twelve and beyond: Contexts, perspectives and meanings* (pp. 119–132). New York: Garland.

Van Hoorn, J., Nourot, P. M., Scales, B., & Alward, K. R. (1999). *Play at the center of the curriculum* (2nd ed.). Upper Saddle River, NJ: Merrill, Prentice Hall.

Van Manen, M. (1977). Linking ways of knowing with ways of being. *Curriculum Inquiry, 6*(3), 205–228.

Vavra, R. (1968). *Tiger flower* (F. Cowles, Illus.). New York: Raynall, Wm. Morrow.

Velichkovsky, B. M. (1996). Language development at the crossroad of biological and cultural interactions. In B. M. Velichkovsky & D. M. Rumbaugh (Eds.), *Communicating meaning: The evolution and development of language* (pp. 1–26). Mahwah, NJ: Lawrence Erlbaum.

Vergeront, J. (1988). *Places and spaces for preschool and primary (OUTDOORS)*. Washington, DC: National Association for the Education of Young Children.

Voss, H-G. (1987). An empirical study of exploration-play sequences in early childhood. In D. Gorlitz & J. F. Wohlwill (Eds.), *Curiosity, imagination, and play* (pp. 152–179). Hillsdale, NJ: Lawrence Erlbaum.

Vygotsky, L. S. (1962). *Thought and language* (E. Hanfmann & G. Vakar, Trans.). New York: Wiley. (Original work published in 1934.)

Vygotsky, L. S. (1978). *Mind in society: The development of higher psychological processes.* (M. Cole, V. John-Steiner, S. Scribner, & E. Souberman, Eds.). Cambridge, MA: Harvard University Press. (Original work published 1934.)

Vygotsky, L. (1987). Imagination and its development in childhood. In R. W. Rieber & A. S. Carton (Eds.), *The collected works of L. S. Vygotsky* (Vol. 1) (pp. 339–349). (N. Minick, Trans.). New York: Plenum.

Waldrop, M. M. (1992). *Complexity: The emerging science at the edge of order and chaos.* New York: Simon & Schuster.

Wanska, S. K., Pohlman, J. C., & Bedrosian, J. L. (1989). Topic maintenance in preschoolers' conversation in three play situations. *Early Childhood Research Quarterly, 4*(3), 393–402.

Weir, R. (1976). Playing with language. In J. S. Bruner, A. Jolly, & K. Sylva (Eds.), *Play—Its role in development and evolution* (pp. 609–618). New York: Basic Books.

Werner, H. (1948). *Comparative psychology of mental development* (rev. ed.). New York: International Universities Press.

Whelan, F. (1992). *Bringing the farmhouse home* (J. Rowland, Illus.). New York: Simon & Schuster.

Whitehead, A. N. (1958). *An introduction to mathematics.* New York: Oxford University Press.

Whiting, B. B., Edwards, C. P. et al. (1988). *Children of different worlds: The formation of social behavior.* Cambridge, MA: Harvard University Press.

Wiener, R. B., & Cohen, J. H. (1997). *Literacy portfolios: Using assessment to guide instruction.* Upper Saddle River, NJ: Merrill, Prentice Hall.

Wilkins, V. A. (1992). *Finished being four* (C. Pound, Illus.). New York: Holiday House.

Williams, V. B. (1982). *A chair for my mother.* New York: Greenwood.

Wilson, E. O. (1998). *Consilience: The unity of knowledge.* New York: Knopf.

Winn, M. (1977). *The plug-in drug.* New York: Viking.

Wohlwill, J. F. (1984). Relationships between exploration and play. In T. D. Yawkey & A. D. Pellegrini (Eds.), *Child's play: Developmental and applied* (pp. 143–170). Hillsdale, NJ: Lawrence Erlbaum.

Wolfberg, P. L. (1999). *Play and imagination in children with autism.* New York: Teachers College Press.

Wolfenstein, M. (1954). *Children's humor: A psychological analysis.* Glencoe, IL: Free Press.

Wood, D. (1998). *Making the world* (Y. & H. Miyaki, Illus.). New York: Simon & Schuster.

Wyeth, S. D. (1998). *Something beautiful* (C. K. Soentpiet, Illus.). New York: Bantam, Doubleday Dell.

Yashima, T. (1970). *Umbrella.* New York: Viking.

Yezerski, T. F. (1998). *Together in Pinecone Patch.* New York: Farrar, Straus & Giroux.

Young, E. (1992). *Seven blind mice.* New York: Philomel.

Zim, H., & Skelly, J. (1969). *Hoists, cranes, and derricks* (G. Ruse, Illus.). New York: Morrow.

Zubrowski, B. (1979). *Bubbles* (J. Drescher, Illus.). New York: Beech Tree.

Zubrowski, B. (1990). *Balloons: Building and experimenting with inflatable toys* (R. Doty, Illus.). New York: Beech Tree.

INDEX